How It Works®

Science and Technology

Third Edition

Marshall Cavendish
99 White Plains Road
Tarrytown, NY 10591

Website: www.marshallcavendish.com

Third edition updated by Brown Reference Group plc.

Library of Congress Cataloging-in-Publication Data
How it works: science and technology.—3rd ed.
p. cm.
Includes index.
ISBN 0-7614-7314-9 (set)   ISBN 0-7614-7321-1 (Vol. 7)
1. Technology—Encyclopedias. 2. Science—Encyclopedias.
[1. Technology—Encyclopedias. 2. Science—Encyclopedias.]
T9 .H738 2003
603—dc21   2001028771

Consultant: Donald R. Franceschetti, Ph.D., University of Memphis

Brown Reference Group
Editor: Wendy Horobin
Associate Editors: Paul Thompson, Martin Clowes, Lis Stedman
Managing Editor: Tim Cooke
Design: Alison Gardner
Picture Research: Becky Cox
Illustrations: Mark Walker, Darren Awuah

Marshall Cavendish
Project Editor: Peter Mavrikis
Production Manager: Alan Tsai
Editorial Director: Paul Bernabeo

Printed in Malaysia
Bound in the United States of America
08 07 06 05 04   6 5 4 3 2

Title picture: Examining a gun for fingerprints, see *Forensic Science*

How It Works®

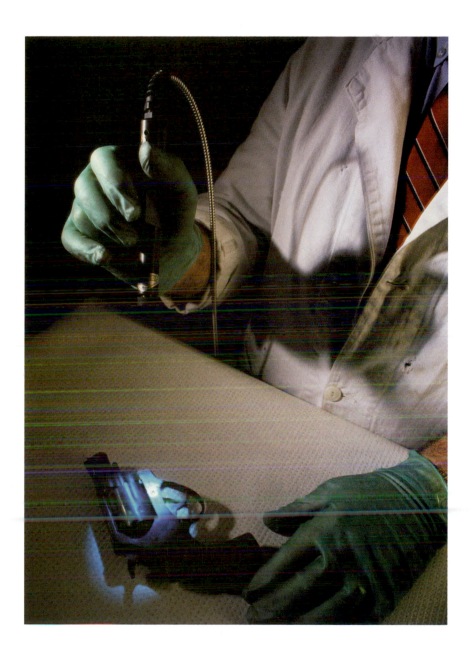

Science and Technology

Volume 7

Firework and Flare

Global Positioning System

Marshall Cavendish

New York • London • Toronto • Sydney

Contents

Volume 7

Firework and Flare

Fireworks probably originated as a consequence of the discovery of gunpowder in China over 2,000 years ago and were possibly used initially to frighten away devils rather than to give enjoyment to the users. The earliest European use of fireworks as an armament (Greek fire) was by the Byzantines in the seventh century, but the development of fireworks for pleasure did not begin until about 1500 C.E. in Italy. The practice spread throughout Europe during the 16th century, and displays gradually became a regular feature of public entertainment on big occasions. Today fireworks are in common use for both public and private displays throughout the world.

Cases and compositions

The cases of fireworks are basically laminated paper cylinders or tubes, the thickness and shape depending on the type of firework and the composition (filling). Most cases are plain cylinders, but there are variations on this shape, such as cone or cube shapes and the specialized cases for jumping crackers and Catherine wheels. The jumping cracker consists of a long thin tube folded back on itself containing a composition designed to give a sequential series of explosions. The tube of a Catherine wheel is wound spirally around a disk of plastic, cardboard, or composite material and is consumed as the composition burns away.

The basic composition of fireworks contains compounds of potassium, carbon, and sulfur. To produce sparks, salts of lead or barium or finely powdered steel, iron, aluminum, or carbon may be added to the composition. Brilliant white flame is produced by the addition of compounds of potassium, antimony, arsenic, and sulfur or powdered magnesium.

Colored flame is created by various metallic salts; strontium and lithium salts produce a red flame, green is produced by barium, yellow by sodium, and blue by copper. Colored stars and similar effects (such as those from a skyrocket) are made by small pellets of color composition that are ignited and ejected from the firework by the force composition. Whistling fireworks contain red gum, potassium perchlorate, and sodium salicylate. When these chemicals burn, they produce a gas that creates the whistling sound.

Fireworks can be extremely dangerous if handled carelessly, and even more dangerous if made by amateurs. Under no circumstances should attempts be made to produce homemade fireworks or to use fireworks in any way other

◀ A firework display taken with a simple camera. The lens is set to a small aperture, and the film is exposed for several seconds. The red cast is given by burning chemicals.

than that specified by the manufacturers. Many unfortunate accidents with fireworks have ruined Fourth of July celebrations.

Displays

Portraits of personalities, depictions of buildings sometimes as much as 600 ft. (180 m) long—and moving outlines of animals or people have long been a feature of firework displays.

Among the most spectacular fireworks are shells, normally round or cylindrical paper or plastic cases projected into the air from a mortar tube sunk into the ground. These shells vary in size from just under 2 in. (5 cm) to 3 ft. (0.91m) in diameter and burst at a predetermined height to produce star, noise, and pictorial effects against the night sky. Daylight shells release slogans or product dummies on parachutes and are used for publicity and product promotion.

The preferred styles of display vary around the world, the Far East generally specializing in attaining perfect symmetry in shell-burst effects, using small short-burning stars and having a wide variety of noise effects, while in America and Europe the stars burn longer and a wider range of effects is normally produced.

◀ A handheld orange flare that is used as a daytime distress signal. It burns for about 30 seconds, can be used safely even in inflatable life rafts, and is visible many miles away.

Flares

The main uses of flares are for signaling (including distress signals) and for illuminating landing strips or target areas. The flares produce a brilliant flame or colored smoke, or they fire rockets into the air that release colored stars or a burning flare carried on a small parachute. The Very pistol, a widely used signaling device, fires colored stars to a height of 250 to 300 ft. (76–91 m) from 1 or 1.2 in. (25–30 mm) diameter cartridges.

The main type of parachute flare is the handheld parachute rocket. This consists of a free-flight rocket made from an aluminum alloy tube, containing the propellant and the payload, which is a parachute-suspended flare. The rocket is fitted into a plastic launching tube and is ignited by means of a striker that fires a percussion cap. The cap in turn ignites a delay fuse and an intermediate charge known as a quickmatch, which ignites the propellant. The rocket motor burns for around 3.5 seconds and drives the rocket to over 1,000 ft. (305 m) before ejecting the parachute flare. The flare burns for over 40 seconds and is carried on a four-string parachute that slows its rate of descent to approximately 15 ft. per sec. (4.6 m/s). On a clear night, such flares can be seen for a distance of about 28 miles (45 km). Illuminating parachute flares may also be dropped from helicopters or low-flying aircraft to light up large ground areas.

Hand stars are used in lifeboats and by other small craft in distress and also by mountaineers. They eject two red stars to a height of about 150 ft. (46 m), with an interval of 3 to 5 seconds between them. Each star burns for about 5 seconds. Distress hand flares produce a bright red flame and burn for about 55 seconds.

Distress flares are always colored red and contain a mixture of magnesium, strontium nitrate, potassium perchlorate, and PVC. Illuminating flares are usually white, and a range of other colors is available for signaling. A recent develop-

▼ Modern firework displays use computer-controlled ignition to ensure the precise timing of explosions.

ment is the radar-reflecting distress rocket, which carries a payload of two red stars plus about 300,000 tiny pieces of silvered nylon that reflect radar signals and so enable rescuers to use radar to locate craft in distress.

Smoke flares

Smoke flares are used for such purposes as daylight distress signals and ground-to-air signals. Orange smoke is used for distress signals, and one type, for use by lifeboats, is designed to float and burns for two to four minutes. The smoke is nontoxic and when burning on oil-covered water it will not ignite the oil. Hand-held smoke flares are also available and burn for about 30 seconds.

An important type of smoke flare used on merchant shipping is the lifebuoy marker. One is carried on each side of a ship's bridge, attached by a line to the lifebuoys. When the lifebuoy is thrown overboard, it pulls the marker out of its mounting bracket, igniting the smoke charges. The flotation collar of the marker contains two electric lights powered by seawater-activated batteries. The smoke burns for over 15 minutes, and the lamps stay lit for over 45 minutes.

SEE ALSO: ALKALI METALS • AMMUNITION • EXPLOSIVE • FLAME AND IGNITION • PARACHUTE • RADAR • ROCKET AND SPACE PROPULSION • SHIP

Fishing Industry

Humans were using hooks and lines, nets, and traps to capture fish for food 20,000 years ago, and the sea is still harvested using these techniques. Fishing from a reed boat or dugout canoe is still common in some parts of the world; a person using these methods can catch up to 3 tons (2.7 tonnes) of fish in a year. Although modern fishing fleets employ methods and equipment that are not very different in principle, the use of modern technology now enables each person to produce 50 or 100 times more fish. This result is achieved by the designing and building of vessels that, size for size, are more expensive than any other except ships of war.

Although some species of shellfish are the most valuable, much the biggest part of the marine harvest comprises various species of finned fish. Pelagic species include the tunas, mackerels, herrings, salmon, and anchovies; most of these have oily flesh. They swim near the surface of the sea, often in dense shoals. Demersal species are those normally found on or near the seabed of the continental shelf; they include cod, hake, halibut, sole, flounder, and sea bream.

Environmentalists are increasingly concerned about the state of many of the world's fish stocks. Species of Atlantic cod have become severely depleted, and many other species are in danger of being overfished. In addition, bycatch, such as dolphins caught in nets intended to catch tuna, causes the needless death of many species that are not even eaten by humans. Some measures have been taken to counter this problem. In the United States, for example, the Marine Fisheries Service insists that larger shrimp boats use turtle exclusion devices on their nets to prevent the death of turtles as bycatch.

Purse seining

The principal method of capture of pelagic species is the purse seine. After detecting a shoal, the skipper maneuvers the ship, taking into account wind, current, and the speed and direction of the shoal, so as to surround the fish with a wall of fine netting suspended from floats, which is fed out over the stern of the ship as it travels. The net is then drawn together at the bottom, and after most of it has been hauled back on board, the fish are scooped or pumped into the ship's hold or refrigerated seawater tanks. Some purse seines are hundreds of yards in circumference, and if there is the slightest breeze, it is often necessary to take steps to prevent the ship from becoming entangled in the net. American purse

◀ Fishers supervising the unloading of a catch of blue whiting as it is emptied into the deck pounds of a typical midwater trawler.

seiners carry a powerful motor skiff, which is used as a tug; European fishing fleets equip their vessels with devices that produce sideways thrust, such as propellers working in transverse tunnels in the hull or rotating cylinder rudders.

Skippers know from experience which sea areas are most likely to yield good catches, according to season; they also may get up-to-the-minute information from colleagues over the radiotelephone. Other indications are water temperature and animal life. Actual shoals may be detected at distances of a few miles by powerful long-range sonar, by the behavior of birds, or by phosphorescence in the water at night. Aerial reconnaissance by helicopter is also used by some of the larger tuna seiners. When the ship has closed the range to a few hundred yards, the sonar is switched to a shorter range to maintain contact with the shoal.

Trawling

Shoaling species can also be captured with a midwater trawl towed at ½ to 5 knots (¾–7½ mph; 1.2–12 km/h) by a single vessel or a pair of vessels. Paired midwater trawling, where the net is towed between two ships, has proved in many cases to be more successful and more economical than a single-boat operation. Single-boat midwater trawls to be effective must be so large and delicate—and thus slow to maneuver—that their successful use depends upon the skipper having precise knowledge of the position of the net in relation to the seabed and the surface. Therefore, vertical echo sounders are attached to the trawl, and the information is then telemetered to the ship by cable or acoustic beam.

A forward-looking sonar may also be mounted on the trawl to enable the skipper to observe the shoal as the net approaches, and other transducers may be used to signal when the net is filling.

Other methods include gill nets (so called because they catch the fish by the gills as they try to swim through) and pole fishing (rod and line); the 20 or 30 people formerly employed on a pole-fishing tuna vessel today can be replaced by mechanical robots. When the tuna shoals are dispersed, floating baited lines 75 miles (120 km) or more in length are employed by trawlers.

Demersal species can also be caught by baited hooks on lines up to 20 miles (32 km) long laid on the seabed, but the most important method of capturing demersal fish is using the otter trawl. A trawl is a tapering bag of netting towed behind the ship, in this case on the seabed. The vertical opening of the mouth is maintained by floats in the headline and weights on the footrope, the lateral opening by two otter boards, wooden or steel plates running on their edges on the seabed, one attached to each side of the net.

Bottom trawling is carried out in depths down to 500 fathoms (3,000 ft., or 900 m) or more (one fathom is 6 ft., or 1.8 m), but the length of the two warps, or towing cables, attached to the otter boards is usually 2½ or 3 times the depth of water. The trawl is hauled up to the surface by winches, which in the biggest vessels may use 500 horsepower motors.

A very effective method on a smooth seabed is bottom seining. A trawl net, without otter boards, is attached to two towing ropes up to 2 miles (3 km) long; ropes and net are paid out on the seabed in a great circle, and as the ropes are winched in from the boat, they move closer together and shepherd the fish into the path of the net. Despite the advantages of bottom trawling, this technique is increasingly criticized by environmentalists for the damage it does to seabeds.

Fishing aids

Important aids in trawling and bottom seining include warp-tension meters, which measure the loads on the towing cables and, among other things, give warning of the net coming fast on an obstruction; the vertical echo sounder, some versions of which can detect a single fish within a few feet of the seabed in 600 ft. (180 m) of water; and radio navigation devices such as LORAN C and DECCA, which are used in conjunction with large-scale charts on which is recorded informa-

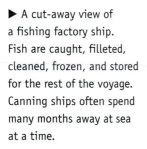

▶ A cut-away view of a fishing factory ship. Fish are caught, filleted, cleaned, frozen, and stored for the rest of the voyage. Canning ships often spend many months away at sea at a time.

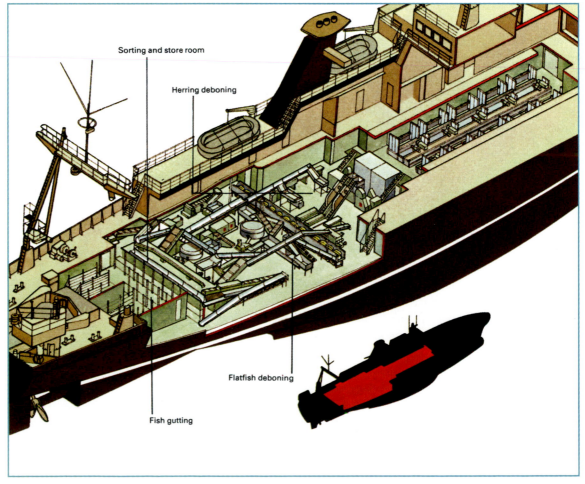

Sorting and store room

Herring deboning

Flatfish deboning

Fish gutting

tion on seabed obstructions, rough ground, and currents and also on the fishing tactics appropriate to the area and season.

Fishing and navigation simulators are available for training the skippers and other officers of fishing ships in how to make the best use of their electronic aids for detecting fish, for navigation, and for other related monitoring systems.

Some trawl nets are longer than the biggest trawlers, which are about 350 ft. (100 m) overall; a midwater trawl may be big enough to envelop St. Paul's Cathedral in London; a purse seine may be 6,500 ft. (2,000 m) long and 600 ft. (180 m) deep. The use of big seines only became feasible with the introduction of hydraulically driven rubber-lined open sheaves, called power blocks, to haul the net on board. Trawl nets used to be hauled on board by hand but can now be wound onto powered drums or reels.

Storage and processing

Once the catch is on board, it is processed and stored according to its intended market and the distance from port. A single haul of sand eel or anchovy may be 100 tons (90 tonnes) or more, but this type of fishing takes place near the coast, and the catch is usually destined for reduction to edible oils and animal feedstuff—about 40 percent of the world catch of marine fish is used in this way—and may simply be stored below in bulk without further treatment. Fish intended for human consumption, if they are to be landed within, for example, one to fifteen days of the time of capture (depending on species, market, season, and climate), are normally stored in boxes or on shelves, and spoilage is retarded by mixing it with melting crushed ice or by storing it in tanks of refrigerated seawater.

Large distant-water trawlers and tuna clippers make voyages of many weeks' or even a few months' duration. Some cod is still split and salted at sea and subsequently dried ashore for consumption in Mediterranean, African, and Latin American countries, but most of the distant-water catch is now quick-frozen at sea and stored on board at temperatures of –20°F (–30°C) or lower.

Tuna can be frozen in tanks through which refrigerated brine is circulated; whole fish are also frozen in cold-air-blast tunnels or in vertical-plate contact freezers between flat, parallel, movable, hollow, refrigerated metal plates. Fillets are usually frozen at sea into regular blocks of 25 to 100 lbs. (11–45 kg) in horizontal-plate contact freezers, and the blocks are destined for reprocessing on shore into fish sticks or standard-sized frozen portions.

◀ Some of the latest freezer and factory trawlers, which make voyages of weeks or months, have automatic fish decks. These enable the crew to gut the huge catches of fish hauled from the sea without bending or lifting. The fish then go into cold storage. Even more modern trawlers are fully automatic and have machines for gutting.

Trawlers equipped to freeze the catch on board are usually of the modern high-freeboard, shelter-deck stern-fishing type, which is fast replacing the low-freeboard, open-deck, single-decked side-fishing trawler that evolved from traditional sail-powered fishing vessels in the 19th century. Mother ships, with attendant catching vessels, are used in some fisheries; the largest is the Russian *Vostock* of 43,500 tons (39,450 tonnes); she carries on board 14 catchers each of which is 60 ft. (18 m) long with a 600 horsepower engine. Some factory ships are equipped to produce fish meal—dried ground fish—for animal feedstuff; some are floating canneries.

Before it is chilled or frozen, the catch will have been sorted and washed and, depending upon species and market, it may be bled, gutted and beheaded or split or filleted. Gutting involves removal of the entrails; some fish livers contain vitamins A and D and are retained for further processing. Filleting is the removal of the edible flesh from the skeleton in one or two large pieces. All of these processes can now be carried out mechanically. Machines for gutting and filleting are extremely complex, not only because of the anatomical problems but also because they must adjust automatically to the size of each successive fish. Some Japanese factory ships are equipped with machines to process the fish flesh into surimi, a frozen minced or ground product that is the raw material for *kamaboko*, or fish jelly, and other manufactured foods.

Crabs and lobsters are caught by baited traps and also by trawls at depths down to 1,200 ft. (365 m). Smaller crustaceans are caught by trawls and dredges, as are mollusks living below low-water mark. Hand gathering is still employed, even in western Europe, for harvesting mollusks in the intertidal zone, but there also exist ship-mounted power dredges fitted with hydraulic digging jets and with jet pumps to deliver the catch continuously on board. Two people so equipped can produce a ton of edible protein in an hour's fishing.

Fish farming

Freshwater fish have been cultivated in Asia since prehistoric times; medieval monastic settlements in western Europe had their carp ponds as farmers still do in countries farther east. Rainbow trout are now farmed in temperate regions and channel catfish in the hot, dry areas of the United States. Tilapia are cultivated in tropical Africa and Asia.

Types of fish farming

Fish farming, or aquaculture, takes many forms. A peasant farmer may keep some fish in a simple pond, or fish may be a subsidiary crop on a flooded rice paddy. American trout farms are elaborate complexes of concrete raceways, pumps, aerators, and equipment that removes waste products and excess nitrogen from the water and restores oxygen and acidity so that it may be recirculated. Some species can live in virtually stagnant water with much plant growth because they require comparatively little oxygen and their diet consists of vegetable matter and small aquatic life.

Cold-water species such as trout require clear, well-oxygenated water, and commercial rearing of carnivorous species like trout, salmon, eels, turbot, and sole depends upon supplies of feedstuff containing a high proportion of animal protein. One source of feedstuff is fish of those species that are difficult to sell for direct human consumption. There is, of course, a net loss of protein, but feed conversion efficiencies are about as good as those of pigs or chickens.

Mollusk cultivation does actually create animal protein, because mollusks feed on microscopic plant life. Oysters are cultivated by arranging for their free-swimming larval stages to settle on strips of wood, plastic, or tiles suspended in the sea near the shore.

Breeding fish

The sea is still harvested mainly by hunting. In nature, however, only a fraction of one percent of the eggs that are spawned by most species ever survive to become fish of marketable size. Abundance, and hence catches, can vary a great deal from year to year; fish farming produces supplies of seafood more abundantly and conveniently.

◄ Fishers on a Scottish trawler casting hawsers around a netted catch as it is hauled aboard the boat in the north Atlantic.

The Japanese have a technique of capturing juvenile wild fish in the open sea and fattening them in netting enclosures fixed into the seabed in shallow sheltered water. Eels are farmed in a similar way. Such techniques, however, still rely upon the natural spawning of wild adult fish.

Hatching in captivity helps to ensure supplies, allows the farming of exotic species, and gives the opportunity for selective breeding. Carp have been deliberately bred for thousands of years for ornament as well as for food, and there are now fast-growing crosses of tilapia species and strains of rainbow trout specially bred for farmers. The Russians have crossed the prized sturgeon, which migrates from the sea up the rivers to spawn, with a freshwater relative.

Only since the 1960s, however, have any marine species been kept alive in captivity throughout the life cycle to the second generation. One problem was feeding the tiny larval stages: algae, microscopic aquatic plants, are now cultivated to feed to oyster larvae in hatcheries; turbot larvae are fed first with cultivated rotifers (*Brachionus plicatilis*) for a few days then naulii (young) of the brine shrimp *Artemia salina*.

The British developed these techniques for hatching oysters and turbot, and similar methods have been evolved in other countries for sea bass

◀ A haul of krill. *Euphausia superba*— Antarctic krill—is a shrimplike crustacean that can grow to lengths of 2.3 in. (6 cm).

and sea bream. The fish are reared to market size either in floating cages anchored in sheltered bays or in tanks on shore through which the warmed seawater from the cooling systems of coastal electricity generating stations is circulated, thus speeding up growth.

Krill

The South Atlantic teems with millions of tiny shrimplike crustaceans called krill, a Norwegian whaling term meaning "whale food." These crustaceans live in large swarms, making them easy for fishers to catch. With swarms as wide as 2,625 ft. (800 m) in the top 656 ft. (200 m) of water, up to 60 tons (54 tonnes) of this high-grade protein source can be caught in a single haul.

Interest in krill as a commercial catch began in the 1960s, when traditional catches were declining in the world's major fisheries. Krill meat is rich in protein, containing up to 60 percent by dry weight—similar to that of beef, shrimp, or lobster. Krill has almost the complete range of vitamins, with the exception of vitamin C. However, as a food product, krill are fragile and easily damaged, particularly when squashed together in a trawl net. They also lose their freshness rapidly and start to deteriorate within four hours of capture unless suitably treated.

Whole, boiled, deep-frozen krill may be the most promising outlet for krill intended for human consumption—and there is already a strong demand, particularly at the luxury end of the market.

FACT FILE

■ Vertical echo-sounders operating between 100 and 200 kHz are used to locate and distinguish shoals of Antarctic krill, the tiny shrimplike crustacean that could be one of the world's largest protein sources. With a potential annual harvest of 60 million tons (54 million tonnes), the krill have to be processed immediately aboard ship, otherwise they rapidly become unfit to eat. The Russians use them to make krill paste, and the Chileans produce a number of products, such as krill sticks.

■ Japanese raw-fish bars specialize in wafer-thin slices of bluefin tuna caught in the northern Atlantic. Sometimes weighing well over 1,000 lbs. (450 kg), the bluefins are caught by purse seiners, long-liners, and rod and line sports anglers and rushed 8,000 miles (12,870 km), packed in ice, by air to Japan from North American east coast ports. The demand is so great that the bluefin is in great danger from overfishing.

SEE ALSO: AQUACULTURE • FERTILIZER • FOOD PROCESSING • NAVIGATION • RADAR • RADIO • REFRIGERATION • SHIP • SONAR

Fission

Nuclear fission is the division of the nuclei of heavy atoms into pairs of nuclei that each have roughly half the mass of the original nucleus. Fission differs from other nuclear reactions in that the changes in atomic mass are much greater than those caused by the capture or expulsion of small particles, such as electrons, neutrons, or alpha particles (helium nuclei). Nuclear fission is accompanied by the release of energy that can be used to generate electricity or to provide the explosive power of atomic weapons.

Discovery of fission

The fission of uranium was first observed in the 1930s, when the German scientist Otto Hahn was attempting to produce transuranic elements by bombarding uranium with neutrons. Hahn detected barium-141 in the products of his tests but hesitated until 1939 to publish his unexpected finding. When he did, the Austrian physicist Lise Meitner realized that barium was being formed by uranium nuclei splitting in two.

Working with her nephew Otto Frisch, Meitner performed a series of experiments that revealed the amount of energy released by the fission of uranium. They also discovered that each fission releases at least two neutrons, which they realized could sustain chain reactions by causing other fissions, themselves releasing neutrons.

The principal applications of the energy released by fission—nuclear weapons and nuclear power—were developed in the 1940s and 1950s. Two atomic weapons devastated the Japanese cities of Hiroshima and Nagasaki in August, 1945, and the first full-scale nuclear power station opened at Calder Hall, Britain, in 1956.

Energy from mass conversion

With the exception of hydrogen nuclei, which are protons, all atomic nuclei are agglomerations of nucleons—protons and neutrons—held together by the strong nuclear force. As a consequence of that force, all nuclei have less energy than their nucleons would have in isolation. The energy difference is called the nuclear binding energy.

As part of his Special Theory of Relativity of 1905, the German-born physicist Albert Einstein formulated an equation connecting energy (E) and mass (m): $E = mc^2$, where c is the speed of light. This equation holds true for nuclei, which have less mass than their component nucleons. According to Einstein's equation, the binding energy is the mass difference multiplied by the square of the speed of light. It is always negative.

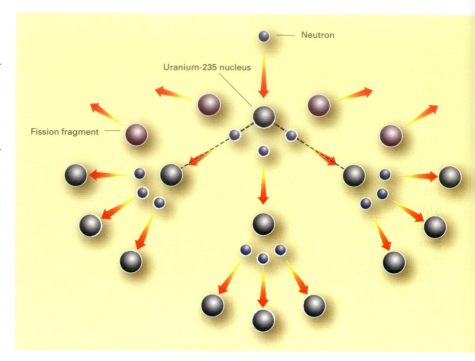

▲ This diagram illustrates the mechanism of a chain reaction. Fission releases neutrons (represented by small spheres) that can collide with fissile nuclei (large spheres) to trigger further reactions. In practice, many of the fission neutrons escape without causing fission. The pairs of nuclei that result from fission reactions (omitted for clarity) have on average just less than half the mass of the fissile nuclei.

Fission reactions release energy because their products have a greater binding energy per nucleon than the original fissile nuclei. The products therefore have less mass than the nuclei that give rise to them, and the energy released by the reaction is equal to the reduction in mass through the course of the fission reaction.

Fission energy is released in various forms, including the electromagnetic energy of gamma rays and the kinetic energies of fast-moving neutrons. Since the release of energy is accompanied by a reduction in mass, fission is an example of energy production by mass conversion.

Chain reactions

A crucial feature of the fission process is the release of neutrons that can initiate other fissions and sustain a chain reaction. If one neutron from each fission triggers exactly one fission, then the rate of fission is stable, as is the rate at which energy is released. This is the type of chain reaction that releases heat in a controlled manner for use in the generation of electricity.

If conditions are created such that more than one fission is triggered by the the neutrons from a single fission, then the chain reaction can soon get out of hand. The increased rate of fission produces more and more neutrons, which in turn boost the rate of fission. This type of chain reaction, which releases vast amounts of energy in a short time, is the basis of nuclear explosions.

If neutrons are somehow prevented from causing fissions, the chain reaction stops and the nuclear reactors will shut down. The spontaneous radioactivity of the reactor contents continues to generate some heat, however.

Criticality

Two factors determine whether a chain reaction can proceed in a given collection of fissile material: the frequency of collisions between neutrons and fissile nuclei and the probability that each collision will cause a fission. If the combination of these factors is favorable, then a chain reaction proceeds and the assembly is said to be critical.

The rate of collisions between neutrons and fissile nuclei depends largely on the amount of fissile material present and the physical form in which it is assembled. The minimum amount of a given fissile material that can sustain a chain reaction is called its critical mass. The atomic bomb that was dropped on Hiroshima consisted of a conical wedge of uranium that was driven by high explosive into a matching hole in a sphere of uranium. Combined, the two masses exceeded the critical mass, and an explosion ensued.

The amount of nuclear fuel necessary for a chain reaction to occur can be reduced by increasing the concentration of fissile material in the fuel. Natural uranium is more than 99 percent nonfissile U-238, with just over 0.7 percent fissile U-235. This is increased to around 3 percent U-235 for use in most nuclear reactors or to more than 90 percent for use in nuclear warheads.

► This photograph shows fuel rods being loaded into the core of a fast-breeder reactor. Note that the level of radiation is so low as to make extensive protective clothing unnecessary. When the critical mass is reached, this reactor will run without a moderator. Its fuel is enriched to 15 to 30 percent U-235 to ensure a sufficient neutron flux for a chain reaction to occur. A blanket of U-238 around the core will absorb neutrons as it changes into plutonium-239 (Pu-239), which can then be used to fuel other reactors.

Moderators and control rods

The amount of material necessary to sustain a chain reaction can be reduced by improving the chances of a neutron causing a fission. Slow neutrons have better chances of interacting with nuclei than fast neutrons, which pass straight through nuclei without causing fission.

Most nuclear reactors use moderators to sustain controlled chain reactions by slowing neutrons released by fission. In pressurized-water reactors, for example, purified water is the moderator as well as being the fluid that carries heat from the reactor. This design has the safety advantage that an accidental loss of cooling water would stop the chain reaction by removing its moderator. The pace of a chain reaction can be slowed or stopped by inserting control rods into a reactor core. These rods are made of boron or cadmium, which are strong neutron absorbers.

Fissile isotopes

The only natural fissile isotope is uranium-235. Its fission produces uneven pairs of nuclei with around 95 and 137 nucleons, respectively—strontium-94 and xenon-140 are a typical pair. Many of the initial products decay rapidly to other elements with the release of more energy.

The other isotope used in some fission reactors is plutonium-239. This material is produced by bombarding uranium-238 with neutrons in fast-breeder fission reactors.

FACT FILE

- In June 1972, technicians of the French nuclear power industry found that a batch of uranium ore from Oklo, Gabon, contained 0.621–0.717 percent of the 235 isotope rather than the 0.720 percent that would have been expected. Further samples showed U-235 contents as low as 0.292 percent— less than half the expected value. These results indicated that some of the fissile isotope had been consumed by a chain reaction. The hypothesis was supported by the relative percentages of neodymium isotopes in the region, which are similar to those produced by fission reactors. It is estimated that the Oklo natural reactor was critical some 1.45 billion years ago, when around 3 percent of uranium was U-235 and there was sufficient water in the ground to moderate the chain reaction.

- The energy released by the fission of 1 lb. (454 g) of uranium-235 is 3.7×10^{13} joules (37,000 gigajoules), equivalent to burning 1,500 tons (1,350 tonnes) of coal.

SEE ALSO: ATOMIC STRUCTURE • BINDING ENERGY • ENERGY RESOURCES • FUSION • NUCLEAR FUEL CYCLE • NUCLEAR REACTOR

Flame and Ignition

Although a precise definition is elusive, a flame is generally recognized as a visible sign of combustion and the release of heat at high temperature. A flame involves chemical processes, in the form of exothermic (heat releasing) reactions that energize molecules and produce light. It also involves the physical processes of transfer of both matter and energy. The heat release arises through changes in chemical bonding. Each molecule of fuel and oxidant is made up of atoms bound together by forces of an electrostatic nature. When the bonds are broken, the atoms become free to rearrange themselves and bind together into a different pattern, releasing their excess binding energy in the process. When the natural gas methane (CH_4), for example, is burned with oxygen, the following reaction takes place:

$$CH_4 + 2O_2 \rightarrow CO_2 + 2H_2O$$
methane   oxygen   carbon dioxide   water

The total energy of the product gases is less than that of the fuel and oxygen before combus-

▲ Above left: The flame of a gas cigarette lighter has a lower premixed zone (blue) where the air for combustion has been drawn in through apertures near the base of the flame, and an upper diffusion zone (yellow) where the air for combustion is derived from the surrounding atmosphere. Above right: A type of burner that produces a large hot flame of the premixed variety. Air is drawn in through inlet apertures, clearly seen as the two small holes in the barrel of the burner, and is mixed with the gas as it passes up to the mouth of the burner. A uniform blue flame is produced.

tion. This energy appears as heat and light. The above combustion equation represents the initial and final materials only; the combustion reaction itself is made up of a continuous series of steps, with the momentary formation of a whole variety of products of partial oxidation, which are themselves unstable and lead to further reaction steps. Flame color is largely determined by these partial products and, in some cases, can be used to identify the material being burned.

Types of flame

Flames are usually classified as either premixed or diffusion. In the former case, the fuel and oxidant are mixed beforehand in ambient conditions and are then introduced to the flame, where they burn rapidly and, if the mixture ratio is suitable, completely. In the diffusion flame, on the other hand, the fuel meets the oxidant only at the flame itself, and the rate of combustion at the interference is then largely controlled by the rate of physical mixing, rather than the rate of chemical reaction.

Both types of flame can be demonstrated with a Bunsen burner. If insufficient air for complete combustion is induced by adjusting the air supply to the gas jet at the base, the gas–air mixture burns with a conical premixed flame which, being fuel-rich, gives rise to an outer diffusion flame owing to subsequent mixing with the atmospheric air. In fact, the two flames may be drawn apart by means of a Smithell's separator, which consists essentially of a glass tube fitted over the top of a Bunsen burner. A wick in a candle or a wick fed from a liquid fuel supply also supports a flame of the diffusion type, the combustion heat that is released being sufficient to promote a continuous supply of fuel vapor from the wick surface.

The most common types of fuel in general use are compounds of hydrogen and carbon, sometimes with oxygen, in gaseous, liquid, or solid states. Their premixed flames tend to be blue, owing to the final phase of combustion of carbon monoxide (CO) to carbon dioxide (CO_2) and their diffusion flames yellow, luminous, and sometimes smoky, owing to carbon particles in the flame. Free carbon is formed by cracking, a disruption of the fuel molecules at high temperature in the absence of sufficient oxygen for immediate combustion. Highly radiant flames are required in heat-transfer devices, such as boilers and furnaces, but are undesirable in work transfer devices, such as heat engines, where the energy is required to remain in the gas stream rather than be transferred to the walls.

Flame propagation

A flame propagates through unburned mixture by processes of transfer of both heat and active radicals; these are energetic fragments of molecules that are capable of energizing and triggering combustion reactions in adjacent layers of fresh mixture. When flames propagate smoothly, they are described as laminar, and the maximum laminar velocity for most hydrocarbon type fuels is remarkably low, being only about 1½ ft. per sec. (0.45 m/s). Laminar velocity is increased by initial heating of the mixture and by breaking up and distributing the flame front by means of turbulence.

Ignition

For the combustion of a material (such as a fuel gas) to take place, there has to be a source of oxygen, and the fuel–oxidant mixture has to have a composition that lies within the limits of flammability. If such a mixture is heated slowly in a closed container, then any heat released by the chemical reaction will be lost through the walls of the vessel. If the oxidation reaction continues when the external heat source is removed, with the heat produced being equal to the heat lost, then a steady state is achieved, this being known as slow combustion with the mixture having ignited. If, however, the rate at which heat is produced is greater than the rate at which it is lost, the temperature will rise above a critical value that depends on both the reactants and the container, and the rate of energy release will increase even further. The stage at which this self acceleration occurs is known as ignition, and the corresponding temperature is the ignition temperature. In this case, it is said that the reaction has become autocatalytic, and its rate will accelerate until an explosion occurs.

When this energy provided to initiate a flame is by means of a pilot flame or spark, the ignition is said to be forced, and the mixture of fuel vapor and oxidant (for example, atmospheric air) is described as flammable. In the case where a liquid fuel is heated in air to produce just enough vapor above the surface to make the mixture of vapor and air flammable, the temperature of the liquid fuel, known as the flash point of that fuel, is important when considering the use of many hydrocarbon fuels and solvents. Standard tests have been devised for flash point determinations.

For most liquid hydrocarbon fuels of practical interest, the mixture of vapor and air just becomes flammable at a fuel vapor concentration of about 1 percent by volume. Although this fuel concentration is common for all these fuels, the temperature at which it is reached depends upon the volatility of the fuel. Hence, heavier and more complex fuels are less flammable, since they require heating to higher temperatures before they can be ignited.

When the ignition energy, however, is supplied as heat or pressure only, in the absence of a pilot flame or spark, the fuel and atmospheric oxygen are able to react spontaneously throughout the mixture. The temperature of the vapor and air mixture is known as the spontaneous ignition temperature (T_{sp}) of the fuel, and lighter and simpler fuels exhibit a higher T_{sp} because their molecules are compact and more able to withstand the thermal agitation that leads to bond breaking. In other words, heavier, more complex fuels are more ignitable, since they ignite spontaneously at lower temperatures and pressures.

There are many ways in which the ignition energy can be supplied, ranging from hot wires to sparks and pilot flames, and the choice really depends on the fuel to be burned and the combustion device being used.

Flame temperature

The temperature reached within the flame is the result of a number of chemical and physical factors. The heat released is a known chemical function of the combustion process (the calorific value of the fuel mixture). If no heat is lost to the surroundings, all this combustion heat is absorbed by the product gases, and the resultant temperature thus depends upon their known physical property of specific heat—that is, the heat required to raise the temperature of unit mass of each product by one degree.

◀ The use of high-temperature flame has a number of applications in engineering and plumbing. For soldering and annealing copper pipe, a portable propane-fueled blowtorch is used.

SEE ALSO: Bunsen burner • Explosive • Flame-retarding agent • Flame thrower • Hydrocarbon • Ignition system, automobile

Flame-Retarding Agent

A flame-retarding agent is a substance or mixture that does not burn or support combustion and that inhibits the combustion of materials in which it is incorporated or to which it is applied. Fabrics that are treated with flame retardants, such as Pyrovatex and Proban, resist ignition and will not support combustion. Consequently, if they are present at the scene of a fire, they do not contribute to the spreading of flames.

In installations where hot or inflammable materials are handled as a matter of routine, such as in some types of factories, completely nonflammable materials such as steel and concrete are the predominant construction materials; potentially inflammable articles, such as carpets and wall coverings, are avoided. In locations where the risk of fire is slight but its consequences could be disastrous—domestic, leisure, and office environments, for example—all decorative finishes and fabrics ideally should be modified or treated to make them resistant to the spread of fire.

Noncombustible fabrics

Few completely noncombustible materials can be formed as fibers. Glass and some other ceramics form noncombustible fibers, but textiles produced from these fibers tend to splinter and are suitable for only a limited range of applications.

▼ In this test of Du Pont's Nomex III aramid fiber, heat sensors in the "skin" of the dummy measured temperatures during a 21-second burst of flame. The results indicated that a person wearing this suit would suffer half the second-degree burns and none of the third-degree burns that would afflict the wearer of a similar suit made of untreated cotton.

Some synthetic fibers have extremely low inflammability. Examples include polyaramids (aromatic polyamides, such as Kevlar), polychloroethene (polyvinyl chloride, PVC) and copolymers of propenonitrile (acrylonitrile, CH_2CHCN) with chloroethene (CH_2CHCl) or 1,1-dichloroethene (vinylidene chloride, CH_2CCl_2). Fabrics produced from these synthetic fibers are similar in textile characteristics to polyamide (nylon), acrylic, and polyester fabrics, but they have several disadvantages. Such fabrics are difficult to color, since they require unconventional dyes, expensive dyeing machinery, and higher dyeing temperatures than other fabrics. They are also awkward to launder, since their thermoplastic nature makes them sensitive to high temperatures; thus, they cannot be boiled to remove stains, and drying at too high a temperature can cause permanent wrinkles.

The most significant disadvantage of such materials stems from their chemical compositions. Although flame-retardant synthetics do not burn as such, the high-temperature decomposition of nitrile-based fibers can produce deadly hydrogen cyanide gas, while chlorine-containing polymers can form highly toxic dioxins.

Flame-retarding additives

The susceptability to combustion of many conventional materials can be greatly reduced by the addition of small percentages of flame-retarding

chemicals, which act by modifying the reaction of the base material to heat so that it burns less well or by interfering in the combustion process in some other manner. The treated material usually suffers some damage in the event of fire, but its contribution to the spread of fire is reduced.

Dehydrating agents

Cellulosic materials, such as cotton, linen, and viscose rayon, can be modified by chemicals that encourage the surface layer of the material to char when heated. Untreated cellulose burns well because its thermal decomposition, or pyrolysis, causes the evolution of inflammable gases at temperatures above 570°F (300°C). Above 660°F (350°C), these gases ignite, producing heat and perpetuating the burning process. The overall formula for this reaction is

$$(C_6H_{10}O_5)_n + 6nO_2 \rightarrow 6nCO_2 + 5nH_2O + \text{heat}$$
cellulose   oxygen   carbon dioxide   water

Some flame-retarding agents function by releasing powerful dehydrating agents, such as boric acid or phosphoric acid, in the heat of a fire. The reaction then proceeds as follows:

$$(C_6H_{10}O_5)_n \rightarrow 6nC + 5nH_2O + \text{heat}$$
cellulose   carbon   water

This reaction, which occurs at 480 to 550°F (250–290°C), releases no inflammable gases; the carbon that results forms a layer of char that burns only at temperatures significantly higher than the burning temperature of untreated cellulose.

Flame-retarding agents that act by dehydration include monoammonium phosphate and dicyandiamide phosphate, which both release phosphoric acid when heated, and mixtures of borax and boric acid, whose active agent is boric acid. Finishes of this type do not affect the normal textile characteristics of treated fabric.

Cellulosic fabrics can also be made fire resistant by reacting them with organophosphorus compounds. These compounds, which release dehydrating phosphoric acid when heated, form chemical bonds with the fiber that make the flame-retarding agent highly resistant to washing and dry cleaning. Yarns and woven or knitted textiles can be treated by immersion in a bath of reactive phosphorus compounds; in the case of viscose rayon, the flame-retarding agent can be incorporated during the manufacture of the fiber.

Flame suppressants

Bromine compounds form a large class of flame-retarding agents that act through three mechanisms that are different from that of the

◀ Fabrics treated with flame-retarding agents are used to make protective clothing for people who work with sources of sparks, such as welding and grinding equipment.

dehydrating agents for cellulosic materials, thus allowing them a wider range of applications than the dehydrating agents. Bromine is a reactive element that can be readily introduced into the raw materials for fibers, plastics, and paints by chemical reaction. The bromine-modified raw materials then render the finished products flame resistant.

The first flame-retarding mechanism is heat absorption: when heated, this group of compounds evolve hydrogen bromide in a reaction that takes in heat from the fire, thereby hindering its propagation. The second mechanism interferes with the burning process directly: hydrogen bromide neutralizes free radicals, which are the reactive molecular fragments that participate in the chemical chain reactions of a fire. Finally, hydrogen bromide gas can form a dense layer that excludes oxygen and therefore stifles the fire.

SEE ALSO: FIBER, SYNTHETIC • FIREFIGHTING • FLAME AND IGNITION • PAINT • PROTECTIVE CLOTHING

Flame Thrower

The first controlled use of flame as a weapon of war is attributed to the Chinese in about 500 B.C.E. In 673 C.E., the Greek architect Kallinikos of Heliopolis invented "Greek fire" at Constantinople. The flame was projected forward from the bows of the Byzantine galleys against Arab ships and rapidly became a war-winning weapon. The Byzantines kept their secret for a long time, but the Moslems finally acquired it and used the fire against the Christians at the time of the Fifth Crusade. In medieval times in Europe, burning oil was frequently poured by defenders of castles and redoubts over attackers outside the walls.

The flame thrower was invented in the 1900s by the German engineer Richard Fiedler. He designed two different versions, a small flame thrower with a range of about 20 yards (18 m) and a larger and less portable weapon with a range of more than 40 yards (36 m). Both used pressurized gas to project the jet of flaming oil.

Weapons such as these were first used by the Germans during World War I against the French at Malancourt in France, in 1914, and against the British at Hooge in Belgium. Flame was also used as a weapon for dislodging troops from strong points. The British and French went on to invent their own versions, but all had a limited range and could fire only for a short period of time. In World War II, portable flame throwers were invented that could be carried on a soldier's back and that had a firing range of about 45 yards (41 m). Larger versions were mounted on tanks and had a range of 100 yards (90 m).

Modern flame throwers

Today, nearly all major armies have been equipped with portable flame throwers. In operation, they act in the same way as most larger equipment. A cylinder containing an inert gas—usually nitrogen—at considerable pressure is let into another cylinder or cylinders containing thickened fuel (petroleum gel) through a spring-loaded diaphragm. This action produces a working pressure of about 280 psi (19 bar), which will force the petroleum gel out of its container to a distance of around 164 ft. (50 m).

The trigger mechanism ignites a magnesium cartridge that lights the fuel to produce a jet of

▼ American soldiers on an exercise in the desert with a tank-mounted flame thrower.

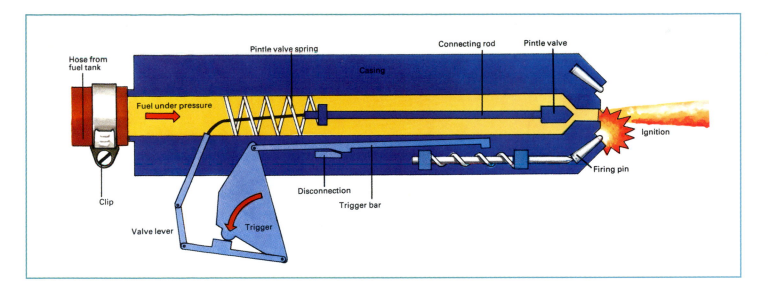

flame. On some models, unignited fuel can be projected to build up a supply around the target, which is then ignited with a burst of flame from the backpack. Unthickened fuel can also be used, but it cannot be projected to the ranges reached by petroleum gel. The U.S. Army and Marine Corps use the M9E1-7 portable flame thrower, which throws thickened fuel 130 to 165 ft. (40–50 m) but unthickened fuel only 65 to 80 ft. (20–25 m). Naturally, owing to its danger, the operator is issued with protective clothing.

The M9E1-7 uses igniter cartridges in a replaceable ignition cylinder to ignite the fuel. This model requires a few seconds between ignition and the time when throwing can begin, but the Italian model T-148/A uses an electronic ignition that is silent, instant, and invisible, and thus the operator's presence is not likely to be betrayed before the jet of flame is thrown.

Uses of flame throwers

All flame throwers are of limited range and are therefore not of much use in fast-moving warfare in open country. They come into their own when attacking an enemy in a confined space—caves, houses, or concrete bunkers. Apart from inflicting burns, flame in a confined space will devour all the oxygen available, suffocating an enemy and scorching oxygen-filled lungs. The use of flame has a strong psychological effect in shattering enemy morale, but it has largely been replaced by HESH antitank rockets, which are very effective against concrete and just as devastating to morale.

In an attempt to overcome the disadvantage of range, the U.S. Army and Marine Corps have the M202A2 multishot, portable flame weapon, which is basically an incendiary rocket launcher. It has a maximum range of 2,460 ft. (750 m) and a reusable launcher that can be fired from a standing, sitting, or kneeling position.

There are also larger flame-thrower weapons that need to be vehicle mounted. One of the most effective of these historically was the tank-mounted British Crocodile of World War II. This weapon could throw flame 390 ft. (119 m) and proved especially effective in operations in urban areas. Few modern armies deploy vehicle-mounted flame throwers today, although the U.S. Army has the M132 weapon, which is mounted on an armored personnel carrier and can be used to support armored infantry vehicle formations.

Napalm

When the Korean war erupted in 1950, the American forces were very much on the defensive, and in an effort to hold up the North Koreans, a new weapon, napalm, was used. First developed during World War II, this weapon was made from an aluminum salt consisting of naphthenic and aliphatic carboxylic acids. When added to gasoline, this salt had a thickening effect, creating a petroleum gel. Napalm was found to burn more slowly than gasoline and could be fired with greater accuracy. In addition, napalm had a sticky quality that caused it to remain attached to the surface of its target, where it would remain burning. When dropped from aircraft, napalm ignited spontaneously and produced a searing curtain of flame that destroyed villages, vehicles, tanks, and life. It was used again in Vietnam with equally effective results; by that time, it had been developed so that even if a victim jumped into a river, the gel would continue to burn down to the bone. The terrifying and destructive use of napalm in Vietnam contributed to demonstrations by antiwar protesters in the United States.

▲ The vintage British Ack-pack flame thrower introduced in 1945. The fuel flows through the nozzle under pressure from a backpack. Pressing the trigger releases the firing pin, which hits a replaceable cartridge, igniting the jet of fuel as it exits.

SEE ALSO: BOMB • FLAME AND IGNITION • FLAME-RETARDING AGENT

Flight Recorder

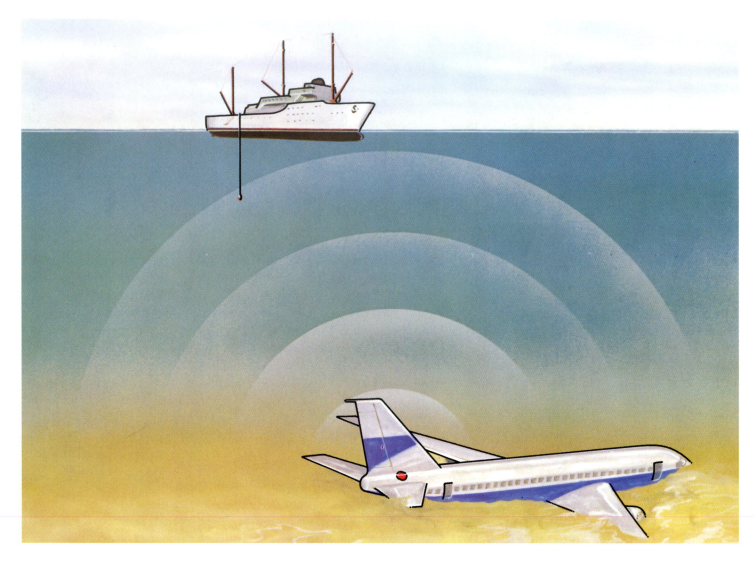

Flight recorders were first developed for military aviation. During World War II, aircraft of Britain's Royal Air Force sometimes carried wire recorders to enable postflight monitoring of radio transmissions. Other kinds of recorders were used to keep a record of a few channels of data while test flying prototype or experimental aircraft. By 1958, flight recording technology reached commercial aviation with the FDR (Flight Data Recorder), which was used to assist in crash diagnosis. Recording only a few parameters, such as airspeed, altitude as pressure, and some control surface positions, the FDR recorded continuously (or when switched on by a crew member in an emergency) and was protected against impact, fire, and water.

The early flight recorders used stainless steel wire or aluminum foil as the recording medium, and the signals were usually analog. These early FDRs were painted black and consequently became known as "black boxes." In 1965, a ruling was made that these boxes must be painted bright orange or yellow to make them easy to find. Despite this change they are still known to the majority of people as black boxes.

Technological developments

In the 1980s, flight recorders began to use digital tape to store the increasing amounts of data that aviation authorities require airlines to record. The moving parts of digital tape recorders are prone to damage, however, and in the 1990s, solid-state digital technology was introduced.

In a commercial airline installation today, there are two recorders referred to as flight recorders. The FDR is supplemented by the CVR (Cockpit Voice Recorder), which records audio signals from the aircraft communications system. The CVR records up to four channels of audio signals, including inputs from the individual crew members' microphones and from a cockpit microphone that is usually situated above the control panel between the two pilots and is used to pick up all the flight deck sounds.

▲ Flight recorders relay a 37.5 kHz acoustic signal when submerged in water to depths of 14,000 ft. (4,700 m). The signal operates for several weeks, giving adequate time for crash investigators to recover the recorder.

In the event of a crash, the FDR and CVR may be subjected to extreme conditions that could damage the sensitive electronic contents. For this reason, flight recorders are placed in the tail of the aircraft, which, in the event of a crash, is the area that usually experiences the least force. Flight recorders are constructed of thick steel with an internal layer of insulation to protect against extremes of temperature. Both FDRs and CVRs must undergo rigorous testing to ensure their ability to remain intact after a crash. They are shot at an aluminum target with a force producing 3,400 g, a 500 lb. (227 kg) spiked steel weight is dropped on them to test their resistance to penetration, they must be able to withstand flames of 2012°F (1100°C) and a crushing force of 5,000 lbs. (2,270 kg), and finally they must remain intact after 24 hours in a pressurized chamber filled with seawater.

Specifications

Some of the most recent FDRs contain 80 megabyte memories and use flash memory chips that are capable of storing data for several years without the need for any power source. This enables an FDR to record 25 hours of flight data while a CVR can record a maximum of 2 hours of voice data. FDRs may have the capacity to record over 300 different flight characteristics such as the position of wing flaps, altitude, and air speed. An underwater beacon called a "pinger" fastened to the side of FDRs and CVRs gives off an acoustic signal of 37.5 KHz from a depth down to 14,000 ft. (4,700 m). These beacons are activated when water reaches the battery inside them. They then transmit their signal for several weeks.

Immediately after a plane crash, both flight recorders must be recovered; then an investigation committee will begin to examine the recorded data. It is possible to use this data to create a computer-animated reconstruction of the final moment of the plane, helping investigators gain a full understanding of what may have happened to cause the crash.

In the United States, a crash investigation committee may be comprised of representatives from the Federal Aviation Administration (FAA), the National Transportation Safety Board (NTSB), the pilots union, the manufacturers of the airplane and engines, and the operator of the aircraft.

▼ A flight recorder must be strong enough to protect the delicate electronic circuitry from the force of a crash. A thick steel case provides strength, while resistance to extreme heat is provided by an internal layer of insulation. Bright orange coloration enables the box to be found easily by crash investigators.

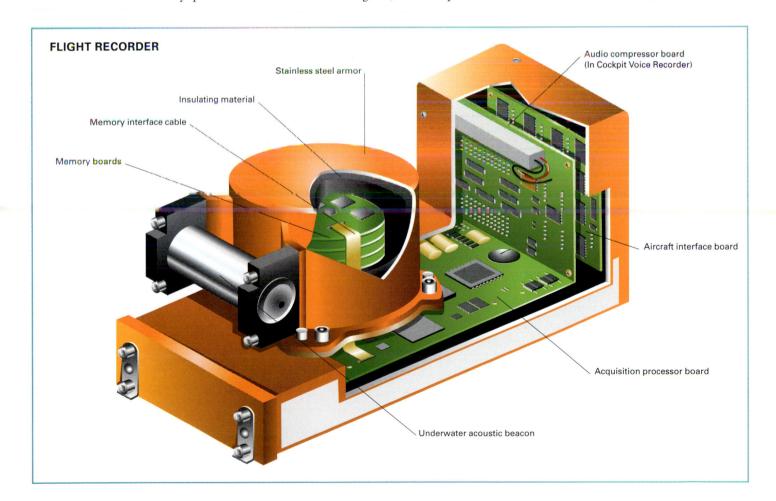

FLIGHT RECORDER

Stainless steel armor

Insulating material

Memory interface cable

Memory boards

Audio compressor board (In Cockpit Voice Recorder)

Aircraft interface board

Acquisition processor board

Underwater acoustic beacon

SEE ALSO: AIRCRAFT-CONTROL ENGINEERING • AIRLINER • DATA STORAGE • ELECTRONICS • INTEGRATED CIRCUIT

Flight Simulator

◄ A flight simulator using the WIDE visual display system. This simulator's complex motion base mechanism gives the pilot a realistic jolt on touchdown.

A flight simulator is a means by which pilots can learn the complex procedures necessary for the flying of modern aircraft without leaving the ground or putting themselves, their instructors, or their aircraft at risk.

When a pilot is in the cockpit or flight deck of a simulator, he or she flies an exact replica of the controls and instruments of a real aircraft, and the precise details of the terrain below are displayed on a screen. During the training exercise, the simulator is controlled exactly as though it were a real aircraft, and thus the pilot can encounter virtually every flying condition, including hazards such as storms, fog, air turbulence, and engine failure.

The pilot is not confined to visual interpretation. The simulator fuselage is mounted on hydraulic jacks or suspended from the frame in the larger systems so as to provide the same motion cues as the pilot would obtain in a real aircraft. Engine noise and other aircraft sounds are also faithfully reproduced. The whole system is computer controlled, usually by means of a high-speed digital computer.

The major use of flight simulators is for crew conversion, that is, the training of crews to oper-

▶ The WIDE visual display projects realistic, wide-angled images onto a mirror. Pilots can be tested for daytime, nighttime, and bad weather flying conditions. Simulators are also useful for practicing takeoffs and landings at difficult sites, such as the old airport at Hong Kong, which required careful piloting through tall skyscrapers, and whose runway ended at the harbor wall.

ate aircraft of types they have not flown before. It is usual for training to be completed with three or four hours of flying time in the actual airplane and the remaining 80 percent on the simulator.

History

Simulation began with the basic trainer of the 1930s, which was used for instruction in instruments and some flying procedures. In the late 1940s, analog computers were introduced, and the first electronic flight simulators were developed. The second major breakthrough came in the 1960s, when the power and speed of digital computers allowed the scope of simulators to be greatly extended.

Fuselage

The fuselage shells are built to the exact specification of the aircraft design drawings with additional structural strength to allow mounting on a base frame attached to the motion system. The cockpit equipment inside the shell consists mostly of genuine aircraft parts obtained from the manufacturer.

Control loading

The flying controls, throttle, pedestal and all the other load-generating units are mounted on a subframe forming part of the fuselage base. They provide exact simulation of both constant and variable control feel. As with a real airplane, the throttle levers need an initial breakout force to move them and subsequent friction as they are moved. In addition, the flying controls have a realistic changing load characteristic according to

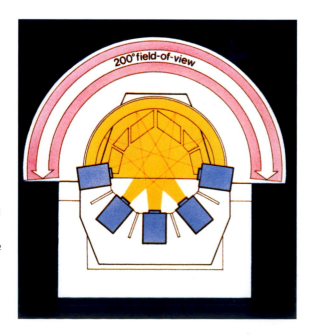

the simulated aircraft's speed. Hydraulic jacks are normally used to enable all these different effects to be simulated.

Instructor's facilities

The instructor has a control station at the rear of the flight deck. From there, he or she can set up the conditions of a training flight by selecting from a list of preprogrammed training exercises and can constantly monitor the program by means of a display screen. The instructor can also record and play back sections of a training exercise. The whole flight can be checked, or an experienced pilot's handling of a given situation may be demonstrated. Radio aids can be simulated for bearings, course selection, and landings, and recorded messages from control towers and ground stations can be used for realism.

Audio system

The audio system faithfully reproduces all the noises normally heard on the flight deck. The noises are generated electronically and correctly mixed and controlled by the computer. These sounds are then replayed through loudspeakers positioned to suggest that the noises are originating from the appropriate instrument or direction.

Computer and interface

Modern flight simulators use digital computers to handle the information that must be stored and made instantly available when required. Such computers are high-speed machines that can carry out, in real time, the calculations needed to make the simulator appear completely realistic.

The required aircraft data are converted into computer programs and are loaded into the computer memory. It is necessary to convert analog signals to digital form, and vice versa, and this conversion is carried out by the interface equipment. An action by the flight crew, for example, adjusting the altimeter setting, is a physical event that generates an analog signal. This signal must be converted to a digital signal so that the computer can process it, and the result of the processing must be converted back to an analog signal that can be used to activate the appropriate instruments on the flight deck. These conversions must be made almost simultaneously to ensure realism, and solid-state interface units capable of making 20 complete conversions per second are commonly used.

Motion systems

The human body is extremely sensitive to changes of speed or direction, and it is essential to provide the pilot with motion cues in the simula-

tor to make the training more complete. This goal is achieved by fitting the simulator cabin onto a motion-generating system that reproduces all the motion effects felt within a moving airplane. Each effect is produced by attaching the cabin to a series of separate hydraulic jacks. These jacks move to provide the cabin motion, the most advanced system giving three rotation cues and three displacement cues. The rotation cues are pitch, roll, and yaw, and the displacement cues are surge (fore and aft motion), heave (up and down), and sway (side to side).

Visual system

There are two main types of visual system in use today, with a third growing rapidly in importance. The most popular is a closed-circuit color television system in which the camera views a three-dimensional scale model of a landscape through an optical probe that scans across it in such a way as to simulate the flight of an aircraft over it in response to signals from the computer.

The second major system uses color photography from an aircraft flying on a particular flight path. Advanced projection techniques allow the images to be distorted so as to simulate movement around the line of the recorded flight path, and the "flying" speed can be varied. Both these systems can be used to simulate day and night flying.

The latest system is known as Computer Generated Image (CGI). A model of the scene, stored in the computer, is continually changed to correspond with the appropriate view as the simulated position, altitude, and speed of the aircraft change.

▲ A Novoview SP1 computer-generated image of the approach to Athens airport, presented to the flight deck of an Orion Airways' Rediffusion B737-300 flight simulator using the WIDE display system.

SEE ALSO:	AIRCRAFT-CONTROL ENGINEERING • AIRCRAFT DESIGN • HYDRAULICS • VIRTUAL REALITY

Flood Control

In 1954, a hurricane in the Atlantic generated a tidal surge that struck the New England coast and resulted in the loss of 60 lives and damage of approximately $600 million. The following year the four major river basins of southern New England experienced devastating floods that killed 90 people and produced damage of $530 million. Farther afield, in 1999, between 10,000 and 20,000 people were killed by mud slides and flash flooding along Venezuela's Caribbean coast. An estimated 150,000 were left homeless. These are typical examples of the havoc that floods, whether from sea or river, can create and are a justification for the massive investment by governments around the world in flood control projects.

An estimated 12 percent of the population of the United States lives on land that is subject to periodic flooding. In Canada, the proportion is similar. The amount of housing and industrial development on flood plains continues to grow as will the damage and loss of life from flooding unless extensive measures to control floods are adopted.

▲ The Thames Flood Barrier spans the river at Woolwich in east London. The barrier, 1,837 ft. (560 m) across, took eight years and cost over $400 million to build. Flood protection for London has become more important as the city slowly sinks and the water level continues to rise, threatening to flood adjoining areas during high tides.

River flooding

Natural river channels are formed by water (usually rain) draining from the land. This water, known as runoff, moves under gravity to the lowest point of the land and ultimately finds its way to the sea. At the low point of the land, where the runoff is concentrated, a channel will be a function of the area from which the runoff is derived and of the rainfall that occurs. It will not grow in size indefinitely but will, after a long period of time, reach a limit and not enlarge itself further.

The discharge (that is the volumetric rate of flow measured, for example, in cubic feet per second) that the channel can accept without flooding the adjoining land, called the bankfull discharge, occurs more frequently than once a year. The exact frequency is not known, but analysis of the discharge records of rivers in Britain has shown that the bankfull discharge is equaled or exceeded once every six months. It is recognized, however, that the bankfull capacity of a channel is less than the maximum discharge that the channel will have to deal with. It is inevitable then that flooding will occur.

When rain sufficient to cause a flood starts to fall on the catchment area of a river, the discharge in the river progressively increases with time as runoff from more distant parts of the catchment arrives downstream. Because a rainstorm lasts for a limited time, the discharge will gradually rise to a peak and start to decrease when the runoff starts to diminish. This variation in river discharge with time is called a flood hydrograph. The flood can be regarded as a large wave, which, as it travels down the river, changes shape, mainly as a result of the volume of water that is stored in the river channel and on the flood plain at any particular moment of time. The peak of the wave becomes flatter and the maximum discharge decreases. This feature is known as attenuation (reduction). It is possible to calculate how the flood wave will attenuate as it travels down the valley (routing the flood) although the computations are complex.

Protection measures against river flooding can be divided into those that lower the flood water levels by reducing the peak of the hydrograph and those that confine the flood to specific, well-defined areas.

Peak flow reduction

One method of reducing the flood discharge is to reduce the rate at which water runs off the contributing catchment area: this can be achieved by land treatment measures such as afforestation, control of soil erosion, and improving agricultural techniques. These measures are intended to delay the direct overland runoff to the river and to increase the amount of moisture stored in the soil.

Reservoirs and flood confinement

Storage can also be provided by constructing a dam across the river to form a reservoir. The dam incorporates an overflow structure—a spillway—

often fitted with movable gates, which is used to control the discharge that is released from the reservoir to the river downstream. At the beginning of the flood season, the water level in the reservoir is at a level that provides sufficient room to store floodwater without overtopping the dam. During a flood, water is released from the reservoir through the spillway at such a rate that serious flooding downstream from the dam is prevented: this release rate will be less than the rate at which water is entering the reservoir, and the difference between the two flow rates will be taken into reservoir storage.

For economic reasons, reservoirs now commonly fulfill a number of different functions, such as flood control, irrigation, hydroelectric power, and water supply, and chains of such multipurpose

reservoirs are to be found on some of the world's major rivers and their tributaries. Because of the multipurpose nature of these reservoirs, it is very important that they are operated efficiently with the aim of maintaining the water levels in the reservoirs as high as possible while providing a sufficient volume of floodwater storage.

In order to operate a chain of reservoirs as an efficient unit, it is necessary to be able to predict when a flood is likely to occur, what its hydrograph will be, and how it will attenuate in its progress along the river to the reservoir so that the inflow into the reservoir can be determined. It is also necessary to know how the water released from the reservoir (which will also act as a flood wave) will attenuate in its passage downstream. This information is required quickly to allow suf-

THE THAMES BARRIER

Half a million tons of concrete were used to build the piers of the barrier and the sills on which the gates rest on the riverbed when being used. When raised, each of the four main gates is as high as a five-story building and as wide as the opening of Tower Bridge (183 ft., or 61 m), with the two gate arms weighing 9,600 tons (8,700 tonnes). The gates are moved by electrically powered "hydraulic power packs." The power packs are housed immediately below the stainless steel shells. Electrical power is crucial for barrier operation, and as well as three alternative supplies, there are three on-site power generators. Since its completion in 1982, the Thames Barrier has been raised more than 30 times, largely as a precaution.

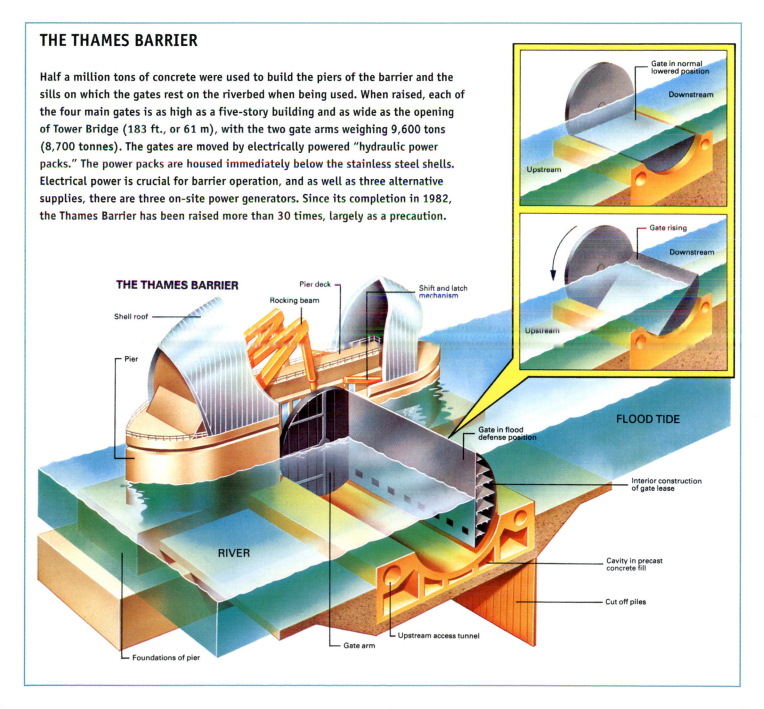

Other methods

In the middle and lower reaches of a river, there is often a lack of suitable sites for large storage reservoirs, and other methods of preventing flooding have to be used.

The channel can be enlarged so that its bankfull capacity is increased. Enlargement sometimes leads to problems with sediment deposition, and often the amount of enlargement that is practicable does not significantly lower the water levels for the more infrequently occurring floods.

Another method is to provide an additional channel at places where it is necessary to lower the water levels, for example, through towns. The additional channel is designed so that it operates only when floods occur—some of the flood water spills into it, the discharge in the main channel is reduced, and floodwater levels are lowered. The flood-relief channel either rejoins the main river farther downstream or is linked to another river that drains away the excess water.

Finally, it is possible to build levees—banks on the flood plain—that run alongside and close to the river channel. When floods occur, they are prevented from spreading over the flood plain.

Now, computer models can predict reasonably accurately the effect of flood-alleviation measures. Small-scale models of rivers continue to provide a means of accurately reproducing the behavior of the river in nature and thus provide a satisfactory way of determining flood-protection

ficient time for releasing water from a reservoir before the flood arrives there, should this be necessary. This used to be an impossible task because of the time required for the calculations, but by using computers it is now possible to plan reservoir operations more efficiently. Development work has been going on to improve the mathematical techniques involved, and computer models of such reservoir systems are now common.

Two types of computer model can be used for studies such as this: a digital model that uses arithmetical operations to solve the equations that are involved and an analog model that uses physical analogies for the variables in the problem, for example, an electrical analogy in which discharge is represented by an electric current, water level by a voltage or potential, and storage by the charge on a capacitor. For certain problems, analog models are faster than digital models.

One of the earliest computer models of such a reservoir system was that of the Kansas River, built in the early 1960s by the United States Corps of Engineers. Digital and analog computer models were both built. Rainfall forecasts were fed to the computers to determine the most effective way to operate the reservoir system—for example, the sequence of water-lowering operations in the various reservoirs. Flood warnings were also given by the models.

In Britain, considerable research has been undertaken to develop long- and short-term control strategies for a reservoir system on the River Dee, one of the aims being flood alleviation.

▲ The Delta Project has shortened the Netherlands coastline by building a series of huge dams and dikes to hold back floodwaters.

▶ The Netherlands has been struggling to hold back the sea for centuries. About half the country now lies behind flood barriers below sea level.

As a result of the 1953 disaster, the Netherlands government undertook its Delta plan, building fixed and movable barriers across the mouths of the Maas and Scheldt rivers: it was designed to protect the Dutch coast against a storm flood that would occur only once every 10,000 years.

In Britain, the Greater London Council built a tidal barrier and raised riverbanks in the Thames Estuary in order to protect the capital city against tidal surges. The barrier comprises four main gates and six minor gates. The main gates lie flat in shallow troughs in the bed of the Thames River. Only when a surge tide threatens are the gates rotated to block the river. The Thames Barrier is sited east of central London at a point where the river is 1,706 ft. (520 m) wide.

After the surge tide has abated, the barrier remains closed until the tide falls to the same height as the trapped upstream pool, ensuring that the opening of the gates causes no erosion to the riverbed or the piers of the barrier.

The barrier has over 50 staff, and computers are used to monitor weather trends and to manage the operation of the structure. Total reliability has been designed into the Thames Barrier—gates can be operated from one end only if necessary, and three separate sources of electricity are available to power the hydraulic gate mechanisms.

requirements. The Hydraulics Research Station at Wallingford in Britain has studied many such problems by means of small-scale models. A model of the Trent River in Britain was used to determine the height and position of flood banks that would be sufficient to prevent flooding from exceptionally large river discharges.

Tidal flooding

The effects of tidal flooding are similar to those of river flooding although the causes are different. Atmospheric depressions (low pressure zones) over the sea can cause the water level beneath them to rise significantly; in addition, they also produce strong winds. As the depression moves or weakens, it and its associated winds may cause a surge to form, and thus create unusually high and possibly dangerous water levels if it coincides with a high tide.

Catastrophic tidal flooding occurred in 1953 when a depression in the North Sea caused a surge to move southward, producing a level in the Thames Estuary, Britain, that was 6 ft. (2 m) higher than predicted and a level at the Dutch coast that was also much higher than predicted. The surge gave rise to disastrous flooding in southeast England and in the Netherlands, and altogether over 2,100 lives were lost. Protection against such tidal flooding can be provided either by the construction of sea defense walls that are high enough to prevent overtopping or, in the case of an estuary, by means of a barrier, usually in the form of movable gates that can be raised and lowered.

▲ Sandbags provide an emergency form of defense against flooding in urban environments. Changes in land use near towns and cities and larger areas of paving and roads have increased the prospect of flooding during heavy rainfall—the rain cannot soak into the soil quickly enough and instead runs off into nearby watercourses or collects in low lying parts of the town.

FACT FILE

- The damming of the Maas River in the Netherlands in 1270 helped cause a major disaster in a later century. The dam was built to protect the surrounding countryside from tidal flooding. The protected areas were drained and reclaimed, and many villages were built. These were inundated with catastrophic effect in 1421 during a freak flooding.

- The regular flooding of the Nile, which created Egypt's fertile earth, sometimes had to be controlled. To this end, the hydraulic engineers of the pharaohs dug a canal parallel to the river into Lake Moeris, which was linked to the Nile by regulating sluices. In time of dangerous flooding, an earth dike was deliberately breached to provide a controlled flood.

SEE ALSO: DAM • HYDRAULICS • LAND RECLAMATION • TIDE

Floor Covering

◄ Complex designs can be created using linoleum. Shapes are carefully cut out of different-colored pieces of linoleum and are then fitted together to form the final design.

Floor coverings can be made from a wide variety of materials, including resins, textiles, felts, and oils. They provide warmth, comfort, and protection as well as enjoyment for their aesthetic appeal. Floor coverings may be hard or soft, smooth or contoured, and they may be attached to the floor or laid upon the surface.

Smooth floor coverings

Linoleum, or lino, is made from linseed oil and various other substances, such as gums, resins, chalk, and wood flour. The oil from linseed, also known as flaxseed, comes from a plant that is closely related to the flax grown to make linen. In the original process for making linoleum, successive thin layers of linseed oil were allowed to oxidize, one on top of the next. This process was repeated until a thick layer of oxidized linseed oil had been built up, which was then fluxed using resin. This process was slow, however, and was eventually replaced by a faster method whereby the linseed oil is heated and stirred in large drums, thus speeding up the oxidation process. When the oil has thickened, resin is added, and this mixture is stirred and heated, making it liquid once more. Other materials, such as wood flour and dyes, may be added at this stage, after which the mixture is rolled out into sheets and a backing is added. The linoleum is then hung and heated in a building called a stove. The heating process, which may take several weeks, hardens the linoleum making it resistant to indentation.

Linoleum has many qualities that make it an ideal floor covering. It is naturally warm and is resistant to fire, staining, and wear and tear. It can also be used very creatively to produce effects such as marbling and can be cut to make colorful and complex patterns.

Vinyl flooring is made using either vinyl chloride or vinyl acetate. These materials provide hard, durable surfaces that may be dyed, patterned with a rotogravure printed surface, or embossed. A protective wearlayer—made of either urethane or polyvinyl chloride (PVC)—reduces risk of damage to the surface. Vinyl flooring is warm and may be made softer by the addition of a foam backing.

Cork floor tiles are made by a process of heating ground cork that causes the granules to stick together. This cork mixture can then be made into tiles that are warm and soft underfoot. Cork tiles, however, lack the durability of either linoleum or vinyl.

Rubber may be used to make a hard-wearing floor covering. In the past, natural rubber was used, but today synthetic rubbers are produced to make this kind of flooring. Though very resilient, rubber flooring can be expensive and may be damaged by grease.

Carpets

Carpets are a comparatively recent innovation in the Western world, and few were seen except in the houses of the rich before the 18th century. They did not become widespread until the invention of mechanized carpet looms during the Industrial Revolution of the 19th century. Carpets had, however, been made on hand looms in the East for a very long time. The oldest carpet known is the Pazyryk carpet, which dates from about 500 B.C.E. It was found in a tomb in the Altai mountains of Central Asia: the log-lined chambers of this tomb had filled with ice, preserving their contents perfectly over the centuries.

Handmade carpets

The Pazyryk carpet is Persian and was made using the Ghiordes, or Turkish, knot, still the most common for handmade carpets. These carpets are made on looms, as for simple woven materials, but instead of one yarn (the weft) simply being woven in and out of the other (the warp), a third yarn, to make the pile, is included. This step is done by knotting the pile yarn on each warp thread in turn, then threading through the weft in the normal way, usually twice or three times for each row of knots. The weaving is then pushed down with the fingers or a comb so that the knots are firmly trapped by the weft. Another row of knots is then made, and so on.

The knots used, such as the Ghiordes and the Sehna, the most common types, are designed so that both ends point outward, taking in one or two warp threads for each knot. By choosing different colors of pile yarn, the intricate patterns of carpets can be built up. The pile is cut to a uniform length when the carpet has been completed.

The Ghiordes knot, used with a longer pile, is the coarser of the two and can be used only for straight-line patterns. Any attempt at a curve gives a stepped, ill-defined appearance. The Sehna knot is more secure and can therefore be used with a shorter pile and a finer mesh. Curved and often more complex designs can be produced using this knot.

Carpet types

The size of the mesh can vary widely, a typical value being about 250 knots per sq. in. (40 knots per cm²), in which case the knots are about 1/16 in. (2 mm) apart. Some carpets may have millions of knots and take several years to make.

Oriental carpets and rugs can be classified according to their pattern and the way they were made. Nomadic tribes make carpets on portable horizontal looms that can be dismantled when moving from camp to camp in search of new pastures for the sheep. These carpets usually have bold geometric patterns with vertical, horizontal, and diagonal lines. Flowers, animals, insects, stars, and so on are rendered in geometric terms. The works nomads produce are usually fairly small rugs, the size being dictated by tent and saddle requirements, and are made of wool with a little camel hair and silk added.

Carpets produced in villages are often stylized, with repeated geometric patterns, more subdued than the nomadic designs. Because the looms are more permanent, the carpets are longer.

◄ A rug loom with revolving beams, but no pedals, set up for weaving.

► Linoleum is made from a combination of different raw materials, including linseed oil, resin, wood flour, chalk, burlap, polyester, and a variety of colored dyes.

The most striking oriental carpets are those made on a large scale in court or studio workshops. They often have intricate floral designs and may be up to 40 ft. (12 m) in length. Many of these carpets, which date back to the 16th century, are impressive works of art. Fine wool, silk, gold, and silver threads were woven by children, whose small fingers were particularly adept at weaving the fine intricate designs. To guide the weavers, a template of squared paper, where each square represented a knot, was frequently used.

Not all carpets have a pile. The Turkish kilim, for example, is a straightforward woven fabric with no knots. In this case, designs are produced by the weft colors; instead of the weft always going from one side to the other, it is doubled back when partway across, so producing small batches of a color.

Dyes

The often brilliant dyes are produced from local vegetation, such as madder root (red), sumac (yellow and brown), and indigo (blue). Pomegranates, walnuts, and other fruits also give stable dyes when fixed with a mordant. These are mineral or vegetable substances that react chemically with the dye, forming an insoluble compound that attaches itself firmly to the yarn. Typical mordants are alum, tin oxide, and iron sulfate.

► A rear view of a gripper Axminster loom showing the lines of pile yarn leading into the back of the machine.

European developments

The art of carpet making by hand spread from the East into Europe, where it became established in France and Flanders. A new technique of nonknotted weaving was developed, known as Brussels weaving; the principles used in this weaving turned out to be suitable for large-scale mechanization and industrial automation.

The pile in a Brussels carpet is formed of loops rather than free ends. The pile yarn is looped over rods laid across the loom during manufacture and later withdrawn. In the simple knotted carpet, there is only one layer of warp and weft, but in the Brussels carpet there are two layers, with two shots of weft sandwiching an extra pair of yarns called stuffers, which strengthen the fabric.

Wilton carpets

Toward the close of the 17th century, persecution of the Huguenot Protestants in Europe forced them to flee to Britain. Some settled in Wilton, Wiltshire, where the Wilton carpet was developed. This carpet uses a Brussels weave but with the rods replaced by blades that cut the loops to form tufts as the blade is withdrawn.

The invention of the Jacquard loom in France in 1801 made it possible to weave Brussels and Wilton carpets in up to five colors. Each color of pile is used over the whole area of one carpet, but only the color that is to be seen at any one spot is brought out as a loop. This extra layer of pile, though wasteful, gives a luxurious thickness to the carpet.

Wilton carpets are still made on large mechanical Jacquard looms. One type of machine weaves two carpets at once, face to face, with the loops going from one half to the other. A single blade is used to separate the two and cut the tufts.

Axminster carpets

In 1755, Thomas Witty, a cloth weaver in Axminster, Britain, set up a factory producing hand-knotted carpets of fine quality. Thus, the use of the word Axminster to describe many carpet processes in which the tufts are inserted individually rather than as a continuous weave.

Both processes in use today for making Axminster carpets are based on inventions of Halcyon Skinner of Yonkers, New York, but were developed by firms in Kidderminster, Britain. The spool Axminster machines have each color required for the pile of the carpet (in theory an unlimited number) preloaded side by side on horizontal spools the width of the carpet. One spool is prepared for each line of pile, and the spools are arranged one above the other on an endless chain so that after a while the pattern is repeated. A typical number of spools is 288, with the pattern reoccurring every yard or meter; a repeat which has come to be standard.

In the gripper Axminster mechanism, a smaller number of different colors, usually eight, is possible. Instead of a separate spool for each line there is a metal strip called a carrier, with a row of eight holes through which each color of pile yarn, loaded on bobbins, projects. There is a row of carriers, each one offering a choice of eight colors, across the width of the carpet, with one carrier for each line of tufts in the finished carpet—usually about seven per inch (2.5 cm). For each carrier, there is a gripper. These are beaklike mechanisms that transfer the pile to the weaving point, where they are woven into the carpet as in the spool Axminster method. Another version, the spool gripper, combines features of both types, with grippers taking the pile directly from the spools.

Axminster carpets are more economical on pile than Wiltons, since none of the pile is lying beneath the visible part, though this is often compensated for by making the pile thicker. They can be cheaper and are therefore more widely used.

Tufted carpets

A large share of the market for carpets has been taken by the tufted carpets. These put soft floorcoverings within the reach of many more people and led to an enormous increase in carpet production. Tufting involves stitching tufts to a previously woven fabric. A needle inserts the pile from what is to be the underside of the carpet in a comparable sewing operation.

It is held by a hook-shaped looper, which has a knife at one end to sever the loops and make the pile. To hold the pile in place, a coating of rubber latex is spread over the underside. A layer of burlap material is often added for stability, which can give the impression that the carpet is woven.

A variety of techniques for producing carpets are based on sticking fibers or tufts onto an adhesive-coated backing. In one process, flocked carpets are made by directing chopped fibers of uniform length onto an adhesive-coated backing using an electrostatic field to project them and maintain their upright position to form a pile.

Carpet tiles

Carpet tiles are a popular alternative to carpet laid in rolls in offices and public places. They are rubber backed and made in exactly the same way as flocked carpet, usually in 15 in. (400 mm) squares, and laid as any other floor tile, usually directly onto the floor.

▼ A tufted carpet loom making a sculptured, patterned pile carpet.

SEE ALSO: ANILINE AND AZO DYES • DYEING PROCESS • FIBER, NATURAL • FIBER, SYNTHETIC • LOOM • PRINTING • RUBBER, NATURAL • RUBBER, SYNTHETIC • SPINNING

Flowmeter

Flowmeters are instruments for measuring the speeds of fluids in general and liquids in particular. As such, they are closely related to anemometers, which measure the flow of gases, and one type, the full bore vortex meter, can be used for measuring either gases or liquids.

Flowmeters measure the rate of flow of fluids in a confined space such as a pipe, although sometimes the flow rate in an open channel is required. Usually the measurement required is the volume of fluid flowing past a point in a given time, and it is calibrated in units such as gallons per hour or cubic meters or cubic feet per second. Flowmeters are used to measure oil and gas flow in pipelines, in automobile fuel lines for fuel gauges, and on seabeds to measure the water current.

Differential pressure meters

Probably the most widely used method of industrial flow measurement are differential pressure ($\triangle$P) meters. They are available in a variety of types, such as orifice plates, venturi tubes, and Dall tubes, but all operate on the principle that fluid accelerated through a restriction has its kinetic energy increased at the expense of its pressure energy, which can then be measured.

With venturi meters, the pipe has a smooth and gradual reduction in cross-sectional area and a similar expansion back to the normal pipe size farther downstream. Because of the smooth contours, as the pipe expands, no turbulence (eddy currents) is created in the fluid; turbulence would lead to a pressure drop. These venturi meters are, however, more expensive to produce than both the flow-nozzle and orifice types.

Flow-nozzle meters have a nozzle-shaped restriction fitted in the pipe that, like the venturi meter, introduces a smooth and gradual change in pipe area. The nozzle, however, ends abruptly with an immediate return to full pipe size. Pressure measurement is taken before and after the nozzle, but the principle is the same as the venturi meter.

The orifice plate is the simplest and cheapest type of the three—consisting of a thin plate with a hole in the middle of it, mounted across the pipe. Pressure measurement, as in the flow-nozzle meter, is taken before and after the plate.

Trapping and passing

Positive displacement (PD) meters operate by trapping a known volume of fluid, passing it from inlet to outlet, and counting the number of fluid "packets" that pass. An output shaft drives through gearing to a local display counter; by selection of suitable gearing, a readout in the required volumetric units can be obtained. A pulse generator, either optical or electromagnetic, may also be fitted for transmission to a remote-control room. Because of their high performance, PD meters are widely used for flow measurement of fuel oils and other hydrocarbon products in small pipe sizes.

Electromagnetic flowmeters

Faraday established that the emf (electromotive force) induced in a conductor moving through a magnetic field is proportional to the velocity of the conductor—and this is the principle on which the electromagnetic flowmeter is based.

An electromagnetic flowmeter consists of a nonmagnetic stainless steel pipe lined with an insulating material. A magnetic field is produced across the tube by exciting coils arranged around the outside. Liquid passing through the flowmeter becomes the conductor; the emf induced by the fluid in the magnetic field is proportional to the fluid velocity. The signal is fed into a unit that amplifies the emf and converts it into a standard mA (milliampere) analog signal.

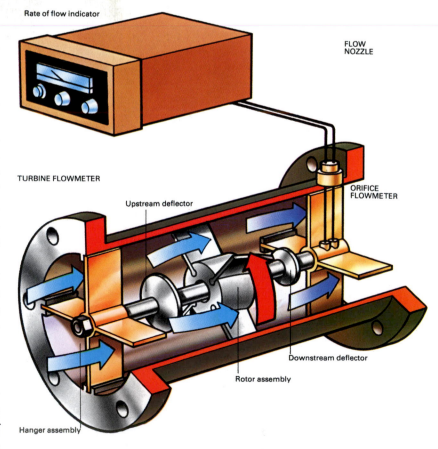

▼ A turbine flowmeter measures flow rates by the speed of rotation of its blades.

Rate of flow indicator

FLOW NOZZLE

ORIFICE FLOWMETER

TURBINE FLOWMETER

Upstream deflector

Downstream deflector

Rotor assembly

Hanger assembly

◀ Four 63 in. (160 cm) detector heads undergoing low calibration at a factory in Britain for use in a water-supply project. Detector heads, as part of an electromagnetic flowmeter system, can be used for measuring the flow rate of virtually any electrically conductive liquid or slurry.

Because electromagnetic flowmeters can be made from materials that are chemically compatible with virtually all liquids, they can be used on many extremely corrosive or aggressive liquids that are difficult or impossible to meter with most other types of flow measurement equipment. The principal limitation with the electromagnetic flowmeter is that the meter is not suitable for gas or nonconductive liquids.

Turbine meters

A turbine meter consists basically of a bladed rotor suspended in a fluid stream with its axis of rotation perpendicular to the flow direction. The rotor is driven by liquid against the blades; its angular velocity is proportional to the volume flow rate. A pickup coil on the outside of the meter body detects rotor motion, and the output signal produced is a continuous sine wave voltage pulse train, with each pulse representing a small discrete volume of the liquid. Turbine meters are widely used for high-accuracy customs and custody transfer measurement of such products as crude oil or petroleum.

Rotameters

Variable area flowmeters—also called rotameters—use the same principle as differential pressure meters—the relationship between kinetic energy and pressure energy. In the $\triangle P$ system, the restriction size is fixed and the differential pressure changes according to flow rate; by contrast, in the variable area meter, the area of restriction changes as the flow rate changes and the pressure differential remains constant.

In its simplest form, a rotameter has a tapered glass tube with a scribed scale, and flow can be read directly. Rotameters are widely used in applications where only local flow indication is required for small volumes of clean fluids.

Shedding vortexes

Vortex meters are based on a natural phenomenon known as vortex shedding. As a vortex sheds from one side of a bluff body (a body with a broad, flattened front), the liquid velocity on that side increases and the pressure decreases; on the opposite side, a velocity decrease and pressure increase occur, resulting in a net pressure change across the bluff body. The entire effect is then reversed as the next vortex sheds from the opposite side. Consequently, velocity and pressure distribution around the bluff body change at the same frequency as shedding frequency. Various methods are used to detect pressure or velocity change.

A capacitance vortex meter is a bluff body with a capacitance detector. A full bore vortex meter combines in one meter many advantages and features that are not found collectively in any other type of flowmeter. One remarkable feature is that the same vortex meter can be used to measure liquid or gas, and the calibration remains the same for either fluid—within normal tolerances. Vortex meters are now being considered as viable technical and commercial alternatives to orifice plates in many applications.

SEE ALSO: ANEMOMETER • HYDRODYNAMICS • METER, GAS • PIPELINE • PRESSURE • VENTURI EFFECT

Fluidics

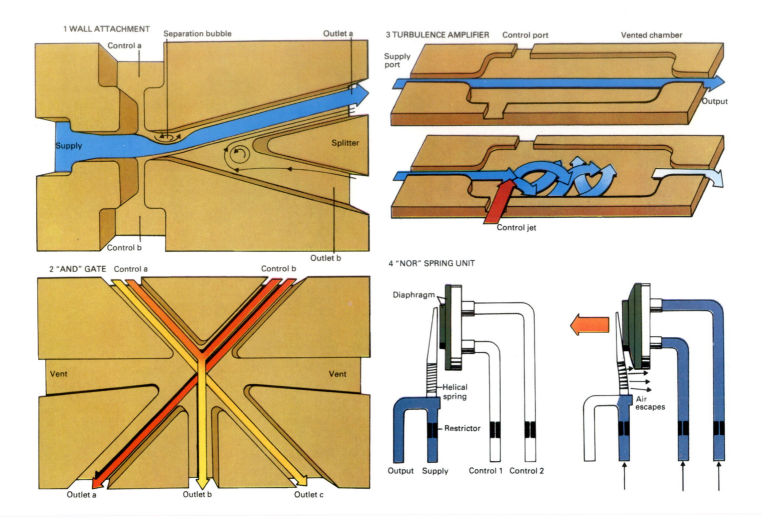

1 WALL ATTACHMENT — Control a — Separation bubble — Outlet a — Supply — Splitter — Control b — Outlet b

2 "AND" GATE — Control a — Control b — Vent — Vent — Outlet a — Outlet b — Outlet c

3 TURBULENCE AMPLIFIER — Control port — Vented chamber — Supply port — Output — Control jet

4 "NOR" SPRING UNIT — Diaphragm — Helical spring — Restrictor — Output — Supply — Control 1 — Control 2 — Air escapes

Fluidics, also known as fluid logic, is concerned with the design and application of fluid-operated switching systems, analogous to electronic logic circuits, which can be used, for example, to control machine tools and industrial processes. The science of fluidics was developed at the Harry Diamond Ordnance Laboratories in the United States and was based on investigations carried out in the 1930s by Henri Coanda, a Romanian scientist living in France.

The fluid used to perform logic operations can be either a liquid or a gas, but in practice gases operate much faster than liquids and are more widely used. There are several ways in which a stream of fluid can be controlled, but the most common systems use the wall attachment, or Coanda, effect.

Coanda effect

The Coanda effect was discovered in the 1900s when Coanda was experimenting with a very early rocket-propelled plane. Forward propulsion of the plane was by streams of hot gases issuing from outlets at the front of the fuselage. The gases were

directed toward the rear at an angle of 45 degrees to the fuselage, and as the plane gathered speed, the slipstream caused these jets to be deflected against the sides of the fuselage, which promptly caught fire, causing a very hasty end to the experiment. In the 1930s, Coanda investigated the reasons why the streams of gas had clung to the fuselage and developed the theories that formed the basis for the science of fluidics.

Water running from a faucet falls in a stream under the influence of gravity, but if a solid object (such as a finger) is put into the stream, the water will run along it, providing the flow is not too fast. Atmospheric pressure acts all around the water, except where it contacts the solid object and presses the stream of water against the surface so that it follows the object instead of falling straight. This is the Coanda, or wall attachment, effect.

A jet of fluid will attach itself to any reasonably smooth surface in this way, unless the angles become too acute. This principle applies to any fluid as long as laminar flow is maintained, that is, as long as the fluid continues to flow in layers, or laminae. Turbulent flow will occur when the lam-

▲ Four types of fluidic devices. Fluid flow in (1) is switched between outlets by a control jet. The AND gate (2) gives an output at outlet b only when there is an input at both control ports. Type (3) uses a control jet to break up the laminar flow, reducing output pressure. In (4) air normally flows from supply to output, but input in either control line will move the diaphragm and bend the spring. Air then escapes through the spring coils.

inar flow breaks up and the fluid flows in a disorganized, swirling manner.

This jet can be deflected by the action of another jet directed against it at right angles so that a jet attached to one wall of a tube, for instance, could be switched to the opposite wall. The deflecting jet need not be continuous; a single pulse will do. The deflecting force can be very much smaller than the force of the main jet, making it possible to build fluidic amplifiers, as a small force can control much larger ones.

Fluidic devices

Detailed research was carried out in the 1950s to develop fluid logic devices that would function reliably in hostile environments, and the uses envisaged were in aerospace and military applications. Fluidic circuits were intended to be used in situations of extreme temperature, humidity, or radiation that would destroy most electronic components. A number of devices were developed that would perform basic logic functions in the same way as electronic circuits, using the Coanda effect or other principles such as the turbulence amplifier. Complete circuits can now be built up that have no moving parts and that require only a low-pressure air supply; this may be anywhere from 0.5 to 25 psi (0.035–1.76 bar) but is usually around 2 to 7 psi (0.14–0.49 bar).

The range of logic devices using the Coanda principle covers all the basic logic functions including bistable amplifiers, or flipflops, AND gates, OR gates, invert OR gates, NOR gates, memories, and shift registers. They can be built up to form integrated circuits, greatly reducing the bulk and also the possibility of connections being broken.

A widely used fluidic device that does not work on the Coanda principle is the turbulence amplifier. It consists of a tube with a flow of air that is just laminar. A very small input from a cross jet breaks the laminar flow and starts turbulence, so there is no longer any laminar output.

As fluidic devices are used for switching and logic purposes, there are also a number of devices for interfacing them with electromechanical or electronic equipment, often types of pressure transducers and valves. Some fluidic devices also have simple moving parts, and these are often used where higher-pressure operation is required.

Uses

As most fluidic devices have no moving parts, they remain trouble free as long as the air supply is kept clean. The most likely fault is a disconnected pipe, but this is easily detected and repaired. In addition, fluidic devices are more easily understood than electronic logic circuits and so do not need highly trained technicians to repair and service them. Fluidic components have also been invented that are modular in design, so that different components can be easily put together to form larger systems. Having no electrical parts, fluidic devices are particularly useful in environments that contain highly flammable materials.

The future of fluidics

Owing to the rapid development of integrated electronic circuits, the advantages of fluidic circuits with respect to cost and reliability have been somewhat reduced. The operating speeds of fluidic circuits are measured in milliseconds, much slower than those of electronic devices, which are a million times faster. Where speed is not of prime importance, however, the robustness, reliability, and convenience of fluidic devices enable them to compete more favorably with electronic logic. Fluidic digital computers have been built, but they were much too slow for any practical purposes. Increasing use is being made of fluidic devices in industrial process control, mechanical handling, machine tools, and other similar applications, but more widespread use will probably not result until the benefits of fluidics have been more fully investigated and publicized.

◄ Example of a pattern arising when laminar flow (entering from left) is broken up by a deflecting jet into turbulent flow.

SEE ALSO: ANEMOMETER • FLOWMETER • HYDRODYNAMICS • INTEGRATED CIRCUIT • LOGIC • TRANSDUCER AND SENSOR

Fluidized Bed

A fluidized bed is a chamber in which an upward draft of gases agitates a layer of solid granules such that their motion resembles that of a boiling liquid. The most important characteristic of this motion is that it promotes surface interactions between the gases and the solid. Consequently, chemical reactions proceed more rapidly and efficiently than they would for larger lumps of the same solid material in a fixed bed.

Fluidized-bed combustion

Fluidized beds are ideally suited to burning solid fuels, such as coal. The behavior of the fluidized bed promotes combustion reactions by ensuring a continuous supply of air to the surface of the fuel particles and by scouring combustion products away from the fuel surface. Furthermore, the flow of gases through the bed efficiently delivers the heat of combustion to heat exchangers, where it can boil water to provide steam to drive turbo-generators or to supply heating systems.

A typical fluidized bed consists of more than 95 percent sand, which serves to maintain the fluid motion and to provide a reservoir of heat that prevents excessive reductions in temperature when fuel is introduced. The bed has to be preheated to start combustion, then the temperature of the bed is governed by feed rates of air and fuel and by the efficiency of the heat exchanger.

The flow of gases through a fluidized bed carries a significant amount of fine particles out of the bed. These materials are stripped from the flue gases in cyclonic separators and then fed back into the bed, where they continue to burn. The flue gases are further cleaned by processes such as filtration and electrostatic precipitation.

Coal-burning beds

Coal is prepared for burning in a fluidized bed by first crushing it until its maximum particle size is no greater than ¼ in. (6 mm). Mixing three parts coal with one part water forms a paste of suitable consistency for pumping into the bed. The coal particles spend around 20 minutes in the fluidized bed, during which time essentially all the combustible material in the coal burns.

Fluidized beds typically burn coal between 1560 and 1740°F (850–950°C). This range of temperatures is much lower than that used in furnaces, where maximum temperatures can reach 2550°F (1400°C). Lower combustion temperatures mean that nitrogen oxides do not form from nitrogen and oxygen in air under the conditions of a fluidized bed. This is an important advantage

▲ Commissioned in May 1987, Unit 1 of the Ohio Power Company's Tidd Plant at Brilliant, Ohio, was the first full-scale example of a pressurized fluidized-bed combustion (PFBC) system in the United States. This picture shows its 70 ft. (21 m) tall pressure vessel, which housed the bed, gas-cleaning cyclones, and systems to feed the bed and remove ash—all at 12 times normal atmospheric pressure. The plant closed in December 1995, having exceeded all expectations of combustion efficiency and pollution control.

since nitrogen oxides generated by the combustion of fossil fuels are implicated in the formation of acid rain and photochemical smog.

Moderate operating temperatures are necessary to avoid the formation of liquid ash, which can solidify and foul the heat exchanging surfaces of furnaces. Moreover, if ash melts in a fluidized bed, it can solidify to form large lumps of clinker, which would interfere with the fluidization of the bed and necessitate regular shutdowns for their removal from the bed material.

Pressurized fluidized beds

The efficiency of a fluidized bed can be greatly improved by operating at several times normal atmospheric pressure. High pressure increases the rates of combustion reactions as well as the rate at which heat transfers from the bed, so a high-pressure plant is equivalent to a much larger plant that operates near atmospheric pressure.

High-pressure beds have the further advantage that their flue gases, after cleaning, can be used to drive gas turbines that contribute around 20 percent to the total output of a power station.

This type of combined cycle (gas and steam) power plant is economically viable for generating plants with a capacity of 50 megawatts or more.

Desulfurization

A useful feature of fluidized-bed combustion is that the sulfur dioxide emissions usually associated with coal-burning furnaces can be significantly reduced by including sorbants in the bed.

Sorbants are alkaline-earth metal carbonates such as limestone ($CaCO_3$) and dolomite ($CaMg(CO_3)_2$), which form metal oxides in the fluidized bed. Those oxides react with sulfur dioxide and oxygen to form metal sulfates:

$$CaCO_3 \rightarrow CaO + CO_2$$
$$SO_2 + CaO + \tfrac{1}{2}O_2 \rightarrow CaSO_4$$

The sulfates produced by this reaction join the residual ash from combustion and are withdrawn from the base of the bed. Trials using Ohio coal with a sulfur content of 2 to 4 percent have shown that more than 95 percent of sulfur dioxide can be absorbed in situ—without it leaving the bed—by adding 1.5 moles of calcium carbonate equivalent for every mole of sulfur in the coal feed.

Alternative fuels, alternative uses

Fluidized combustion beds are remarkably flexible systems. Apart from coal, the fuel stream can consist of wood chippings, various forms of vegetable waste, or even sewage. The bed material contains sufficient heat to vaporize the moisture content of such feeds so that combustion can begin, but the available heat output diminishes accordingly. In the case of sewage treatment, practically all the heat developed in the bed is used to evaporate the moisture content of the feed, but the reduction in volume from feed to ash is so great as to make the process useful.

Once fine particles have been removed, flue gases from fluidized beds are remarkably clean, consisting mainly of carbon dioxide, nitrogen, oxygen, and water vapor. They can be used to dry grass, clay, chalk, and stone, for example.

Fluidized beds can even be used to destroy toxic chemicals in contaminated soil. By recirculating flue gases through the bed and adding lime (calcium oxide, CaO), practically all traces of polychlorinated biphenyls and dioxins can be eliminated. Nitrogen-rich feeds can be prevented from forming nitrogen oxides by injecting ammonia into the bed so that nitrogen gas results.

If steam and air are fed into a fluidized-combustion bed, the output gases are a mixture of hydrogen, carbon monoxide, and nitrogen. This mixture can be used as a fuel gas or as a raw material for the production of synthetic gasoline.

▶ A pilot-scale fluidized-bed combustor allows engineers to assess the performance of a given combustor design before a full-scale plant is built. By varying parameters such as bed composition, fuel mixture, and air flow rate, technicians can determine the influence of such factors on the thermal power output and the composition of the waste gas stream, for example.

▲ This bed operates near atmospheric pressure. A fan draws hot waste gases through the pipes of a boiler and expels them through an exhaust flue.

Fluidized catalyst beds

The intimate mixing of gas and solid in a fluidized bed is ideal for using a solid catalyst to promote a reaction between gases, such as catalytic cracking, and for growing solid polymers from gaseous monomers. Fluidized beds are also used to pretreat or regenerate solid catalysts.

SEE ALSO: CATALYST • ENVIRONMENTAL SCIENCE • FURNACE • GASOLINE, SYNTHETIC • POLLUTION MONITORING AND CONTROL

Flywheel

All flywheels are essentially energy-storage devices that use a mass, usually in the form of a metal disk, which can be spun. While spinning, the flywheel stores rotational kinetic energy. In normal usage, a power source, such as an electrical motor, supplies energy to the flywheel, and a mechanical load, such as a machine tool, uses the stored energy at a later time. By using the flywheel as a reservoir of energy, the motor does not have to supply energy at exactly the rate required by the machine tool: if the motor supplies energy faster than it is being used, the flywheel will speed up to absorb the excess; if usage exceeds supply, the flywheel will slow down as energy is taken from it.

Stored energy

A flywheel stores energy in the form of rotational kinetic energy. This depends on the total mass of the wheel, its distribution about the axis of rotation, and its angular velocity. If the mass of a wheel were to be doubled, but distributed in the same way about the axis, and the wheel were spinning at the same angular velocity, the stored energy would be doubled. If the wheel's diameter or angular velocity were to be doubled, without increasing the mass, the stored energy would be quadrupled. The distribution of mass in an object rotating about a fixed axis is described by a quantity called its moment of inertia, which is calculated taking into account the distance of each mass element from the axis. The rotational kinetic energy of the spinning wheel is equal to one-half of its moment of inertia times the square of its angular velocity.

In order to achieve the greatest energy storage for a given mass, diameter, and rotational speed, most of the mass should be concentrated at the rim. Some high-performance flywheels consist of a massive rim supported on a few slender radial spokes. At rest, the rim is not perfectly circular, having a maximum radius where it meets the

▼ A typical four-cylinder, five main bearing automobile engine. The flywheel is designed to form part of the starter and clutch mechanisms.

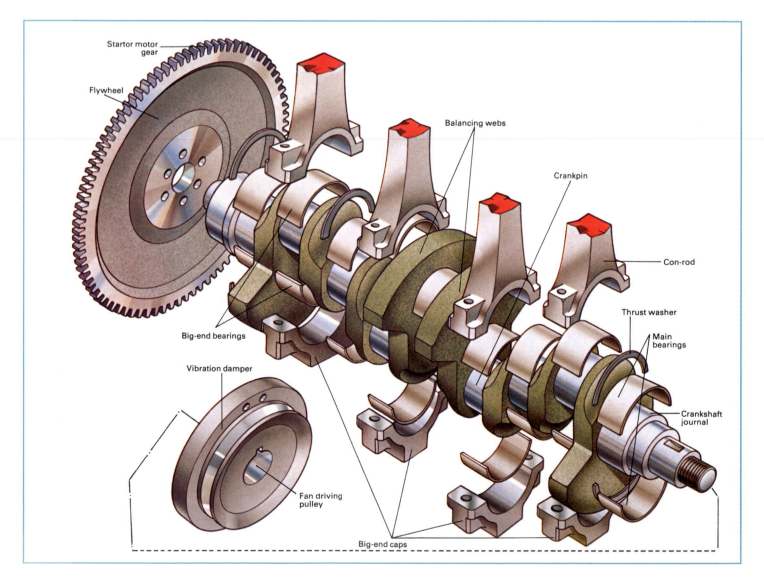

spokes and a minimum radius midway between spokes. At operating speeds, the rim is distorted by centrifugal reaction into a true circle.

Flywheel balancing

If a flywheel is not properly balanced, it will impose extra stresses on its supports. There are two methods of flywheel balancing: static balancing relies on adjusting the weight distribution of a flywheel until it does not take up a preferred rest position when allowed to rotate freely on a horizontal spindle; dynamic balancing is a more complex system, relying on measuring the out-of-balance forces that are generated as the flywheel is spun and adjusting its weight distribution until these forces are minimized.

Dynamic balancing is more accurate than static balancing and thus is used for products where the cost of the more complex testing equipment can be justified. The weight distribution of a flywheel may be adjusted by adding extra small weights around its periphery, as is done when balancing car road wheels, but it is more likely to be achieved through selective removal of small amounts of metal from the flywheel, often done by drilling a series of holes in its rim.

Uses of flywheels

A flypress is a machine tool that makes use of energy stored in a flywheel to perform cutting or bending operations. Energy is fed into the flywheel from an electric motor by hand turning or

▶ Although largely superseded by CDs, hi-fi turntables are still used by enthusiasts and by disc jockeys. Almost all hi-fi turntable systems rely on the flywheel effect to smooth out minor speed fluctuations. In some cases, a turntable motor may twitch erratically instead of spinning smoothly if its platter is removed.

by falling weights. When the flywheel is turning at maximum speed, its momentum is quickly transferred to the press tool where most of the available energy is dissipated in a fraction of a second as the tool hits its workpiece. If a flywheel were not used, far less power would be available at the press tool during that fraction of a second.

The flywheels in car engines are used to match engine power—produced by the cylinders as a series of short bursts—to transmission load, which is fairly constant. They are often designed to form part of the starter and clutch mechanisms, thus saving the cost, space, and weight of separate components.

Fluid flywheel

Cars fitted with automatic or semiautomatic transmissions may include a device called a fluid flywheel. In its simplest form, it consists of a sealed chamber containing two sets of blades, one connected to the engine and the other to the transmission. The space between the blades is partially filled with oil. When the engine is turning slowly, it merely stirs the oil, passing little power to the transmission. As the engine speed increases, the oil is forced to spin with the engine-driven blades, forming a liquid flywheel.

FACT FILE

- Bicycle frames have been adapted for use as stationary power units in developing nations. The Dynapod consists of a clamped frame and pedaling unit with a flywheel made from a bicycle wheel with cement filling between the spokes. A rotary water pump operated by this means can lift the same volume of water that would take the efforts of four people using traditional methods.

- Some drag racing cars in the United States are constructed with a large flywheel connected to the engine so as to build up a massive power surge potential for racing starts. The energy buildup is so great in these flywheels that they have frequently pulled the vehicle apart when the transmission was first engaged.

SEE ALSO: ENERGY, MASS, AND WEIGHT • INERTIA • MATTER, PROPERTIES OF • TRANSMISSION, AUTOMOBILE

Food Preservation and Packaging

When a vegetable is harvested or an animal slaughtered for a source of food, microbiological and chemical changes occur in it over a period, limiting the time for which it remains acceptable and safe to eat. Not all the changes that take place in the food after killing or harvesting are undesirable, and in some cases, advantage of naturally occurring changes may be taken to prepare food for future use and enjoyment.

For example, the conversion of sugars to alcohol in wine and beer making and the souring of milk to make cheese have been practiced for many centuries without the knowledge of scientific explanation for these processes. In general, however, most of the postharvest changes in food will lead to spoilage, and thus, various methods of food preservation are used to prolong the length of time for which it retains its quality and appeal.

In the days of simple farming communities, it was possible to live on locally grown produce, and no highly organized methods of food preservation were necessary. When food preservation was practiced, it would have been of a very elementary kind, as in the case of the Inuit who preserved fish by burying it in frozen ground and ice so that it could be subsequently dug up and eaten many months later. In the modern world, the situation is entirely different because the centers of world population are in towns and cities, often many miles from the main areas of food production. In such circumstances, unless the food is preserved before shipment, it will have deteriorated by the time it reaches the consumer.

Many staple foods, such as vegetables, can be harvested only on a seasonal basis, even though the demand for them is perennial, as they provide the vitamins and other nutrients essential for a well-balanced diet the whole year round. Modern techniques of food preservation, such as canning, freezing, and dehydration, ensure that seasonal foods can be preserved to meet the demand for the whole year and that the waste of harvest surpluses is avoided.

Food spoilage

When a plant or animal tissue dies, it is unable to prevent the attack of microorganisms, such as bacteria, yeasts, and molds, which break down the food structure and produce "off" flavors and odors. The number of organisms in an ounce of food can range from several hundred to 20 million or more, and they can multiply so rapidly that under optimum conditions their numbers can double every 15 or 20 minutes.

▲ Farmhouse cheddar cheeses are left to mature for many months to develop their traditional flavor and texture. During this time, they form a hard rind, which frequently becomes covered with a harmless mold. Both are removed before the cheese is cut and packaged for eating.

Bacteria are minute microorganisms varying in size from 0.001 mm to 0.003 mm and they are the most common cause of food spoilage. Sometimes the effect of bacteria can be beneficial, as in the case of cultures of *Lactobacillus bulgaricus* and *Streptococcus thermophilus*, which are used to manufacture yogurt from milk. Generally, however, bacteria will either cause spoilage of food so that it is unpleasant to eat or, in the case of pathogenic bacteria such as *Staphylococcus aureus* or *Clostridium botulinum*, it will have far worse effects, giving rise to food poisoning.

Bacteria are often divided into three groups on the basis of their optimum temperature range for growth. Thermophilic bacteria flourish between temperatures of approximately 108 to 167°F (42–75°C); mesophilic bacteria prefer temperatures between 50 and 104°F (10–40°C); and the optimum range for psychrophilic bacteria is between temperatures of 59 and 68°F (15–20°C), though several have been reported to grow at temperatures as low as 23°F (–5°C). Many bacteria also form spores capable of surviving at high temperatures; the spores then grow and produce spoilage. Thus, in canning, for example, it is essential to heat the food enough to destroy all spore-forming bacteria.

Most foods contain many different types of bacteria, and the nature of the spoilage will depend upon the temperature at which the food has been held. For example, proteolytic bacteria predominate in milk held below 50°F (10°C), and they cause spoilage by attacking the protein in the milk and turning it alkaline and smelly. On the other hand, above 59°F (15°C) another type of bacteria in the milk will ferment the lactose sugars present to form lactic acid, with the result that the milk curdles.

Molds and yeasts

Food spoilage caused by molds and yeasts is not normally so dangerous as with bacteria. Most molds are readily destroyed by the heat treatment given to canned foods, though the spores of the molds *Byssochlamys fulva* and *B. nivea* have been responsible for spoilage occurring in canned fruit. A temperature of 195°F (91°C) is usually necessary to stop this type of spoilage. Yeasts are oval-shaped cells about 0.007 mm long; they have a very low heat resistance, and a few minutes' exposure at 165°F (74°C) is usually sufficient to kill them.

Food spoilage may also be caused by chemical substances known as enzymes that are always present in minute quantities in living materials. In fruits and vegetables, for example, enzymes are the chemical catalysts that bring about the changes of flavor and texture associated with ripening. Enzymes are often responsible for the deterioration of fruits and vegetables after harvesting, and the browning of the cut surface of apples, pears, and potatoes is caused by the oxidation of phenols by the enzyme phenolase. Enzymes can be inactivated by blanching the food in boiling water or steam or by the action of sulfur dioxide: the cut fruit or vegetable is dipped in a weak sodium sulfite solution.

Principles of food preservation

A number of methods are available for destroying or inactivating the microorganisms and enzymes responsible for food spoilage, and the major techniques are canning, curing, dehydration, freezing, pasteurization, and pickling.

Canning is a process of sterilization in which the microorganisms and enzymes are completely destroyed by heating the food in hermetically sealed cans. It was patented in 1810 by the French inventor Nicholas Appert, who succeeded in preserving foods by heating them in sealed glass jars. Having no knowledge of bacterial activity, he incorrectly assumed that the food was preserved because of the absence of air.

The most important factor in determining the degree of heat treatment required is the acidity, or hydrogen ion concentration, as indicated by a quantity known as the pH. At pH values below 4.5, the food is sufficiently acidic to limit the growth of microorganisms, and a heat treatment with steam or boiling water at 212°F (100°C) gives the required sterilization. Canned fruit is a good example of an acidic pack.

With less acidic packs such as meat, fish, and vegetables, the pH is above 4.5, so a more severe heat treatment is required. The most dangerous pathogenic (disease-producing) bacterium is *Clostridium botulinum*, which is extremely heat resistant and produces a toxin (poison) so lethal that a spoonful would be sufficient to kill thousands of people. *Clostridium botulinum* can be killed by heating at 250°F (121°C) for at least three minutes, and cans of low-acid foods must be given at least an equivalent heat treatment at their lowest heating point to ensure that they are microbiologically safe.

Curing is a method of preservation applied to products such as bacon and ham, and in many parts of the world fish is preserved by this method. Salt is added to the food, which withdraws the water molecules to form hydrated salt ions. If sufficient salt is present, enough water can be withdrawn from the food to control the growth of microorganisms. In bacon curing, the salt concentration in the curing tank is about 25 percent, with about 1.7 percent of sodium nitrate and a small quantity of sodium nitrite to develop the color. After fish are cured by being soaked in brine, they are often placed in a smokehouse for a period of time. Smoking gives a characteristic flavor and color to the food as well as helping to preserve the surface texture.

When the moisture content of a food is reduced by dehydration to about 8 to 25 percent,

▼ Curing the famous Bayonne hams in France. The Basque region's Bayonne salt is used to preserve the meat, which is then hung from the ceiling beams of traditional kitchens, restaurants, and shops alongside strings of garlic and colorful dried red peppers. Fish may also be cured by this method, using salt to remove water and control the growth of bacteria.

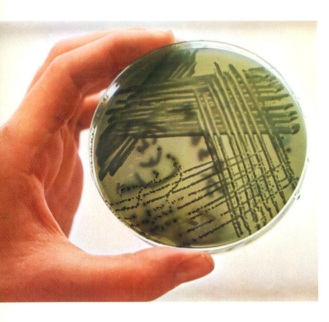

▲ Colonies of *Salmonella* bacteria grown on a bismuth–agar culture medium. Food companies have to do regular microbiological tests to ensure that the food leaving their factory is safe to eat.

depending on the product, the water levels are too low for microorganisms and enzymes to operate. Spray drying is one method of producing dry powders from liquid concentrates of a wide range of commodities varying from milk and coffee to fruit juices and tomato paste. The droplets in the spray are only about 0.15 mm in diameter, and they give rapid rates of drying when put into a stream of warm air. The product is usually very hygroscopic (it absorbs moisture rapidly), so spray-dried powders are often packed under a dry gas such as nitrogen or carbon dioxide, which also protects against oxidation. Dehydrated foods also have the advantage that they are light and hence reduce transportation costs during distribution.

The growth of microorganisms does not usually occur at temperatures below 23°F (–5°C), and food can be stored for several months at deep frozen temperatures of –4°F (–20°C), provided the enzymes have been inactivated by blanching prior to freezing. Freezing does not destroy the microorganisms, and once the food is thawed they will begin to multiply again.

During the 1920s, an American, Clarence Birdseye, discovered that the quality of frozen foods could be improved by quick freezing. One of the main reasons for this is that during slow freezing large ice crystals are formed, which damage the cells and cause valuable nutrients to drain away when the food is thawed. When a food is quick frozen, it passes through the zone of maximum ice crystallization, 32°F (0°C) to 23°F (–5°C), in 30 minutes or less, minimizing the mechanical damage to the cell.

Pasteurization is a process of mild heat treatment developed around 1860 by Louis Pasteur, who showed that unwanted fermentation in wine could be prevented by raising the temperature to 140°F (60°C) for a short period of time. Today most milk for domestic consumption is preserved by pasteurizing it at 165°F (74°C) for 15 seconds. This process ensures that pathogenic organisms such as tubercle bacillus, streptococci, and salmonellae are destroyed. The milk will keep for three days in a domestic refrigerator before nontoxic spoilage by other bacteria takes place.

Pickling is a process of soaking food in an acid solution such as vinegar. The acetic acid present limits the growth of microorganisms rather than destroys them, so its action is bacteriostatic rather than bactericidal. Most pickles are pasteurized

▶ One method of preserving crops is drying. This farmer is using a solar drier, which traps the heat of the Sun, to dry his harvest of chili peppers. In hot countries, this type of technology is environmentally friendly and cheap to operate.

because some microorganisms, such as the yeast *Saccharomyces bailii* and the mold *Moniliella acetoabutans*, are able to tolerate acetic acid (the acid in vinegar).

The microbiological keeping properties of the pickled product are expressed as the preservation index, which is the amount of acetic acid in the product expressed as a percentage of the volatile constituents (including water). Normally a preservation index in excess of 3.5 percent is required in an unpasteurized product to give freedom from most forms of spoilage.

The proportion of product to pickling solution is about 70 percent, and if the packing liquor has an acidity of 5 percent, the final overall acidity of the product will be about 1.6 percent, with a salt content of approximately 0.6 percent.

Food additives

Asthma attacks, rashes, numbness and palpitations can all be caused by allergies to some of the chemicals that are routinely added to a vast number of the packaged and processed foods we eat today. For most people, permitted food additives are harmless, but during the past few years, it has become clear that several of the most widely used additives can make susceptible individuals ill.

The commonest reactions are wheezing or itchy swellings on the skin. One of the main culprits has been found to be the yellow dye tartrazine, which is still added in some countries to literally thousands of food and drink products but has been outlawed for some years in the UK and other parts of Europe. Valued by food manufacturers for coloring and preserving packaged foods, it nevertheless causes problems for about one person in 100. Tartrazine was first suspected as a cause of allergy over 30 years ago by a U.S. physician, Stephen Lockey, though little notice was taken of his research at the time.

Monosodium glutamate can also cause side effects. Symptoms were first reported in 1969 by a Chinese-American doctor, Robert Kwok, who suffered from effects that resembled those of a heart attack after eating Chinese food. Symptoms include numbness at the back of the neck radiating to both arms and the back, with general weakness and palpitations. Further research showed the symptoms had been found in others, also after eating Chinese food, and the link to monosodium glutamate (MSG) was made. Monosodium glutamate is used generously in Chinese cooking and is also added to canned or frozen food to enhance its flavor.

Food manufacturers argue that it is impossible to keep our mainly urban societies fed unless they add preservatives to keep foods from going bad and emulsifiers and stabilizers to keep the various

◀ Sausages hanging at the end of the production line in a German factory, before packing. Air drying reduces the moisture content of the meat, prevents it from spoiling, and imparts flavor and texture to the sausage.

ingredients of processed foods bound together so that they do not separate and become unsightly and unpalatable. All additives are kept under scrutiny by government agencies, and occasionally some are struck off the list of permitted substances. Cyclamate sweeteners, for instance, were banned when animal experiments showed that large amounts could cause tumors.

Although chemically treated foods are still commonplace, a considerable interest is developing in organic varieties, which have no artificial ingredients added and where the product has been grown without the aid of pesticides or artificial fertilizers. There is a strong movement in Europe, characterized by protests against genetically-modified crops, towards less-processed food and drink despite the obvious disadvantages in terms of color and size compared to foods that have been highly processed and that have added colors and flavorings.

Other additives also have substantial disbenefits—sugar has no nutritional value except as a source of energy. The average consumer eats 2.5 lbs. (1 kg) per week, a habit that has been proved to increase tooth decay, obesity, and the risk of heart disease. Sugar is present in foods that might not be considered sweet—most brands of tomato ketchup, for instance, are almost 50 percent sugar.

Excessive salt increases blood pressure, yet average consumption is four or five times more than doctors regard as safe and ten times as much as required by the body. Salt is an almost universal additive, and like sugar, it is used as a preservative.

One of the best examples of permitted adulteration is a loaf of white bread. It contains refined flour (from which the bran and wheatgerm have been removed), milk, egg, water, preservatives, lard, vegetable oil, calcium propionate (a mold preventer), salt, sugar, synthetic vitamins (to replace those removed when the flour was refined), and bleach, as well as chemicals to make the flour run smoothly through the machinery and help the loaf "mature."

Food packaging

Food can be packed either for transport or preservation in many different ways. One popular form of packaging is the cardboard carton, often called the Tetra Pak, after the name given to this type of packaging by the Swedish company of the same name that invented it. The Tetra Pak was so called because the original, developed in 1943, was a tetrahedron-shaped carton. The idea was to create a milk package that required a minimum of material and provided maximum hygiene and that would remain solidly based however it was placed on a surface.

Development of the package involved, among other things, the introduction of new techniques

for coating paper with plastics and for sealing packages below the level of the liquid.

In 1953, polyethylene was introduced as a plastic coating on the cardboard and by 1957, 1¾-pint (1 liter) cartons were being produced. In 1959, development began on the Tetra Brik, a brick-shaped carton still commonly used for fruit juices and long-life milk. In the late 1960s, the Tetra Rex package, a "gable-top" container was invented. This is still the most popular format used for ordinary milk cartons.

▲ An operative attends a machine that automatically slices, shingles, and packs sausage slices.

Foods are also packaged in such materials as shrink wrap, a thin, flexible plastic film. Shrink wraps are generally applied over foodstuffs or other products as a primary wrapping to prevent contamination. The shrink wrap process completely encloses the item in plastic film. A further development, skin packaging, forms a very tight sheet of plastic film that is adhered by vacuum onto the product, which is normally further protected by a stiff card backing. More recent packaging products for foods include specialized pouches for liquids, from wine to fruit juice, that are made from laminated film that has barrier properties. Packaging for frozen vegetables is commonly made from polyethlyene or nylon, laminated for gloss and strength when frozen.

Wax is a more traditional packaging material, used in order to preserve the food in question. Although a number of types of food have occasionally been packaged by adding a wax coating, the most common recipient of waxing is cheese. Waxing is mainly applied to hard varieties that have a well-defined insoluble rind to prevent the wax from infusing into the cheese itself. The life of cheeses such as Dutch Gouda, Edam, and many Cheddars are extended and transportation made easier by coating the thin, natural rind in odorless, colorless paraffin wax. Gouda is traditionally coated in yellow paraffin wax, whereas Edam's distinctive coating is red.

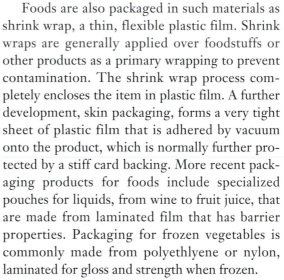

FACT FILE

- Until recently, some Inuit tribes preserved large numbers of snared birds, such as starlings, inside the skin of a seal, packing them in and sewing up the skin so that the birds absorbed the heavy subcutaneous fat. Pemmican, a preserved food of the North American Indians, was similarly treated by packing strips of lean, dried meat into rawhide sacks containing melted fat and certain dried berries.

- It is possible to sterilize the surface of certain foods such as meat and bread by subjecting them to ultraviolet light of wavelengths below 300 nanometers. Penetration is shallow, and the process is useful for short-term preservation only.

- Salting and drying fish, the earliest method of preservation used as far back as 3500 B.C.E. in the river delta civilizations of the Indus Valley in Pakistan and the Nile River in Egypt, is still widely used. Some peoples have become so used to the taste that they prefer the preserved flesh to that of fresh fish. Salt cod, for instance, has become a gourmet ingredient of some French, Indian, and Portuguese cuisines.

SEE ALSO: CANNING AND BOTTLING • ENZYME • FOOD PROCESSING • NUTRITION AND FOOD SCIENCE • PACKAGING • REFRIGERATION

Food Processing

Food processing is mainly concerned with the technology of preserving foods in such a way that they retain nutritive value and are acceptable to the consumer. Some idea of the extent of food processing can be obtained by considering the main methods available to the food manufacturer.

Cooking

Cooking is a basic form of heat treatment used to destroy the enzymes and bacteria that lead to food spoilage and make food more appetizing and palatable. Cooking must be thorough enough to ensure heat penetration through the center of the food, with the maximum cooking temperature reached as quickly as possible because the enzymes become increasingly active as the temperature rises. When it reaches a certain level, typically 158 to 176°F (70–80°C), the enzymes are destroyed, most after a few minutes of exposure at 212°F (100°C).

Bacterial action also increases until the temperature is high enough to kill the microorganisms, but more prolonged heating may be necessary to destroy all the pathogenic spores. Spores are destroyed quickly in acidic foods, such as fruit, but in more neutral foods, especially pork and seafood, prolonged cooking times are necessary.

Canning

A popular example of a canned food is baked beans in tomato sauce. The beans—dried pea beans or small white navy beans—are graded, sorted, and soaked in cold water for 12 to 18 hours. They are then blanched to destroy enzymes prior to canning.

The beans and sauce (tomato paste, sugar, salt, flour, and spices) are machine filled into the cans at about 176°F (80°C) to give a high final vacuum in the can after closing and heating. The ends of the can are made from lacquered tinplate, and after filling and seaming on the lid, the cans are processed in autoclaves at 240°F (115°C) or higher. Since the product is fairly viscous, the rate of heat penetration would normally be very slow and result in overcooking, so the cans are agitated while they are processed.

Curing

The use of salt for the curing of bacon is well known, but this method of preservation can also be applied to fish. An appreciable quantity of the

▲ Perishable foods, such as salmon, need to be processed quickly to ensure the product is in peak condition when it is sold or sent on for preservation by canning or smoking.

world catch of cod is salted in countries such as Canada, Norway, and Iceland. The fish is packed in layers with solid salt, which takes about 24 hours to penetrate to a depth of ¾ in. (18 mm).

Eventually the fish becomes saturated with salt to give a salt content of 18 percent by weight and a moisture content reduced from 80 percent to about 55 percent. After washing off surplus salt, the fish is placed in mechanical warm-air dryers to reduce the moisture content to less than 15 percent to prevent the growth of molds. Salted fish is susceptible to bacterial contamination, which can cause a pink coloration and unpleasant odors, but it can be checked by storing at below 38°F (4°C).

Dehydration

Many fruits and vegetables are air dried using a variety of equipment, including tunnel dryers, continuous conveyor-belt dryers, and air-lift dryers.

When potatoes are dried to make instant mashed potato flakes, for example, they are cooked, mashed, and mixed with previously dried potato powder—35 percent mashed potato to 65 percent dried powder—to obtain a blend with 35 to 40 percent moisture. Sulfite, used to prevent browning, and other additives, such as antioxi-

dants, are added at this stage. The mixture is then cooled to 77°F (25°C).

From here, the product passes to the primary dryer, often a thermal venturi type, where a powerful hot-air stream lifts the product through a tower-shaped duct into a collecting cyclone, which rapidly reduces the moisture content to 12 to 15 percent. Approximately two-thirds of the powder is returned to mix with the mashed potato in the first process. The remainder of the powder passes to a secondary dryer, which is either a fluidized bed or rotary louver type, to reduce the moisture content to 6 to 7 percent.

Spray drying is used extensively for coffee and milk powder. The liquid product is atomized at high pressure, about 250 to 500 psi (17.5–35 bar), through several nozzles into a stream of hot air in a large column approximately 60 ft. (20 m) high. The dried particles collect at the bottom. Instant-milk granules are made from spray-dried, skimmed milk powder that has been subjected to steam to form porous clumps with 15 to 20 percent moisture then redried to 6 percent moisture in a pneumatic dryer.

In freeze drying, the food is frozen to 0°F (–18°C) or lower and placed in a vacuum chamber whose pressure is at 0.036 psi (0.0025 bar). Under

▼ The processing of potatoes to produce a pack of frozen French fries includes many quality-control checks before they are frozen and packed.

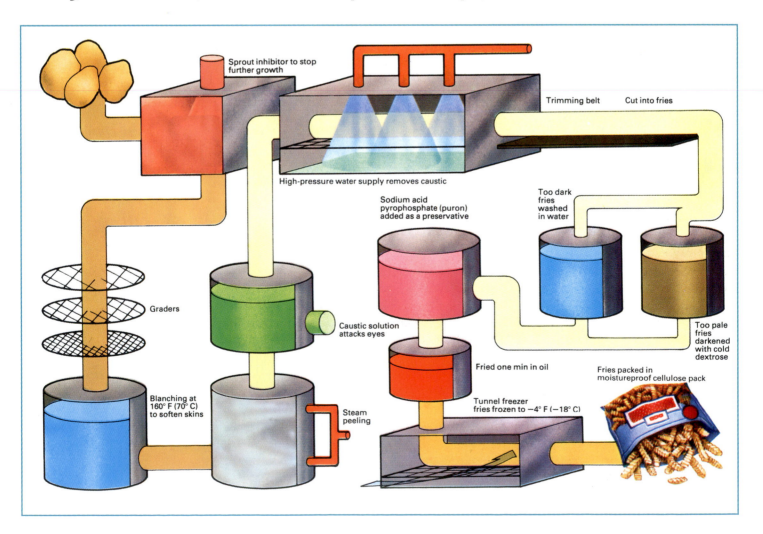

these conditions, the ice sublimes directly to water vapor, which is condensed out on the coils of a refrigerator. The low drying temperature causes very little heat damage, and the product is so porous that it rehydrates extremely well.

Freezing

Frozen foods manufacture is now a major industry, whose products range from vegetables to meat products and precooked meals. A typical example is frozen French fries. Graded potatoes are blanched at 160°F (70°C) to inactivate enzymes and soften the skins, which are removed using a caustic solution. The potatoes are cut into fries by a revolving drum with blades.

The sugar content of the fries is corrected by adding a cold dextrose solution if it is too low, which would give pale fries, or by immersion in water at about 185°F (85°C) if it is too high, giving dark fries. The fries are fried for about one minute in peanut oil and cooled before freezing in a tunnel freezer in which cold air at –22°F (–30°C) is blown upward through a mesh belt. After about 20 minutes, the center of the fries has frozen to 0°F (–18°C) and they are packed.

Irradiation

Microorganisms and enzymes in food can be destroyed by gamma rays from a radioactive isotope such as cobalt-60. Unfortunately, at high doses, the rays can initiate chemical reactions that produce unpleasant flavors in the food and lower the nutritional value by destroying vitamins and the amino acids in the proteins.

Irradiation is measured in Grays (GY), and 1 GY is equivalent to 1 joule of energy absorbed per kilogram of food. A dose of 40 kGY destroys spores of *Clostridium botulinum*, but tests on beef protein have shown that levels of 56 kGY cause losses in the amino acids, ranging from 25 percent in the case of glycerine and methionine to 75 percent for serine and glutamic acid. Even a level of 30 kGY in beef causes a 63 percent loss of the B vitamin thiamine.

Pasteurizing doses between 3 and 10 kGY reduce the bacterial load significantly and extend the storage life of some foods. Tests on pork sausages, at a dose of 10 kGY, have delayed the onset of microbial spoilage at 59°F (15°C) from 7 to 24 days.

Pasteurization

Pasteurization is a mild heat treatment process at temperatures normally less than 212°F (100°C); although it destroys pathogenic organisms, it cannot provide indefinite protection against microbiological spoilage. The pasteurization of milk is

◀ Potato chips emerging from the oven. The potatoes are first peeled and washed then graded and checked for blemishes. After cutting, they are washed again, drained, and finally cooked. They are then sprinkled with salt or other flavorings.

well known, but even an acid such as vinegar requires protection from spoilage organisms, such as *Acetobacter*, which can lead to cloudiness. Spoilage can be eliminated by pasteurizing or passing the vinegar through a sterilizing filter.

The cloudiness in some citrus juice products is due to pectin, which occurs naturally in some fruit and helps to maintain the viscosity of the juice. If the natural pectolytic enzymes of the fruit are not destroyed, however, they degrade the pectin so that it clarifies and often gels. If a cloudy citrus juice is required, it is essential to destroy the pectolytic enzymes by flash pasteurizing in a plate heat exchanger at 203°F (95°C) for 30 seconds.

Some pasteurized, cured canned hams are vacuum packed and heat processed until a temperature at the center of the can of 151°F (66°C) is reached. The cans must be rapidly cooled to 70°F (21°C) and then refrigerated.

Pickling

Preservation of pickled foods such as beets is achieved by the presence of acetic acid in the vinegar used for the pickling liquor. Washed beets are first cooked in boiling water or steamed until tender. The beets are then salted if necessary and skinned and immediately immersed in the packing liquor prepared from malt vinegar with 2 percent salt if steam cooking has been used. After cooling, the liquor is drained off, filtered, and used for packing when the jars are filled. The cooled beets are now ready for machine slicing.

The sliced beets are packed in glass jars and topped up with liquor to give an ⅛ in. (3.2 mm) headspace. After filling, the jars are closed with an acid-resistant metal cap, capable of providing a vacuum seal, and pasteurized in a steam cabinet so that the liquid in the center of the jar is held at 165°F (74°C) for at least 25 minutes.

Sugaring

One of the most common uses of sugar as a preservative is in the manufacture of jelly, which is basically a gel formed by boiling fruit pulp with the common sugar sucrose until a sugar content in the range 65 to 70 percent is reached. The high sugar concentration produces an osmotic pressure that causes water to diffuse from the cells of any microorganisms present, thus inactivating them by what is virtually a process of dehydration.

The gel structure of a jelly is due to pectin, which, under the correct conditions of acidity and sugar concentration, can form a network of interlinked molecules holding the jelly together. Some fruits, such as apples, plums, and damsons, are rich in pectin whereas others, such as cherries, pineapple, and rhubarb, have low pectin contents. Thus, the jelly processor should always prepare a test jelly to determine the amount of pectin required.

Traditional jelly manufacture is carried out by boiling fruit pulp, sucrose, and pectin at atmospheric pressure in steam-heated kettles of 40 gallon (182 l) capacity. During the boil, some of the sucrose is converted to two other sugars, glucose and fructose, by a process known as inversion. Approximately 30 to 40 percent of the sucrose should be inverted in jellies, with a final sugar content of 65 to 70 percent. After adjustment of the acidity, the jelly is cooled to about 181°F (83°C) and placed in jars whose headspace is sterilized with steam prior to machine capping.

Jelly is also made by boiling under vacuum at a temperature of 140°F (60°C) to reduce flavor and aroma losses. Because of the low temperatures involved, the degree of sucrose inversion is much less, and either preinverted sucrose or glucose syrup must be incorporated in the jelly recipe. The low boiling temperature also prevents the addition of pectin at this stage, otherwise prejelli-fication would occur. When the jelly has reached the required sugar content, the vacuum is broken and the temperature raised to 185°F (85°C) for the addition of pectin as a 3 percent solution. Subsequent filling follows the same pattern as for jelly prepared for atmospheric boiling.

UHT processes

Traditional sterilization involves heating a food in a can or bottle for long enough to kill all the microorganisms at the slowest heating point. The food in the outer part of the container will therefore be more likely to overcook and lose heat-sensitive vitamins. Canned meat has a slow heating rate, and 56 percent of the B vitamin thiamine can be lost. Even a liquid product, such as sterilized milk, loses 20 percent of thiamine and 60 percent of vitamin C.

Sterilizing at high temperatures in short time has been shown to reduce the heat damage. This method is good for liquids with a low viscosity because rapid heating is necessary—the production of UHT (ultra-high temperature) milk by sterilizing at 280°F (138°C) for two seconds is an example. UHT sterilization reduces thiamine losses to 10 percent and vitamin C losses to 25 percent. More viscous liquids are sterilized in a scraped surface heat exchanger, which is a rotor blade spinning at 1,000 rpm inside the heating tube. Nonacid foods, such as soups, can be sterilized by heating at 286°F (141°C) for eight seconds followed by cooling to 90°F (32°C) and placing in presterilized containers. Acid foods, such as fruit juices, can be sterilized in heat exchangers at about 221°F (105°C).

Cereal processing

Some of the most interesting and versatile processes deal with breakfast foods. Cornflakes are made by cutting cleaned and degermed corn into small granules. These are cooked with salt and malt in a pressure cooker, followed by "conditioning" for up to 36 hours to modify the starch cells. Finally the corn is steamed, formed into flakes by passing through rollers, and toasted in a revolving oven. Puffed wheat is cleaned, dehusked, and heated to reduce its moisture content to about 8 percent. It is then heated to 240°F (115°C) and placed in a "gun" pressure chamber, where the heat is increased to 800°F (427°C) and steam at 200 psi (14 bar) is introduced. The gun is then "shot" off, the steam is released, and the difference in pressure between the chamber and the atmospheric pressure outside causes the starch cells to expand suddenly. Later, the puffed wheat is sprayed with syrup and dried. Extrusion is also used, with the cereal made into a dough, forced through an extruder and shaped.

◀ Part of a maturometer, a machine that automatically assesses the maturity of peas by measuring the amount of force needed to push metal rods through them.

◄ One of the causes of milk spoilage is the action of proteolytic bacteria that attack the milk proteins. These bacteria can be destroyed by sterilization. In this process, pasteurized homogenized milk is bottled and then steam-heated to 212°F (100°C) for up to 30 minutes.

Synthetic foods

Not all the foods we eat are in their natural form—some are produced artificially. The more common approach to producing synthetic food is to modify an existing foodstuff into a more palatable form, for example, artificial meat made from soybean. A second approach involves the actual synthesis of foodstuffs from nonedible materials, such as the production of single-cell proteins (SCP) from natural gas or the manufacture of vitamins identical to natural ones.

Artificial meats

Artificial meat products look like meat and have a fibrous structure similar to meat but are made from vegetable protein (usually soybean or wheat protein) rather than meat protein. They are more properly called textured vegetable protein products. The vegetable protein is treated to make it look and feel like meat by two main methods.

In the simplest method, an extrusion process, the raw material is defatted soybean flour containing 50 to 70 percent protein. To this is added wheat protein (gluten), a binder such as egg protein (albumen), casein (milk protein), flavors, salt, spices, and colors to form a dough. The dough is fed into an extruder, down a heated cylinder, and through an extrusion nozzle.

The combination of heat and pressure in the cylinder helps to unwind the protein molecules into protein chains. When the dough is forced out through the extrusion nozzle, the protein chains are aligned so they are roughly parallel. As the dough leaves the nozzle, it is subjected to a rapid drop in pressure of about 1,000 psi (69 bar), causing the water to boil off rapidly. The water bubbles burst through the dough, puffing it and drying it at the same time. The dried dough is then cut into chunks or ground into small pieces.

A development of this process is used to produce more sophisticated foodstuffs, such as synthetic crabmeat. This is the dual extrusion process, in which the material produced by the first extrusion is put through a second extrusion sequence that further refines the protein structure.

The second method is called spinning and is similar to the techniques used for the production of artificial fibers such as rayon. The texture and appearance of the product can be adjusted to appear like different types of meat. The starting material is a pure vegetable protein extract, such as soy protein isolate, containing 95 percent or more protein. The protein is made into a viscous dope solution in a highly alkaline medium (such as sodium hydroxide, caustic soda) that causes the protein molecules to unwind into chains. They are then forced through fine holes in a stainless steel die called a spinneret to produce filaments $\frac{1}{1000}$ in. (0.025 mm) to $\frac{3}{1000}$ in. (0.075 mm) in diameter. These filaments emerge into an acid (such as acetic acid) coagulating bath that sets the fibers and neutralizes the alkali.

◄ Food technologists evaluate different seasonings, as ingredients must meet stringent requirements in most developed countries.

The protein molecules are aligned in a parallel fashion by the action of the spinneret and then reinforced by stretching the filaments. This stretching also controls the degree of chewiness. The individual strands are gathered into tows, washed, and the acid neutralized before they are passed through a bath containing flavors and colors. Finally the tows are cut and dried.

Single-cell proteins

Protein produced by yeasts, algae, and fungi has been used as a foodstuff for thousands of years. The preconquest inhabitants of Mexico used to prepare cakes (apparently with a cheesy flavor) from the algae *Spirulina maxima*, which grows in the alkaline waters of Lake Texcoco. Similarly, yeasts are commonly used in bread and other foods and can be eaten by themselves.

In one process—the ICI Pruteen process—methanol produced from natural gas is used as a feedstock for a continuous fermentation using the bacterium *Methylophilus methylotrophus*. The protein consists of the (dead) bacterium cells and is used as an animal feedstuff. Other animal feed proteins are produced by growing yeast on oil-based chemicals. Such proteins are not currently used for direct human consumption.

Similar concern has restricted the application of SCP for animal feedstuffs, though a more important factor restricting its use is the cost of manufacture. To produce SCP on a commercial scale requires considerable capital investment, and the raw feedstock is relatively expensive. Given current agricultural efficiency, it is usually cheaper to grow, for example, soy as a protein source than to produce protein using microorganisms.

However, the economies of SCP production alter considerably if the feedstock used is a waste that would otherwise have to be disposed of. For example, the sulfite liquor produced as a waste product in paper making is difficult to dispose of but can be consumed by *Paecilomyces* molds to produce SCP for animal feed. Other processes are being developed that will be able to utilize waste materials from a number of industries, including forestry and agriculture.

Food additives

Although true synthetic foodstuffs are not generally available for human consumption, some of the additives used to improve flavor are produced synthetically. One example is artificial sweeteners, which impart a sweet flavor although they have no food value and pass through the body unchanged. Saccharin is the best known of these and has been used for many years as a sugar substitute. It is approximately 400 times sweeter than sucrose (common sugar). Cyclamates have also been used as a sweetener, but their use has been restricted by safety fears. Another artificial sweetener is aspartame (some 200 times sweeter than sucrose), which is a combination of two amino acids and can be manufactured using a microbial fermentation process.

The food industry also makes wide use of fructose (fruit sugar) as a sweetener. It is a natural sugar found in fruit and honey. It is also manufactured, by using an amylase enzyme to convert starches into glucose and another enzyme, glucose isomerase, to convert the glucose to fructose.

Biotechnology processes are used to produce a wide range of other food additives, an outstanding example being monosodium glutamate (commonly known as MSG), widely used as a flavor enhancer. Production exceeds 0.5 million tons (0.45 million tonnes) a year, and its production is based on the fermentation of glucose using the bacterium *Corynebacterium glutamicam*.

The taste of food products—and particularly those produced by synthetic processes—is also improved by the use of flavorings, and although most flavorings have natural sources, a high proportion are replaced by artificial substitutes. These are highly refined pure chemicals and are used in very small quantities, with only a few parts per million being added to the food.

Vitamins

Many foods, such as margarine, have vitamins (A and D in margarine) added to them during manufacture as normal practice to improve their nutritional value. These vitamins are produced artificially but are chemically identical to the natural ones. In addition to their nutritional use, some vitamins are used in the food industry to improve the texture of a food.

SEE ALSO: Canning and bottling • Food preservation and packaging • Nutrition and food science • Vitamin

Forensic Science

The word *forensic* means "pertaining to the courts of law," so forensic science means science applied to legal matters. This definition covers not only criminal and civil courts but also quasi-judicial bodies, such as veterans' administration appeals and insurance claims, and medical aspects of administrative law, such as the burial of people who have died from infectious diseases.

The sciences involved in forensic science include chemistry, physics, botany, zoology, and biology, especially medicine. Forensic medical science is especially concerned with pathology and is a very old branch of forensic science, going back thousands of years to the Greek courts. More recently, forensic science was developed in the United States in 1812 with the founding of a research department in New York City initiated by the College of Physicians and Surgeons. In France in 1910, a doctor, Edmund Locard, founded a small police laboratory dedicated to forensic science that subsequently became a university department. It was Locard who first put forward the theory that a criminal almost always leaves behind at least one physical clue at the scene of the crime—a fiber, a fingerprint, or a bullet—that is a vital pointer to the criminal's identity.

From Locard's research springs the modern study of forensic science, and as the crimes themselves have grown more complex, so has the technology used to resolve them. The popular image of the forensic scientist as one who can unravel anything from a shootout to a poison case is a myth, largely perpetuated by crime-fiction writers. In fact, forensic science is multidisciplined, calling on the very specialized skills of the pathologist, the forensic toxicologist, the ballistics expert, the forensic biologist, and the chemist.

Human evidence

In the 19th century, a Belgian biometrician, Adolphe Quetelet, published a hypothesis that stated that no two human beings had the same physical measurements. This theory spurred a French police clerk, Alphonse Bertillon, acknowledged as the father of modern identification systems, to devise a criminal record system based on measurements of the human body that included data such as the circumference of the head, the length of the feet, and the width of the ears. Although Bertillon's system is antiquated by today's standards, the underlying principle—that the human body is unique and that certain clues may only belong to a certain individual—is as important now as it was then.

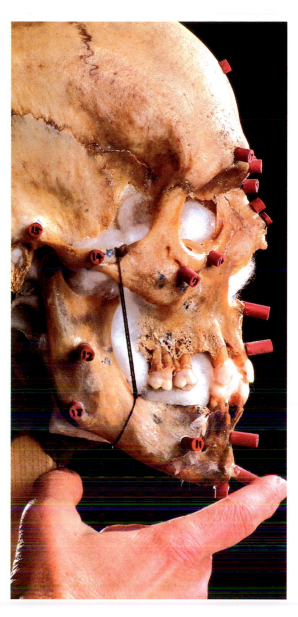

◀ The reconstruction of a human face from a skull has been one of the most dramatic advances in forensic pathology. A forensic sculptor works from 26 key points on the skull to which rubber cylinders are attached. These cylinders are of various lengths and will determine the thickness of soft covering tissue. The sculptor then applies pieces of clay, building up the surface of the face to the height of the pegs.

Today, analysis takes the form of blood testing, voice prints, speech spectrograms, forensic dentistry, and fingerprints. Of these, fingerprints are one of the most reliable forms of evidence. Unlike the probability of blood group identification (usually accurate to a fraction of one percent), the evidence of the fingerprint is indisputable. Even people with identical genetical makeup (such as identical twins) will have different fingerprints.

The forensic value of fingerprints was first recognized by Sir Edward Henry, Inspector General of Police in Bengal, India, in the late 19th century. The Henry classification of fingerprints is based on the distinctive ridges that appear on the bulbs of the inside of the fingers and thumbs. They have definite contours and appear in four general pattern types—the arch, the loop, the composite, and the whorl—each with general and specific variations of the pattern.

The Latent Fingerprint Section of the Federal Bureau of Investigation (FBI) deals with the identification of both obvious and hidden (latent) fingerprints at the scene of a crime. Fingerprints can be compared with the FBI records, but they are of little help if a first timer is involved, because only criminals, government workers, and people working for certain private employers have been finger printed. These prints may, however, be kept and matched up in due course.

Fingerprints fall into three categories: visible prints left by a bloody or dirty hand; impressions left in malleable materials, such as soap; and those that cannot be seen by the naked eye, such as perspiration marks, called latent prints. The police no longer use powder dusting techniques to locate latent prints but instead use a form of ultraviolet scanning. Once located, the prints are dusted with aluminum powder to develop them and then photographed.

Other parts of the body that leave distinctive prints are the ridges of the palms of the hands. Even the soles of the feet closely resemble the fingerprint and can be used to assist the police in tracing criminals. Unfortunately, prints from the scene may be blurred or gloves may have been worn, and legal evidence requires at least 16 points of resemblance between prints from the scene and prints on file to give a legal identification. Such evidence may not always be used in court, but it may give the police a good lead to the suspect and allow them to produce further evidence during interrogation.

Although the system of identifying fingerprints used by the FBI is based on the system devised by Edward Henry, it has been necessary to extend the system with many additions. To be considered a complete classification, all ten fingers are considered as a unit. This classification is written as a formula consisting of letters and numerals in combinations. There are 200 million records in civil and criminal categories on file at the Latent Fingerprint Section of the FBI, and a complicated cross-reference system has been designed for locating a record within minutes.

Another effective means of identification is human hair. The scene of a crime often reveals one or many hairs left by the criminal. To study hairs, an electron microscope can be used. It will give great detail but is imperfect when it comes to comparison. Possibly the most controversial means of identification is the voice pattern. This test is carried out by performing speech spectrograms on a number of selected words and phrases and comparing the pitch and intensity of speech over fractions of a second. But, while voice prints evidently show some idiosyncrasies of speech, their findings are not conclusive and are not accepted as definitive evidence. However, the State of Michigan has regularly been using voice identification techniques since 1968 with a considerable degree of success.

Forensic ballistics

The 20th century saw the rise of a new sort of homicide, that of gun death, and with it has come a whole new branch of forensic science. The field of ballistics, as it is loosely called, is now one of the busiest disciplines in forensic science. Ballistics is not simply the study of projectiles in flight but also includes specialized knowledge of the mechanical design of different firearms, the sort of wounds they make, and the analysis of the chemicals they leave behind. As soon as a bullet is fired, a telltale sign is left behind that helps point the finger at the suspect.

Most guns, except the smooth bore types, such as shotguns, flintlocks, and homemade replica guns, are rifled. Rifling means that a spiral groove has been cut into the bore of the gun barrel to impart spin to the bullet and thus make its flight path more accurate. In turn, these grooves mark a bullet when it is fired. These marks are called striations and, depending on the number and angle, can help pinpoint a particular make of gun.

Moreover, if the user of a gun is careless enough to throw down a spent cartridge, this too will bear striations. The extractor and ejector

◀ This face is the result of the forensic sculptor's art. As the superstructure is built up, an anonymous skull becomes a complete and identifiable likeness of a once-living person and can be dressed to give an idea of what the person may have looked like in a normal daily context, especially if fragments of clothing were found with the body.

mechanisms will also tend to leave scratch marks, as will the breech face, which the cartridge is slammed against when it is fired. Another important point of identification is determining whether the shell has a rim. Revolvers and shotguns normally have rimmed cartridges to prevent them from sliding through the breech, while a self-loading pistol is rimless and instead has a groove to provide grip for the extractor. Because of the popularity of pump-action shotguns within the modern criminal fraternity, the job of the firearms examiner has been made slightly easier. These guns have a magazine of up to five cartridges and are fitted with extractor and ejector devices, which leave distinctive and unique markings. Also, the ejectors tend to throw out the spent cases with some force, making it more difficult for the person firing the gun to collect them.

Two of the most important tools in the forensic ballistics laboratory are the helixometer and the comparison microscope. The former, which is a modification of a medical instrument used for examining internal organs, is a hollow probe fitted with a lamp and magnifying apparatus used for inspection of the gun barrel. The comparison microscope, invented by an American chemist and photographer, Phillip O'Grovelle, allows two bullets to be compared under a single viewing lens. Other new technology has allowed for advances in the analysis of blow back, the chemical deposits left after a gun has been fired. They include scanning electron microscopy and microprobe analysis, both of which aid minute examination of the suspect's body and clothes.

Fragment analysis

If a fragment of something can be found and later matched by comparison testing, it could implicate a criminal. For example, in a hit-and-run accident, careful analysis is made of both the victim and the automobile bodywork, to match any samples. Glass found at the scene of a hit-and-run accident could be analyzed and compared perhaps with a suspect vehicle's broken light. Analysis of the glass is obtained by a technique that compares the refractive indexes of the two fragments. Refractive indexes are the extent to which the glass fragments bend the rays of light passing through them. In the past, determining the exact index of refraction of glass shards found on a suspect and comparing them with fragments at the crime was subject to human error. Now, with the help of computers, more accurate, objective analysis can be made.

One application of comparing substances arose in New Zealand in 1982, when 12 suitcases full of marijuana were seized by police. It was

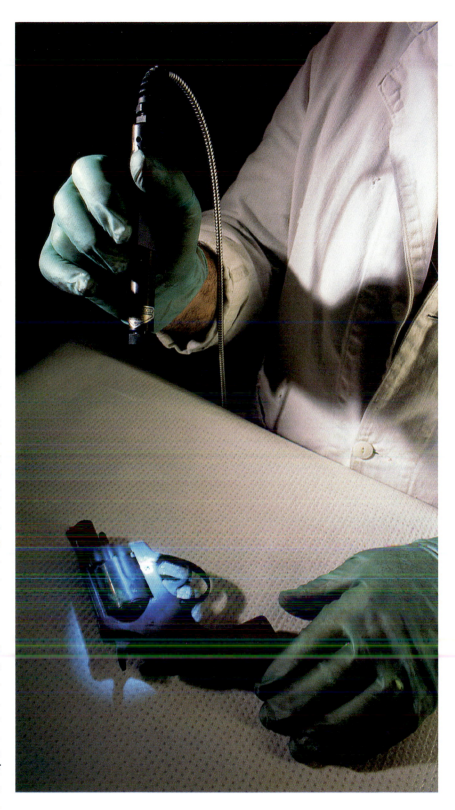

▲ A forensic technician uses a laser to look for fingerprints on a gun.

obvious who had possession, but the more important factor was to prove that the accused had attempted to transport the drug from Southeast Asia to New Zealand.

Chemical tests were made using a technique called chromatography. This involved creating a solution of the drug and allowing the solution to climb up strips of absorbent paper. Since the constituents will do so at different rates, they separated themselves into bands; these could then be compared with a chromatographic analysis of the

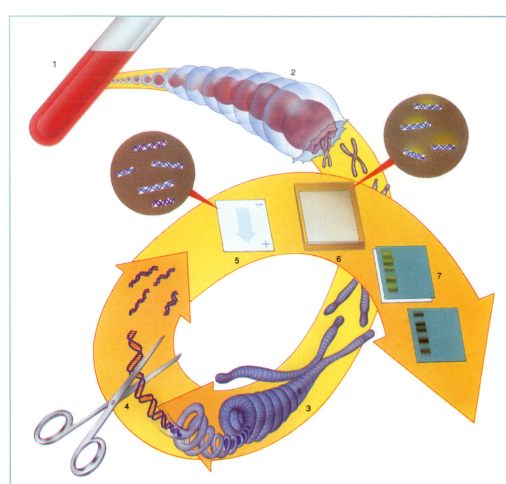

GENETIC FINGERPRINTING

The development of DNA testing, or genetic fingerprinting, has had a significant impact on the field of forensic science. Minute samples of blood and other bodily fluids, as well as hair, skin, and fibers, can enable scientists to determine the most likely suspect in a case with amazing accuracy.

The process involves taking, for example, samples of blood (1), from which DNA can be extracted (2). Each strand of DNA is isolated (3) and chemically sliced into fragments and radioactively labeled (4). These fragments of DNA (5) are placed on a sheet of polymer gel and separated by electrophoresis. The sheet is then covered by an X-ray plate (6). Different plates, for the suspects, victim, and any evidence found at the scene of the crime (7), are checked against each other to see if any match.

Southeast Asian cannabis. If the color bands were similar, then it could be shown that the drug had been imported and not homegrown. Unfortunately, the ratios of active ingredients in the samples varied considerably, and no distinction could be made between the homegrown New Zealand plants and the Asian variety. There were, however, a considerable number of tiny insects, captured during the marijuana manufacturing process, that could be seen with powerful microscopes. Entomologists, experts in insect classification and identification, checked the samples and found the bodies of 60 insects. Only one, a rice weevil, had ever been found in New Zealand. Eight of the species were indigenous to Asia. Thus, not only was the continent of origin established, but scientists were able to pinpoint the source of the marijuana to an area 150 miles south of Bangkok, Thailand. Such was the convincing weight behind the evidence that one of the guilty changed his plea to admit the charge.

Other substances that can be compared are paints, which are found in flakes made up of several layers. One method is to compare the flakes edgeways on under a microscope. Another method is gas chromatography, in which the paint flakes are burned and a comparative analysis made of the hot gases that are produced. One of the most common applications of gas chromatography is in measuring the alcohol content of blood. A stream of nitrogen is used to blow the alcohol out of the blood into and through a long tube packed with a material that holds back other variable constituents. The alcohol is thus measured electrically as it emerges. Alcohol-related road accidents are increasing, and British forensic toxicologists have found a substance in the blood that may identify the worst and most persistent offenders. Chronic drinkers have an increased amount of an enzyme called gammaglutanyl transferase in the blood, no matter how much alcohol has been taken or when.

Poisons

Poison now accounts for only a tiny percentage of homicides in the United States, but since the days of the great Victorian poisoners, such as Dr. Crippen of London, there have been several deadly newcomers to the scene. The herbicide paraquat has claimed many lives, both in accidents and in murders. Forensic pathologists are now very familiar with the subsequent pulmonary hemorrhage. New poisons, however, require new techniques to determine their use in criminal situations. This new challenge has led investigators to the specialized field of molecular biology, which can help to trace poisons, determine other causes of death, and even identify human remains.

Both criminal and civil courts receive forensic evidence in cases of suspected unnatural death. All state and local governments establish by law a procedure for forensic investigation. In most states, a medical examiner is appointed to conduct these investigations. In determining how, when, and where the deceased died, the medical examiner draws upon a range of evidence, including the medical record of the deceased, reports on the circumstances surrounding the death, and if required, an autopsy report. In other states, a coroner is elected to conduct investigations, sometimes with the help of a coroner's jury, which hears the forensic evidence but does not try the case.

Forensic medicine

The specialty of forensic medicine, broadly defined, covers any aspect of medicine that relates to the law. Clinical forensic work is concerned with living patients, from measuring the level of alcohol in the blood of those accused of drinking and driving to the examination and taking of samples from rape victims. Those doctors who practice forensic pathology, by contrast, occupy themselves with dead bodies.

Related fields are forensic serology, the study of blood groups and other inherited elements of the blood in relation to crime and the law, forensic toxicology, which is the study of poisoning in relation to crime and the law, and forensic odontology, where dentists advise on problems such as identification of corpses (by correlating their teeth with dental records) and deciding whether a suspect may have been responsible for a bite left on a murder victim.

Forensic pathology

Forensic pathology is the most famous branch of forensic medicine. The forensic pathologist will be called in to investigate deaths that are the result of accidents, that are associated with medical treatment, that are sudden or unexpected, or that are criminal or suspicious. It is the cases in the last category—people who may have been murdered—that often attract enormous publicity in the media. At the scene of a murder, police will want the forensic pathologist to help them establish key facts, such as the cause and time of death. If the body is badly decomposed, they may need help in identifying the body.

Numerous new methods help forensic pathologists to provide more accurate answers to these questions. It may be possible to determine the cause of death simply by inspecting the scene of the murder or by carrying out an autopsy.

One technique makes it possible to confirm that someone who apparently drowned was in fact still alive when he or she became submerged, ruling out the possibility that murder had been carried out by some other means and the body disposed of in water. This method involves looking for diatoms, microscopic algae found in both salt and fresh water. If someone takes water into his or her lungs when drowning, diatoms can pass from there into the bloodstream and be carried in the circulation to another organ, such as the liver. Tests on the liver at autopsy can show that diatoms, which have walls impregnated with silica, are present. But diatoms will not enter the circulation if the person's heart has stopped beating before his or her body enters the water. Diatoms can even provide clues to the place of death: different types are found in fresh and salt water and even in different localities.

Time of death

Establishing the time of death has always been a problem for police and pathologists. Three factors may be of help: the drop in temperature of the body, the order of decomposition of the various organs, and the onset and passing away of rigor mortis. But such characteristics are of only limited use in estimating the time of death and are of no use at all after three or four days have passed.

At this stage, the somewhat unlikely specialty of forensic entomology may be able to provide some clues as to the time and place of death. Particular species of flies will arrive on the body after it has cooled sufficiently for them to lay their eggs on it. These will hatch into maggots, whose age can be assessed. So if the maggots are five days old, then death must have occurred at least five days earlier—assuming the body was exposed soon after death. If the temperature outdoors is very cold, yet blowfly maggots are present on a body found outdoors, this suggests that death took place in an environment warm enough for flies to be active, probably indoors, and the body was then disposed of elsewhere. As time elapses after death, the type of insects that feed or breed on the body changes. Bluebottles, blowflies, and greenbottles, which are attracted early on, are absent during the later stages of the body's decomposition. Three to four months after

▼ A pathologist checks DNA samples for evidence of matching. The patterns on the plate are complex, and the analysis is often done manually.

FACT FILE

- Genetic fingerprinting has revolutionized much forensic work. Developed by Professor Alec Jeffreys of Leicester University in the United Kingdom, it makes it possible to identify an individual by examining his or her DNA.

- Genetic fingerprinting can be used to determine whether a blood stain found at the scene of a crime belongs to a suspect, whether a child is the offspring of its mother's husband or her lover, or whether a potential immigrant to a country really is related to his or her alleged family residing there.

- The method relies on the fact that there are highly variable regions within the DNA that consist of short sequences repeated many times. No two people (except identical twins) share the same set of these so-called hypervariable regions. A child shares about half of its hypervariables with its biological mother and the rest with its biological father. Jeffreys identified short sequences within these regions that were the same in many different people. This discovery made it possible to develop a test for the regions that would demonstrate different individuals' patterns of them.

- The first step in the technique is to obtain DNA from the tissue being tested. Enzymes added to the DNA act like chemical "scissors," chopping the molecules into pieces of unequal size. Adding pieces of DNA that are radioactively labeled and that bind to the hypervariable regions of the DNA in the sample makes it possible to show the pattern of the regions in the sample being tested. The result is a unique pattern of stripes, which looks something like a supermarket bar code.

- The method can be used to test very old forensic samples. It can also be applied to tiny samples of material that have been amplified with the polymerase chain reaction. In a development in 1992, the race of a person was able to be deduced from a sample, thus narrowing the range of suspects.

death, the tiny maggots known as cheese skippers are commonly present.

Methods to help identify the corpse have improved greatly in recent years. Study of the skeleton, provided it is complete, makes it possible to determine the person's sex and their height. In young people, the extent to which the long bones have progressed in their gradual change from cartilage to calcified bone makes it possible to provide a good estimate of age.

Characteristic features of the teeth can give clues to age and race. Scientists can detect the identity of a body from a single tooth. It is possible to use the pulp inside the tooth to determine a whole range of genetic information and in turn identify the body. Scanning electron micrographs of the teeth show that their surface becomes smoother as people age. People of Asian origin have distinctive pits on their teeth, visible under high magnification. It may also be possible to make the identification by superimposing an X ray of the skull onto a photograph of the person thought to have died. If the photograph is of the same person, key "landmarks" on the face, such as eye sockets and the position of the chin, will match up with those on the X ray.

Starting with the skull, artists have tried to make models of what people looked like when they were alive. They have used clay to build up the muscles of the face according to the positions and sizes of the areas where the muscles were originally connected to the skull.

Computer portraits

Such techniques are now being superseded by computerized methods. Laser scanners can produce a very accurate series of measurements describing the dimensions of the skull. Fed into a computer, the measurements can be translated into a three-dimensional image of the skull, which can be rotated on the screen and viewed from any angle.

Although this work is still in its early stages, it is now possible to "flesh out" the image of the skull on the screen, using software that provides information on the average thickness of the skin and muscles at each point on the face. Researchers hope eventually to collect enough data about the average thickness of the facial tissues in people of various ages and races in order to produce accurate images of what the person to whom the skull belonged looked like when he or she was alive.

 SEE ALSO: BALLISTICS • BIOTECHNOLOGY • DENTISTRY • DRUG AND ALCOHOL TESTING • GENETIC ENGINEERING • PATHOLOGY

Forestry

Forestry can be defined as the the science of managing woodlands, along with the associated wastelands and waters, for the benefit of humanity. Forestry's main aim is to raise and harvest crops of timber, but the aims of the science have become bound up with conservation of resources, such as soil, water, and wildlife, and with recreation.

Less than one-third of the world's land surface is covered in forests and woodland. However, this proportion is changing. In temperate countries, forest cutting and regeneration are more or less in balance; a few countries have even increased their forest cover this century through sustained tree planting. But in the tropics, forests are disappearing rapidly and are not being replaced. In 1999, the United Nations estimated that around 34 million acres (13.7 million hectares, or ha) of rain forest were being cleared or burned every year, the equivalent of about one football field every second. At the current rates of clearing, the Amazon forests will not last till the end of the 21st century. Estimates of the global loss vary, but by comparing old and new infrared images taken with the *Landsat* satellite, scientists have found precise figures for some areas.

All uses of wood—for fuel, pulp, lumber, and panel products—total about 8.26 billion board feet (3.5 billion m³) per year. The world is well able to supply this quantity of wood since it roughly equals annual new growth. It is local imbalances in wood demand and land clearance for other uses that cause deforestation.

Population increase is often made a scapegoat for deforestation, but the causes are mainly social and political. People clear forests to plant subsistence crops, then exhaust the nutrients in the soil and move on; governments sometimes encourage this by moving people into forest areas to save other land for cattle ranching or export crops that will bring in cash to pay foreign debt. The need for cash has also encouraged excessive logging.

Deforestation affects the livelihoods of forest dwellers and those living around forests who depend on them for food and fuel. In 1980, the Food and Agriculture Organization of the United Nations reported that 96 million people in Africa, Asia, and tropical America lacked enough wood to meet their heating and cooking needs. When wood is too scarce to use for boiling water, disease takes hold. Clear-cutting—removing all

◀ A typically lush equatorial rain forest in Guyana. Despite often infertile soil, rain forests are the densest on Earth —the foliage of trees 180 to 270 ft. (55–82 m) tall forms a thick canopy above lower, distinct levels of vegetation.

trees at one time—speeds erosion, diminishing the productivity of the soil and silting downstream reservoirs.

Forest biodiversity

Approximately 1.75 million species have been identified worldwide, and some scientists believe there may be as many as 12.5 million yet to be discovered. The majority of species live in tropical forests, but deforestation means that many plants and animals are being forced into extinction before they can even be discovered. Less than one percent of tropical forest plants have been tested for their medicinal value, yet that small number has produced drugs to treat such diseases as glaucoma, heart disease, and cancer. Perhaps most important, the destruction of forests increases the amount of carbon dioxide in the air, contributing to global warming.

Alarm over tropical deforestation and its consequences led to the International Timber Trade Agreement in 1984 and the formation of the Tropical Forest Action Program in 1985. Countries attending the U.N. Conference on Environment and Development in June 1992 in Rio de Janeiro agreed on a nonbinding statement of principles for a global consensus on the management, conservation, and sustainable development of all types of forests.

Social and community forests

Forests are no longer just timber factories. Developing countries, for example, have launched social forestry programs that encourage local peoples to create tree plantations to provide products such as fuel wood, poles, fodder, and even organic fertilizer in the form of nutrient-rich leaves. Forestry research can assist these projects; foresters in Costa Rica, for instance, have tested over 150 species of trees to see which are best suited to reforest former cattle pastures. Such tests have shown that native species of hardwoods will grow rapidly even without forest cover.

However, research is useless unless the political and economic forces behind deforestation are dealt with. Many experts believe the best way to preserve forests is not to leave them alone but to manage them to produce medicines, fruits, nuts, and other products besides timber, making them valuable enough to compete with other land uses. Using forest selectively, preserving some woodland cover, and sensitively managing plantations to enhance edge effects and preserve stream and river margins and areas of natural woodlands all enhance biodiversity. Wood production from forests is sustainable; the priority today is to make sustainable these other values, as well.

▲ In a typical tropical rain forest, the vegetation rather than the soil is the nutrient bank.

Forestry is both a very old and a very young science. Humans have been managing woodland to a greater or lesser extent from prehistory. Today, the aims of the science of forestry are far more extensive.

In prehistory it is almost certain that the greater part of the land masses was covered with forest. The natural life cycle of the trees in these forests had young trees replacing old trees after they died and disappeared. The area of forest has been reduced because of a number of factors: domestic animals have interfered with life in the forest; forests were cut down in order to gain pasture and agricultural lands; and most recently, there has been large-scale cutting of timber for commercial reasons.

Forestry in the United States

There are five principle types of forest found around the world, of which three are found in the United States. In the north around the Rocky Mountains and down the Pacific coast from Alaska to California can be found evergreen coniferous forests. At the northern edge of this kind of forestation is the timberline, where trees struggle to survive and become no more than prostrate shrubs, eventually giving way to mosses and lichens. In contrast, the trees in the Rockies and along the Pacific coast are among the finest to be found anywhere in the world. Douglas firs and western red cedars are often centuries old and from 200 to 300 ft. (60–90 m) tall. Evergreen coniferous forests supply the greatest proportion of the world's softwood timber, and important types of tree include Sitka and silver spruce; Lawson cypress; Nootka cypress from Alaska; and ponderosa pine, sugar pine, Western white pine, and Engelman spruce from the Rockies.

To the south of the evergreen zone is temperate hardwood forest. The two zones merge into a large area of mixed softwood and hardwood forest. Temperate hardwood forests can be found in the northeastern United States. The important kinds of trees include oak, ash, elm, beech, sweet chestnut, and sycamore, with species such as maples, hickories, red gum, and the tulip tree being found exclusively in the United States.

The third type of forest in the United States is subtropical evergreen forest, which is typical of Mediterranean climates. The types of tree found in this kind of forest include certain species of pine and fir trees, and evergreen oaks. Florida is one example of a region with this kind of forest, where trees such as the persimmon, dogwood, and southern yellow pine are to be found. Subtropical evergreen forests, starting in the more temperate climate of Virginia and the Carolinas and extending through Florida to most of the Caribbean, have been severely depleted by overcutting during the last 100 years but are still an important source of high-quality softwood timber.

The earliest American foresters, including Gifford Pinchot, received their training in Europe, where Germany had become the center of expertise in the 19th century. In the 20th century much legislation was passed to protect woodlands from irresponsible exploitation by those seeking short-term profits. The establishment of national forests in the United States in 1905 was the first attempt to transfer the techniques built up over hundreds of years in Europe to large-scale forest areas. It was not until the 1930s, however, that forest management really came of age.

In the United States, forests are owned by both the federal and state governments, and worldwide, governments have taken large stakes in the ownership of forests. It is interesting that every developed country, almost without exception, has deemed forestry important enough to establish a special forestry department with associated research stations and training for foresters, who are seen as valuable professionals within society. On an international level, cooperation between nations is governed and assisted by the Forestry and Forest Products Division of the UN Food and Agriculture Organization, which is based in Rome.

Trees as crops

In biblical times, trees were raised from seeds or cuttings, but it was not until 1460 that William Blair planted the first planned forest in the grounds of the Abbey of Coupar Angus in Scotland. Over the succeeding centuries, landowners in Scotland found that trees were a profitable long-term investment when planted on poor land.

The first book on forestry was published in 1664. Titled *Sylva*, it was written by a courtier of Charles II of England, John Evelyn. The following centuries have seen forestry take over the forests of Britain to the extent that most of the 4.5 million acres (1.8 million ha) of woodland are artificially planted. Throughout the world, the 20th century saw a great growth in artificial plantations, planned to meet the ever-growing demand for both timber and paper.

Forestry's objectives

The key to modern forestry lies in the multiple-use concept. No country has an excess of land that can be devoted purely to forests. Timber and other marketable products are the primary concerns of forest managers, because they give the highest returns. In addition to the hard-edged commercial demands of production, recreation has become a major consideration for foresters. Forests are gaining in importance as areas for city dwellers to visit. With careful planning, people are able to hunt, shoot, fish, walk, and pursue other outdoor activities without either the forest or its commercial objectives being harmed. The cost of facilities and supervision that visitors need can sometimes be recovered through camping and car parking fees.

Wildlife preservation is important and is controlled by legislation. By putting a halt to deforestation, forestry preserves the habitats of many wild animals—the northern coniferous forests are the habitat of wolves, bears, elks, and lynxes, for example. Rare plants can also be safeguarded by careful forest management.

The demands of sports enthusiasts, conservationists, and farmers are often directly opposed to each other, but the forest manager must try to reconcile their interests against a background of considering what is best for the forest. Forest managers, then, must have a thorough understanding of the flora and fauna that inhabit the woodlands.

Aside from the day-to-day direct considerations of running a commercial concern, forest managers have wider issues to consider. The environment must be protected. For example, in mountainous regions, woodlands are sometimes more important for protecting the watershed and preventing soil erosion than they are for commercial products and providing recreation.

Trees protect all types of soil from the effects of weathering and help enrich it by conserving moisture and providing a rich supply of fallen leaves. In climates with heavy snowfalls, trees are protection against avalanches, as they trap snow until the thaw.

▼ This tree is well adapted to the poor rain-forest soil. The massive buttress roots support the tree and absorb nutrients.

◀ A technique invented in Japan uses a giant microwave oven to make logs pliable. They can then be compressed by a simple ram into a square shape. The method squeezes out moisture, thus improving the wood's hardness and quality. Crooked logs are straightened, and waste at the sawmill is reduced by up to 50 percent. The squeezing process takes less than seven minutes.

Crop control

Treating trees as an agricultural crop has its parallels with conventional farming, but with one crucial difference—the timescale considered by foresters is far longer than that considered by farmers. Crop rotation is as important a concept in forestry as in conventional agriculture, but the shortest rotation periods are at least ten times longer than those for arable crops. The shortest rotation periods are for pulpwoods in the tropics—10 years for eucalyptus and 20 years for pines.

Away from the ideal growing conditions of the tropics, rotation periods extend significantly. Pulpwood in North America and northern Europe needs 50 years, whereas softwood sawlogs usually need about 100 years to attain a commercially viable size. The longest periods of rotation, which may be as long as 200 years, are encountered with broad-leaved trees, such as oak and beech.

Modern forests are economical only on a continuous-operation basis, which ensures a sustained yield. Over these long growing periods, a small part of the planned yield is obtained by clearing a fraction of the forest each year. The rest of the yield—some of it only really suitable for paper manufacture—is obtained by systematically thinning out the forest, each section being treated in turn after a gap of a predetermined number of years. How this system works in practice can be seen in the following example: A forest producing softwood sawlogs has a 100-year rotation. Just one percent of the forest would be cleared each year, but a further 20 percent would be thinned. The complete forest is then completely thinned at the end of five years.

Sustained-yield principles are also applied to other products from the forest. Products such as turpentine, pitch, cork, and rubber are harvested systematically over suitable time periods. Foodstuffs such as maple syrup and nuts are a source of seasonal income for the forest.

Forest management techniques

Forest management is at the core of forestry. Forest managers are concerned with everything that affects the area in their charge. They have to have a thorough knowledge of the scientific and technological aspects of the forest as well as the business and social aspects.

One of the most important concerns of forest management is silviculture, the tending of growing trees. Silvicultural systems come in two types—those employing natural regeneration and those employing artificial regeneration. Natural regeneration is the simpler of the two, requiring little investment in labor, as the forest is renewed by natural seeding. Balanced against the labor advantage is the drawback that, left to its own devices, forest regeneration is slow and irregular.

Artificial regeneration, on the other hand, raises trees from seeds or cuttings. The technique is labor intensive but can prove more profitable in the long run because regeneration is quicker and more even. Artificial regeneration also allows new varieties of trees to be introduced into the forest.

The land

Until the 20th century, foresters did not concern themselves with the land itself, planting less-difficult trees on less-fertile land and accepting the lower returns. The modern forest manager has a different attitude. Borrowing from research into plant nutrition and soil chemistry and the twin technologies of mechanical aids and artificial fertilizers, the forest manager can attend to improving low-quality soils.

Drilling deep drains and plowing are two weapons that are becoming more important as their advantages become better understood. Fertilizers based on nitrogen, potassium, and phosphorus have also been successful in boosting yields. The most popular is calcium phosphate, used at about 5 tons (4.5 tonnes) per acre.

Hazards

A forest is vulnerable to many hazards, of which the most dangerous is fire. However, not all types of forests are vulnerable to fire. Tropical rain forests and temperate hardwood forests are generally insufficiently dry for fires to occur. The story is different in hot dry zones, where conifers and evergreen broad leaves are extremely vulnerable to fire in conditions where air, smoke, and combustible gases rising from the forest floor mix and ignite in the strong sunlight. Forest fires may travel at frightening speeds—up to 10 mph (16 km/h) with a prevailing wind. The year 2000 saw some of the most devastating forest fires in the history of the United States—nearly seven million acres of forest were lost.

A forest manager, in areas where fire is a hazard, has to be expert in fire prevention techniques, including the use of natural and artificial fire breaks and organizing effective firewatching. Putting out forest fires can be a problem and demands almost military-style precision to bring together bulldozers, land-based firefighters, and special firefighting helicopters used for dumping large quantities of water.

Pest and disease control applies to every kind of forest but can be both difficult and expensive to implement. Prevention is far better than cure in forestry, so foresters aim to plant only those trees that have been proven resistant to pests and diseases. Rigorous quarantine measures are also imposed on imported trees. Once a quarantine barrier has been breached, little can be done to eliminate the danger.

Where foresters have to resort to chemicals to eliminate pests and diseases, undesired side effects can result, such as the killing of naturally occurring predatory insects that protect the trees. Birds also suffer considerable casualties from many pesticides. For these reasons, large-scale chemical treatments are usually avoided. Plant pathologists and entomologists are engaged in continual research to understand the vulnerability of trees to attack, and to minimize tree losses.

▶ A California pine seedling nursery. Forested areas in temperate regions are increasing, according to a 1992 survey. As overproduction of cereals creates "grain mountains," more land is being set aside for forestry.

In 1980, the explosive force of the eruption of Mount St. Helens in Washington State leveled trees for miles around and laid a thick blanket of fiery ash over a vast area of approximately 160,000 acres (64,500 ha). The land could have recovered on its own; it had done so after previous eruptions in the 1800s and countless other times throughout prehistory. However, foresters saw an opportunity to make the whole area a laboratory to learn how to deal with similar disasters in the future.

To study the natural restoration process, 110,000 acres (44,400 ha) were left untouched. The other 50,000 acres (22,000 ha) were divided into test plots to compare various approaches to reforestation. Some trees were planted with fertilizer, some with upright cedar shingles to shade the seedlings, some with no assistance at all. Over six years, more than 25 million trees were planted.

Scientists found the young trees grew faster than expected, probably because there were no tall trees to block sunlight and, at first, no animals to browse on the seedlings. At least 20 types of shrubs and 80 different varieties of soft vegetation have returned on their own. Animals and birds that formerly inhabited the area also came back, helped by the U.S. Forest Service, which installed bird houses and drilled holes in fallen trees to provide habitats. Still, it will be many years before the reforested area returns to its former vigor and decades before the natural area completely recovers.

FACT FILE

- The English furniture industry depended in the 18th and 19th centuries on the auctioning of small forest sections to "bodgers," makers of chair parts who lived for months on site, shaping timber with primitive pole lathes. It encouraged the cultivation of close-set, tall young trees, grown and cut by rotation and ideal for making chair legs and stretchers.

- Cork producers on the Mediterranean shores of North Africa, Spain, and Portugal strip the outer bark of the evergreen cork oak. New growth for the cork crop takes 20 years, and the groves are methodically renewed according to a long-term plan of clearing and replanting.

SEE ALSO: AGRICULTURAL MACHINERY • LUMBER • WOOD COMPOSITE

Forklift

Forklift trucks are established today as the universal means of handling materials in factories and in storage or warehouse operations. The goods are normally placed on pallets, which are platforms, usually made of wood, designed to accept the forks of the truck. This system provides a convenient means of moving, lifting, stacking, and storing loads weighing 3 tons (2.7 tonnes) or more. Forklift trucks fall basically into two main categories: general-purpose vehicles and high-density storage trucks.

General-purpose trucks

In this category, trucks are called counterbalanced fork trucks because the weight of the load is counterbalanced by the weight of the truck itself. They may be battery powered or driven by an internal combustion engine, which can be fueled by diesel oil, bottled gas, or gasoline.

On electric trucks, the lead-acid battery may weigh 3 tons (2.7 tonnes) or more, thus providing much of the counterbalance. Advanced systems of electronic solid-state control enable continuous operation for up to 18 hours before recharging. For round-the-clock operation, two batteries can be used, one is recharged while the other is in use. Electric trucks are especially useful in close quarters indoors or where food or medical supplies must be handled, because they are quiet and emit no polluting exhaust. Smaller electric trucks may be operated by a pedestrian, rather than a driver riding on the vehicle, by means of a handle similar to a lawn mower handle, with the controls built into the handle grip.

Engine-powered trucks are used for large warehouse and stock-handling applications, for general yardwork, and for loading and unloading of vehicles. Torque converter transmission provides smooth operation; power steering and all-weather cabs are options available.

Forklift trucks for general purposes have pneumatic or solid tires. The lifting mechanism is hydraulic. An electrically driven hydraulic pump, or mechanical pump driven off the engine, supplies oil pressure through control valves to a hydraulic cylinder, or lift jack. The forks are mounted on a double or triple section mast, which extends upward as the lift jack raises the forks through a system of chains and rollers. The mast can be tilted forward and backward by

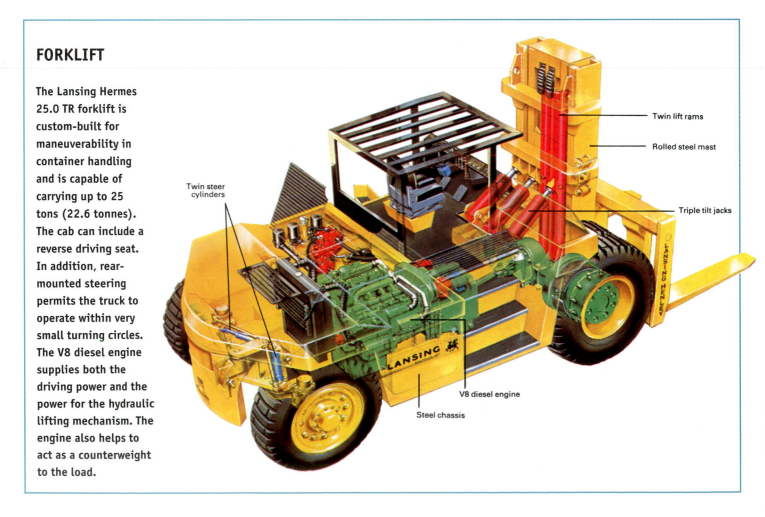

FORKLIFT

The Lansing Hermes 25.0 TR forklift is custom-built for maneuverability in container handling and is capable of carrying up to 25 tons (22.6 tonnes). The cab can include a reverse driving seat. In addition, rear-mounted steering permits the truck to operate within very small turning circles. The V8 diesel engine supplies both the driving power and the power for the hydraulic lifting mechanism. The engine also helps to act as a counterweight to the load.

Twin steer cylinders

Twin lift rams

Rolled steel mast

Triple tilt jacks

V8 diesel engine

Steel chassis

A turret truck rotating the load within a narrow aisle. The rails are on the storage racks.

means of smaller tilt jacks. Accessories can be fitted for lifting awkward loads, such as reels of newsprint or barrels.

Lift capacities of counterbalanced trucks range from about 1,000 lbs. (454 kg) to 10,000 lbs. (4,540 kg) for electric models and 4,000 lbs. (1,814 kg) to perhaps 100,000 lbs. (45,400 kg) for the engine-powered trucks. (The largest models are used in container handling.) Most forklift trucks have the steering positioned on the rear wheels, which allows the truck to operate with a very small turning radius.

High-density storage

The high-density storage, or narrow-aisle, forklift trucks are called reach trucks and turret trucks and are electrically powered. The electric and hydraulic systems are the same as for general-purpose trucks, but reach and turret trucks are used in storage systems designed to use the maximum amount of space, with narrow aisles and goods stacked as high as possible.

The reach truck is so called because the whole mast and fork unit reaches out to pick up a load. The wheelbase of the truck is the same length as in an ordinary forklift truck of comparable size, but the size of the body of the truck is considerably more compact; reach legs extend from the body of the truck to the front wheels, and the mast travels back and forth on these. Once the load has been picked up, it is brought backward to within the wheelbase of the truck, thus reducing

the length of the truck and its load by as much as a third of the length of the conventional truck. The truck has an extremely short turning radius, and the driver sits sideways, since in a narrow-aisle situation, he or she is driving backward as much as forward. The truck can also be used for ordinary forklift truck applications and can be fitted with attachments for special lifting jobs.

On a turret truck, the mast is fixed and does not reach, but the truck is fitted with a turret mechanism that turns the forks through 90 degrees to either side of the truck. Then the forks reach out on a pantograph arrangement to pick up a load. The truck itself does not have to turn to face the load, thus, the aisle width required for operation is even less than for the reach truck. The aisle width is governed by the diagonal size of the load and can be as little as 62 in. (1.6 m).

Because of the narrowness of the aisle, the truck is guided by rails on each side of the gangway at the base of the storage racks; the rails locate with side rollers on the truck. This relieves the operator of the necessity of steering, unless the truck is being operated outside the aisle. Because turret trucks can lift load to heights in excess of 30 ft. (9 m), beyond accurate judgment by eye, the driver can preselect the correct operating height by pushing a button.

▶ A versatile modern electric forklift truck, which can lift to a height of 20 ft. (7 m) or more and has a special hydraulic attachment for handling cylindrical bulk paper reels.

SEE ALSO: FREIGHT HANDLING • HYDRAULICS • WAREHOUSING

Freight Handling

Sea transport of bulk cargoes, especially coal and grain, is at least as old as iron ships, which began to come into use in the 1860s. Loading and unloading of these vessels required a large, cheap labor force equipped mainly with baskets and shovels. These were followed in time by mechanical hoists that elevated railway trucks and tipped their contents directly into the ship's hold; cranes equipped with grabs were used for discharging the cargo from the holds.

Many materials that are today bulked were transported in sacks or barrels until well after World War I. Such methods still called upon a large labor force—one gang to enter a ship's hold and manhandle the separate units onto a cargo net, a crane to lift the full net over the ship's side, and a second gang to transfer the contents of the net into waiting trucks, which were then driven into the warehouse where a third gang built a stack. It is not surprising therefore that loading and discharge costs could account for as much as 50 percent of the cost of an entire voyage.

In comparison with ocean-going vessels, bulk transport by road and rail vehicles, per carrying unit, has been insignificant. Rail vehicles are always limited in size by existing tunnels, gradients, track curves, and signal gantries. Road haulage, despite the advent of the motor age, did not develop much for many years, partly because the only roads available were those built for horse-drawn vehicles and were unpaved, so it was quicker to send goods by rail.

Common bulked materials

A wide range of liquid and free-flowing solid materials are today successfully transported in bulk. These materials include solids such as metal ores, fertilizers, coal, limestone, cement, whole grains, flour, chemicals, and sugar. Liquid materials include petroleum products, vegetable oils, latex, liquefied gases, chemicals, wine, fruit juices, milk, water, and beer.

Crude oil and petroleum products account for the largest annual tonnage shipped in bulk. Grain shipments stand second, although ore cargoes are ever increasing as the demand for metals rises and ore deposits in manufacturing countries are worked out, making it necessary to import ores from overseas.

The reasons for bulked, rather than packaged, transport are clearly economic since bulk handling requires no labor for packing or unpacking and no packaging materials and a relatively small labor force is needed to control

▲ The largest supertankers can measure a quarter of a mile in length. The powerful pumps aboard such a vessel can load and discharge a full cargo in 24 hours. For inspecting the decks, the crew are sometimes provided with bicycles.

loading and unloading. Bulked cargoes can be handled relatively quickly, and therefore ships spend less time in dock.

Ships

The most spectacular bulk-carrying vessel today is the tanker; before 1939, the typical tanker did not exceed 12,000 deadweight (dwt) tons (11,000 tonnes); by 1972, the popular size was around 250,000 tons (225,000 tonnes). By comparison, one modern bulk tanker, the *Seawise Giant*, is rated at 565,000 tons dwt (509,000 tonnes). The deadweight tonnage is the difference, in tons, between the amount of water displaced by the ship when unloaded and its displacement when fully loaded with cargo, fuel, and stores.

The advent of these very large crude carriers (VLCC), or supertankers, was due partly to a new policy of refining at the marketing end of the haul rather than at the loading end and partly to the temporary closure of the Suez Canal, which meant that oil from the Arabian Gulf had to be carried all the way around the coast of Africa instead of through the canal and the Mediterranean Sea. In addition, it was found that oil transportation costs fell dramatically when the tanker size was increased above 70,000 tons (63,000 tonnes). Apart from other factors, crew costs do not rise proportionately with the size of the tanker. Despite loading and discharge jetties being built well out into deep water, the draught of the largest tankers is often too great to permit direct approach to many jetties when the vessel is fully laden. Part of the cargo, therefore, has to be transshipped to a smaller vessel in some sheltered deep-water area.

Apart from oil products, there are a vast number of wet- and dry-cargo carriers at sea today. Some vessels are built specially for conveying a single product, for example, liquefied methane gas. For this cargo, the hull is filled with a number of separate, insulated, refrigerated tanks, and the vessels can operate only between specified ports having the necessary handling and storage equipment. Such vessels typically have a cargo capacity of 12,000 to 14,000 tons (7,000–12,500 tonnes). Other products shipped in tankers include molasses, vegetable oils, whale oil, bitumen, grain, various chemicals and solvents, wine, and caustic soda.

Road and rail

Although there are fundamental limitations to the size of freight cars, with modern track design, improved vacuum and compressed-air brakes, and increased locomotive power, larger train loads and bigger freight cars are being used. In the United States, maximum train loads can be as high as 30,000 tons (27,000 tonnes). Some rail tankers in service in the United States can carry over 30,000 gallons (114,000 l). In other parts of the world, tank cars carrying between 16,000 gallons (61,000 l) and 25,000 gallons (95,000 l) are in use.

Apart from oil and petrochemical products, specialized tankers are used for the bulk transport of many liquids and chemicals and for powdered or granular materials, such as cement, lime, flour, starch, and plastic pellets. These products are usually unloaded from the tankers using pneumatic or suction conveyors or by gravity discharge through the bottom of the tanks.

For some applications the tanks may be refrigerated or heated. In Spain, for example, tankers for liquid asphalt are heavily insulated and have heating systems to keep the asphalt at 480°F (250°C). Within iron and steel works, the hot liquid metal from the furnaces and converters is often moved from one area to another in custom-built rail tankers that can hold over 250 tons (225 tonnes). Hopper cars, with a capacity of as much as 110 tons (100 tonnes), are used to carry bulk loads of many solid materials, including coal, ores, grain, wood chips, limestone, and aggregates.

Road vehicles carry the same range of bulked goods as the railways, and the size of the loads has increased steadily. Trucks capable of hauling 40 to 50 tons (36–45 tonnes) are common, but many countries are restricting the size of vehicles for environmental reasons and developing their rail freight services to encourage shippers to send long-distance loads by rail instead of by road.

Handling equipment

A growing number of ports are now extensively adapted for handling bulk cargoes. For full efficiency, fast transport must be matched by rapid loading and discharge methods, and this requirement has led to the introduction of numerous specialized handling devices. Whereas packaged goods create a need for pallets, forklift trucks, cranes, and slings, bulk handling methods rely on more expensive but much faster pumps, compressors, conveyors, or pipelines. Pipelines are used for conveying liquids and gases, the best known and most important of these being water, crude oil, refined petroleum products, natural gas, and coal gas. In the case of refined petroleum products such as diesel oil, heating oil, and gasoline, they can be sent in batches at the same time because the amount of mixing can be kept to a minimum or prevented.

Choice of a method is governed by the characteristics of the material: flowability, abrasiveness, corrosiveness, dampness, presence of dust or noxious fumes, or sensitivity to contamination. Liquids are usually loaded and discharged by pumps that are part of the equipment of a ship or road vehicle: a large oceangoing oil tanker has pumps capable of delivering 10,000 tons (9,000 tonnes) per hour, and complete loading or discharge can be finished in 24 hours; the crew required for the operation is minimal.

◀ Molten steel will remain liquid for long journeys in a well-insulated container, so the metal can be formed in specialized plants many miles away from its point of production.

Grain flows easily, and modern handling equipment, normally shore based, includes compressor operated suction pipes and Archimedes' screw conveyors. A grain ship can be unloaded at a rate of 2,000 tons (1,800 tonnes) per hour at a modern terminal. When bulk loads of grain, flour, or other granular and powdered solids are being handled, great care must be taken to avoid the buildup of static electricity, because the dust-laden atmosphere created is highly combustible and the spark from a static discharge could easily cause a serious explosion.

Pumping, suction, blowing, and screw conveyors are methods of continuous handling. Discontinuous methods include aerial cableways, which can run many miles from a mine and discharge by gravity directly into a ship's hold. Other discontinuous methods include the giant crawler cranes, used on opencast mineral deposits, which have a shovel capacity of 60 tons (54 tonnes) or more.

Container handling

Container handling consists of stowing large amounts of cargo into strong, standard-sized, reusable metal containers and transporting the sealed containers to the consignees.

Using the traditional (or break bulk) methods, an average loading rate for a seagoing vessel is 10 tons (9 tonnes) per hour. With containerization, 30 tons (27 tonnes), the maximum capacity of a single container, can be loaded and stowed in ten minutes. Containers also offer other advantages. The cargo, which is sealed inside its container, cannot easily be stolen, and it arrives at its destination in a better condition than formerly. Furthermore, the lower levels of stacks of cargo cannot be crushed. Labor, packaging costs, and insurance charges are reduced, and ships can effect a much faster turnaround. The five days required for break bulk methods is reduced to one day or less by containerization, with a corresponding increase in revenue earning capacity. In the ports, warehouses are no longer required, as the containers are weatherproof.

Although the concept of transporting goods in sealed containers was not new, the container revolution started in the 1960s following the establishment of standard sizes for containers. Standardization meant that the various interested agencies—shipping lines, road and rail transport companies, and port authorities—could tailor their carrying facilities to suit the containers. The

▲ Containers being moved by crane onto a railroad transporter at a distribution center. Some industries, such as coal mining and power plants, have their own dedicated rail terminals for easy loading and unloading of raw materials.

advantages of container shipping has led to its widespread adoption on major routes, rapidly displacing conventional methods of cargo handling. A particular feature has been the development of hub center shipping networks, where main ports act as distribution centers. Here containers are shipped in from a number of smaller ports and consolidated into full loads for shipping on the main trade routes, such as across the Atlantic.

The container

The standard container is either 20 or 40 ft. (6 or 12 m) long—although there are a small number of 30 ft. (9 m) containers—and 8 ft. (2.4 m) high by 8 ft. wide. These dimensions are a development of the container dimensions used to supply U.S. forces in Europe, being such that ammunition boxes fit in perfectly. The standard box container has rigid corner posts and a rigid steel frame with steel infill panels. Standard reinforced lifting apertures are built into the four top corners. The container is durable and can be heated, ventilated, or refrigerated. It must be loaded so that the contents cannot move—interior restraint devices, such as webs or shoring bars, are therefore provided, to be clipped or slotted into side, floor, and roof racks.

Special-purpose containers are also produced such as open-top units for heavy machinery, tank units for liquids, and side-opening designs for rail use. Half-height, 4 ft. (1.2 m) high, containers are used for heavy materials, such as steel, where the load restrictions mean that a standard-sized container could not be filled.

The maximum loaded container weights are 20 tons (18 tonnes) for 20 ft. (6 m) containers and 30 tons (27 tonnes) for 40 ft. (12 m) containers. A 40 ft. (12 m) container weighs approximately 5 tons (4.5 tonnes) when empty.

Loading and terminal handling

Although goods are often loaded piecemeal into containers with the aid of hand trolleys, mechanical loading systems are also used, including pneumatic extending roller conveyors and low-profile forklift trucks that can be driven into the interior. Prior to being loaded, the container may be mounted on a flatbed road trailer or rail chassis, ready for transport to a container depot or terminal; sometimes it is more convenient to employ self-loading road vehicles that can lift a 40 ft. (12 m) container with their own lifting gear.

A swap-body system is also used for container movement. This system requires a rigid leg fitted to each corner of a container so that a road transporter can temporarily park it, support it on jacks, then drive away from beneath it.

On reaching the container terminal at the docks, a 40-ton (36-tonne) capacity ship-to-shore container crane straddles the road or rail vehicles, lifts the containers, and transfers them along a 120 ft. (36 m) boom directly into the ship's hold or onto its deck.

Container stacking in the terminal area and the loading of road or rail vehicles from a stack (which may be three containers high) are accomplished by a terminal handling crane; this is of similar straddle and carrying capacity to the ship-to-shore crane, but without its long reach. This crane is usually rail mounted. For moving containers about the parking area, the more mobile straddle carrier or forklift trucks are used, which can also stack the containers three high.

These types of container-handling equipment have telescopic spreader attachments to suit 20 ft. (6 m), 30 ft. (9 m), or 40 ft. (12 m) containers; the attachments incorporate locking fasteners that locate positively into the top corner fittings of the

▶ Straddle carriers position containers for handling by wharf cranes. The cranes then load directly into the container ships. Most ports will have a number of different types of cranes to handle the variety of cargoes being shipped.

container, which are specially reinforced. The specialized container ship accommodates stacks perhaps six containers high in the hold and two high or three high on the deck. Usually a complete row of containers can be locked together.

Container ship capacity is measured in twenty-foot equivalent units (TEU) so that a 40 ft. (12 m) container represents 2 TEU. The majority of modern container ships have capacities of less than 5,000 TEU, but an increasing number of new ships are being built to carry even more units—the highest-capacity ship on order in 2000 will be capable of transporting 7,200 TEU.

The volume of container traffic is also expressed in terms of TEU. In 1998, the volume of container traffic being shipped around the world reached 156 million TEU, about half of which passed through the Asian ports of Singapore, Hong Kong, Kaohsiung (Taiwan), and Tokyo. However, the busiest container port is Rotterdam, with a movement of over two million TEU compared with just under two million TEU for New York, which is the second biggest.

Another form of containerization is the roll-on, roll-off (ro-ro) system by which a 30-to-40-ton (27–36 tonne) loaded trailer is driven onto a ship through bow or stern doors and driven off, direct to its ultimate destination, from its port of arrival. Although originally developed for short sea routes, the advantages of rapid loading and unloading have led to the use of ro-ro ships on longer routes, such as across the Pacific. Nearly one-quarter of the general cargo fleet around the world is now made up of ro-ro type ships.

Air containerization

With the introduction of wide-bodied aircraft, such as the Boeing 747, the Douglas DC10, and the Lockheed L1011, and the use of all-freight flights, the use of airborne containers has expanded considerably. Some 6 million tons (5.4 million tonnes) of air freight was shipped by airlines to and from the United States in 1995.

Although much of the traffic uses nonstandard containers, often tailored to suit the space available in specific aircraft, increasing use is being made of a lightweight version of the 20 ft. container. These containers are normally made of aluminum alloy or glass-reinforced plastic and typically would have a maximum gross weight of 12 tons (8.4 tonnes) with the container itself weighing 1 ton (0.9 tonnes).

Use of aircraft offers the advantages of speed of shipment and is particularly good for transporting fresh produce, such as vegetables and flowers, which would perish if shipped by conventional means. Often air freight provides the only means for some countries to export their goods abroad.

▲ A ship docked at the British port of Manchester, showing two of the ship-to-shore container cranes. The turnaround time for a ship like this is little more than a few hours.

SEE ALSO: CONVEYOR • CRANE • DOCK • ELEVATOR, GRAIN • RAILROAD SYSTEM • RAILROAD YARD • SHIP • TANKER • WAREHOUSING

Friction

Friction is the resistance to motion that occurs when an attempt is made to slide one surface over another. This frictional resistance is a force, but a purely reactive one; that is, it does not arise by itself in isolation. It always arises as a reaction to the force trying to create such a motion.

When there is relative motion between two surfaces (known as slipping), the frictional force opposing this slipping is called kinetic friction. Before slipping occurs, the frictional force is called static friction. Usually, for any two surfaces, static friction is greater than kinetic friction.

Uses and disadvantages of friction

A useful consequence of friction is that a ladder can be placed against a wall without slipping down. It is the static friction force between the ladder and the ground and wall that keeps it in its place. Braking systems harness kinetic friction to slow down a moving vehicle or machine. In the process of braking, heat is generated in the brakes, and this heat energy equals the amount of kinetic energy lost as the vehicle or machine slows down. Also, without rolling friction between the tires and the ground or road surface, a vehicle would not be able to brake or turn corners.

In many mechanical systems, however, friction can be a nuisance and sometimes destructive. Machines that must periodically stop and start have to overcome static friction each time they start up. If this force becomes too large, the machine may not start up at all—a permanent stall condition. The kinetic (rubbing) friction between the piston and cylinder of an engine must be reduced to a safe limit if overheating and destruction of the finely machined surfaces is to be eliminated. In such circumstances lubrication may be required.

Limiting friction

Consider a block of wood on a horizontal table. A small sideways force on the block will do nothing; thus, the static frictional resistance between the block and the table is equal and opposite to the applied force. Frictional resistance cannot, however, continue to restrain the movement of the block if this force is made bigger. A point is eventually reached—called limiting friction—when the block will "break away" from its position. It then starts to move (slip).

Limiting friction is the critical point considered in many calculations concerning friction. For example, a ladder against a wall is stable at steep angles of lean, but it will slip down at shallow angles. The critical angle at which this begins to happen is determined from the value of limiting friction of the ladder against ground and wall.

The laws of friction

The first systematic observations of friction were performed by Leonardo da Vinci in the 15th century. His findings were developed by the French physicist Charles Coulomb in 1781. The empirical laws describing mechanical friction that they formulated still form part of classical mechanics.

The first law states that the value of limiting friction between two solid bodies is independent of the (apparent) area of mutual contact. That is, the maximum frictional force that can occur between the block of wood and the table is the same whether the block is standing on its largest or smallest face.

The second law states that, for two given materials, such as wood on wood, the maximum (limiting) frictional force is directly proportional to the load one material puts on the other. Therefore, doubling the weight of the block of wood doubles the limiting frictional force between it and the table.

From this second law, it can be seen that the ratio of limiting frictional force to load for any two materials is a constant. Furthermore, this constant—called the coefficient of friction and

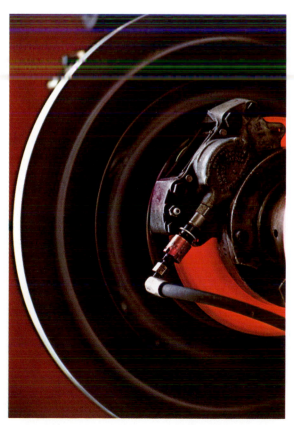

◀ Although glowing red hot, this disk brake on test remains intact at temperatures in excess of 1112°F (600°C). Brakes convert the kinetic energy of a vehicle into heat to slow it down.

◀ Friction welding, in which friction created between two surfaces is used as a heat source. Two chucks hold the parts to be welded. One rotates while the other presses the second half of the workpiece against the rotating end. The joint heats up in seconds, and the rotation is stopped. An axial force, which may be over 250 tons, is applied to make the weld.

usually assigned the Greek symbol of μ—is a property of the two materials alone and is in no way related to the shape or size of the objects concerned. Substances with a low μ value, such as ice on ice (μ = 0.02), have slippery surfaces—the maximum frictional force in this example is only 4 lbs. (2 kg) for a 220 lb. (100 kg) block of ice. Some typical values of coefficient of friction are bronze on bronze (μ = 0.2), wood on steel (μ = 0.5), and steel on steel (μ = 0.1).

The physics of friction

Under the high magnification provided by the electron microscope, even the flattest surface is, in fact, quite irregular. It consists of troughs, or valleys, and asperities, or peaks. Thus, any two surfaces apparently in good physical contact will actually touch at only a few points.

When one surface is bearing the weight of another, the local pressures at these points of contact can be enormous. These high pressures cause virtual welding of one point to another with the formation of weak chemical bonds between the surface atoms. These interactions are termed surface adhesion. It is the strength of these bonds, limited though they are, and the work done in continually having to break them that is observed as frictional resistance to motion. For chemically clean surfaces, the force required to break adhesions is very high, but often contaminants, such as oxide films, which considerably weaken the bonding, are present.

Rolling friction, such as occurs between a wheel and the road surface, is much less than kinetic friction because the bonds are "peeled" away by the rotary motion of the wheel rather than ruptured or sheared over the entire length of the surface. For this reason, vehicles have wheels rather than runners. Bearings also exploit this property to produce nearly friction-free motion.

Since it is the behavior of the surfaces that is important, and as already mentioned the introduction of a cushioning layer of some impurity will reduce the surface bonding, lubricants are often used to reduce friction. A solid body moving through a fluid, such as air, water, or oil, also meets frictional opposition, but this type of friction is usually expressed in terms of the fluid medium's viscosity.

One substance, helium-4, exhibits zero viscosity. Below a temperature of –455°F (–271°C), it makes the transition from a normal liquid to a superfluid. Unlike any other natural substance, superfluid helium-4 flows without any apparent friction. There is no classical explanation; the theory of superfluids rests entirely on quantum mechanics.

Maglev trains

Maglev trains are monorails that hover above the surface of the track on powerful magnetic fields. These systems have the advantage of much reduced friction—the only friction remaining is in the form of air resistance—and the potential for much greater speeds. However, though much experimentation has occurred in Europe, Japan, and the United States, few passenger-carrying maglev trains have actually been built. Increased speeds on conventional trains combined with the greater building costs of maglev trains have discouraged governments from investing in this form of transport.

SEE ALSO: BEARING AND BUSHING • CHEMICAL BONDING AND VALENCY • LUBRICATION • MONORAIL SYSTEM • VISCOSITY

Fuel Cell

A fuel cell is a device that produces electrical energy directly from the chemical energy released when a hydrogen-containing fuel is oxidized. Fuel cells resemble electrochemical power cells in many respects; the main difference is that fuel cells are designed to use a continuous supply of fuel, whereas a cell contains a fixed amount of fuel that is consumed as the cell provides energy. A functioning fuel cell produces pure water, which is a useful by-product in isolated vehicles such as spacecraft and submarines.

A fuel cell can produce around 15 times as much power as a lead–acid automobile battery of the same weight, which is useful where space is limited. Fuels cells are also extremely robust and require little maintenance, making them good power sources for remote locations.

Principles and early models

The inventor of the fuel cell is generally held to be the British physicist William Grove, whose gas battery of 1838 used a reaction that is the basis of modern fuel cells. Grove's device comprised two platinum electrodes dipped in sulfuric acid. Hydrogen bubbles played over one of the electrodes, while oxygen bubbled over the other.

Platinum catalyzes the dissociation of hydrogen molecules (H_2) into hydrogen ions according to the following equation:

$$H_2 \rightarrow 2H^+ + 2e^-$$

The electrons released by this reaction passed into the platinum electrode of Grove's cell. When he connected the two electrodes through an electrical circuit, a current flowed and the electrons that passed into the other electrode took part in the dissociation of oxygen:

$$O_2 + 4e^- \rightarrow 2O^{2-}$$

Oxide and hydrogen ions combine immediately, so the overall reaction was an oxidation of hydrogen to form water. Most of the heat energy that would have been released by burning hydrogen was instead converted into electrical energy.

Early drawbacks

Grove's gas battery had three major failings that prevented it from being a commercially viable power source. First, the cell's output was limited by the small contact areas between gases, electrolyte, and electrodes. Second, by-product water gradually diluted the electrolyte, reducing its effectiveness and eventually halting the reaction. The third failing was the high cost of platinum.

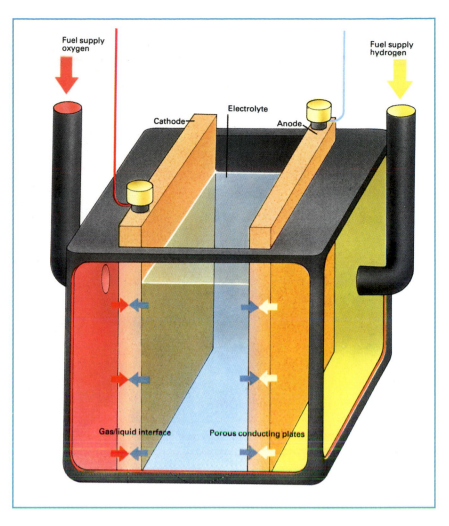

Fuel supply oxygen

Fuel supply hydrogen

Cathode

Electrolyte

Anode

Gas/liquid interface

Porous conducting plates

Developments

Modern fuel cells, developed since the 1950s, resolve the problems of Grove's device in various ingenious ways. First, their electrodes are porous membranes that separate the electrolyte from the fuel gas and oxygen while providing a large surface area per unit volume, which facilitates the interactions between the gases and the electrolyte. Second, by-product water is removed by evaporation from a hot electrolyte or by simple drainage from the fuel-gas side of the electrode where it forms. Finally, many fuel cells use relatively cheap electrode materials, such as carbon or nickel.

Several limitations remain, however. The electrodes and electrolyte of a fuel cell may eventually decompose. This process is much slower than the breakdown of the equivalent components of conventional power cells, in which the electrolyte and sometimes the electrodes are consumed by the energy-providing reaction.

The pressures of the fuel gas and the oxidant (air or oxygen) are critical to the efficiency and power output of a cell. Too little pressure allows the electrolyte to escape through the porous electrodes; too much pressure forces the electrolyte from the electrodes' pores, reducing the vital area of contact between gas, electrolyte, and electrodes.

▲ This diagram shows the layout of a three-chamber fuel cell. Hydrogen is fed into one chamber, from which it diffuses into a porous electrode and interacts with an electrolyte. Hydrogen molecules release electrons as they form positive hydrogen ions, giving the electrode a negative potential. A positive potential develops at the other electrode, where the process that forms hydroxide ions from water and oxygen consumes electrons.

One type of fuel cell uses solutions of alkali-metal hydroxides, such as potassium hydroxide (KOH), as electrolytes. The hydroxide ion acts as a carrier of oxide ions in these cells, and the electrode reactions are as follows:

$$2H_2 + 4OH^- \rightarrow 4H_2O + 4e^-$$
$$O_2 + 2H_2O + 4e^- \rightarrow 4OH^-$$

Variations of this type of cell use hot, molten metal carbonates, in which the carbonate ion (CO_3^{2-}) is the oxide-ion carrier, or even solid modified zirconium dioxide (ZrO_2), which conducts oxide ions through its lattice at operating temperatures of around 1800°F (1000°C).

Other types of fuel cells use acidic electrolytes, such as phosphoric acid or sulfuric acid. The electrode reactions in such fuel cells are identical to those of the Grove gas battery.

Alternative fuels

Hydrogen is not the only fuel that can be used in fuel cells, although most fuels are compounds of hydrogen. Alternatives include methane (CH_4) and methanol (CH_3OH), which are oxidized to form carbon dioxide and water, and hydrazine (NH_2NH_2), which forms water and nitrogen. Fuel cells that use molten carbonate electrolytes can even use carbon monoxide as fuel, converting it into carbon dioxide and producing no water.

Fuel cells that can use the complex mixtures of hydrocarbons found in gasoline are in development, as are reformers—devices that produce hydrogen from gasoline. Such systems will improve the acceptability of fuel cells as power sources for electric road vehicles, since they will allow such vehicles to use the extensive infrastructure of gas stations that already exists.

Operating efficiency and costs

The electrochemical reaction in a fuel cell releases around 95 percent of the chemical energy theoretically available from a fuel, the remaining energy being lost to the internal resistance of the cell. Some of the power output is diverted to heaters and pumps that keep the fuel cell operating, and the typical efficiency is around 60 to 65 percent once these demands have been met.

Fuel cells are considerably more efficient than conventional fossil-fuel power plants. A large coal-fired power plant can convert around 35 percent of the thermal energy of burning coal into electrical energy, while a natural-gas-burning power plant converts up to 45 percent of the total thermal energy into electricity. Nevertheless, the relatively high costs of the fuels and components used in fuel cells make them uncompetitive for power outputs greater than around 100 megawatts.

Applications

One of the earliest applications of fuel cells was in the *Gemini 5* spacecraft, which undertook a nine-day flight in 1965. The advantages of the fuel cell for space flights include their lack of harmful emissions and their by-product—water—which astronauts can drink and use for washing. Fuel cells were also used in the Apollo missions, when efficiencies around 75 percent were attained, and they continue to be used in NASA's space shuttles.

The complete lack of harmful emissions also makes fuel cells attractive for use with electric motors in vehicles. One such fuel cell, General Motors' HydroGen 1, produces 80 kilowatts of power at 53 to 67 percent efficiency. The power output and compactness of the HydroGen 1 are sufficient for it to be used to power the motor of an electric automobile. On a larger scale, the first of 25 prototype fuel-cell powered electric buses went into service for the SunLine Transit Agency of Palm Springs, California, in September 2000.

Many of the current projects related to expanding the exploitation of fuel cells focus on making hydrogen cheaper and more readily available. One such scheme uses concentrated sunlight to convert water into hydrogen and oxygen by thermal decomposition. This system has the advantage over conventional solar power that the hydrogen and oxygen can be stored and used in fuel cells to provide power according to demand. Another project aims to develop a domestic electrolysis cell for producing hydrogen for fuel-cell vehicles from electricity and water.

▲ A rechargeable aluminum–air fuel cell in test for potential use in quiet, pollution-free electric road vehicles.

SEE ALSO: BATTERY • CATALYST • LOW-EMISSION ROAD VEHICLE

Fuel Injection

Fuel-injection systems introduce fuels, such as gasoline, diesel, or alcohol–gasoline mixtures, into internal combustion engines. Some types dispense metered doses of fuel into the cylinders of piston engines; other types spray continuous streams of fuel into the combustion chambers of gas turbines. Together with an effective engine-management system, fuel injection increases the efficiency of such engines, as well as improving the quality of their exhaust gases.

Fuel injectors were developed at the end of the 19th century for diesel engines, which require a pressurized fuel input. Gasoline engines of that time used a fuel–air mixture from a carburetor, in which fuel vaporized and mixed with air. In such a system, the fuel–air mixture is drawn into the cylinder during the induction stroke of the engine cycle. In that stroke, the piston moves away from the cylinder head and creates a partial vacuum.

In the 1930s, fuel injection was introduced for gasoline-burning aircraft engines; this type of engine was fitted to a large number of World War II aircraft, where it proved its worth under demanding flight conditions. Nevertheless, the possibility of using fuel injection systems for gasoline-burning automobile engines continued to be overlooked for several years.

Car manufacturers started to use fuel injection for gasoline engines in the mid-1970s, when increasing fuel costs made the fuel-saving potential of such systems attractive. The earliest gasoline-injection systems were mechanical, as were the diesel-injection systems of the time.

By the end of the 20th century, most new cars—gasoline or diesel—were fitted with electronic fuel-injection systems, usually commanded by an electronic control module (ECM), sometimes called an electronic control unit (ECU). By injecting fuel in doses and with timing suited to an engine's operating conditions at any instant, this combination improves performance and fuel economy while reducing harmful emissions.

Coal injection

When the German engineer Rudolf Diesel built the first example of the compression-ignition engines that would later bear his name, he intended it to use powdered coal as its fuel. Its fuel-injection system was a blast of air that blew coal into its cylinders. Unfortunately, Diesel's choice of fuel made the engine difficult to control and prone to clogging, which soon caused it to explode. Air-blown pulverized-coal injectors are now used to feed many large industrial furnaces.

▲ This picture shows the main components of a mechanical gasoline-injection system: a rotor-and-sleeve metering device (left) and an electrical fuel pump (right).

▼ A close-up view of a mechanical injector. The bright metal tip is part of a spring-loaded valve. When fuel enters the injector under pressure, it forces the valve out of its seating and issues around its edge, forming a fine mist of fuel.

Early diesel injectors

In a diesel engine, fuel is admitted to the cylinders after a charge of air in the cylinder has been compressed to make it hot. The high temperature then ignites the fuel–air mixture. Fuel injection is necessary because of the high pressure in the cylinders at the time of injection.

After trying powdered coal as the fuel for his engine, Diesel experimented with liquid petroleum, still using a blast of compressed air to spray fuel into the engine's cylinders. Although this approach was less fraught with problems than his attempts with coal dust, the expansion of compressed air as it entered the cylinder chilled the fuel–air mixture and delayed its ignition, reducing the efficiency of the engine.

The first practical fuel-injection system for diesel engines was developed around 1912 by the German engineer and entrepreneur Robert Bosch. Based on a single pipe that supplied diesel fuel, pressurized by a pump, to valves at each cylinder head of an engine, Bosch's invention was the first example of a common-rail injection system ("rail" meaning "pipe" in this context).

Mechanical diesel injection

Mechanical diesel-injection systems have a low-pressure pump that draws the fuel from the tank and forces it through a filter to remove any solid matter that could otherwise cause blockages. A high-pressure pump then pressurizes the fuel to between 1,000 and 10,000 psi (7–70 MPa) for injection into the engine, and injectors dispense the fuel as a fine spray. A metering system that controls the amount of fuel in each injection provides a way of varying the engine's power output.

There are two main types of injection pump: the in-line multicylinder pump and the distributor pump; both are engine driven. The in-line pump has a separate pumping element for each cylinder. Each element consists of a barrel in which a plunger slides up and down, driven by a cam on a shaft connected to the engine. When the plunger is at the bottom of its stroke, fuel enters the the barrel through an inlet port. As the plunger rises, it covers the inlet port and forces the fuel in the barrel through a pipe to an injector.

Fuel enters an injector through a pipe that leads to a point near the spray orifice. As the fuel pressure rises, it forces a spring-loaded valve out of its seating in the spray orifice. Fuel then passes through the orifice, forming a fine mist of fuel. As soon as the charge of fuel has been sprayed, the pressure falls and the valve closes.

The top of the plunger is so shaped that the point at which it cuts off the fuel inlet depends on the angular orientation of the plunger within the barrel. Covering the inlet late in the upward stroke traps less fuel in the barrel than an earlier cutoff, so the amount of fuel delivered is less. The angular orientation of the plungers is controlled by a mechanical linkage to a speed governor or other control. The pumping elements are mounted in line in a single unit, and a common camshaft drives their plungers.

Distributor-pump systems use a single high-pressure pump to feed all injectors; their function is described in the box below. The injectors of this type of system are identical to those used in combination with in-line multicylinder pumps.

Mechanical gasoline injection

Gasoline-injection systems deliver fuel at lower pressure than do diesel-injection systems, because they spray fuel into air that is close to atmospheric pressure rather than compressed.

A typical mechanical system uses an electrical fuel pump to supply gasoline from the tank, through a filter, to a metering distributor. Pressure in the fuel line is maintained at around 100 psi (700 kPa)—the injection pressure—by a relief valve that returns excess fuel to the filter.

The device that meters and distributes fuel to each injector in turn consists of a hollow rotor in a sleeve. The metering occurs in the central bore of the rotor, which houses a shuttle. When fuel enters at one end of the bore, it drives the shuttle to the other end, forcing the fuel behind the shuttle through an outlet to an injector. The next stroke admits fuel at the opposite end of the bore, driving the shuttle back and feeding another injector. As the rotor turns, grooves in its periphery align with inlet and outlet ports in sequence so as to direct incoming fuel to alternate ends of the central bore and guide outgoing fuel from the other end of the bore to the appropriate injector.

A movable stop at one end of the bore adjusts the volume of fuel delivered by altering the travel of the shuttle. The position of this stop is determined either by the throttle position or by the partial vacuum in the manifold air intake.

DISTRIBUTOR-PUMP SYSTEMS

One form of mechanical fuel injector uses a distribution pump, whose rotor turns in time with the engine. The pump is charged with fuel when an inlet duct in the rotor lines up with the feed pipe. Two plungers that turn with the rotor separate at this point to allow the entry of fuel. As the rotor turns further, the inlet port is closed off and the plungers are pushed together by cams (smoothed ridges) in the pump casing. This action pressurizes the fuel, which is released as the outlet duct of the rotor aligns with a port that feeds the injector of a cylinder. The cycle is repeated as many times in a rotation as there are cylinders in the engine. A low-pressure pump forces the fuel through a filter to a transfer pump that pressurizes the fuel. A metering valve between the transfer and distributor pumps controls the rate at which fuel is supplied to the engine.

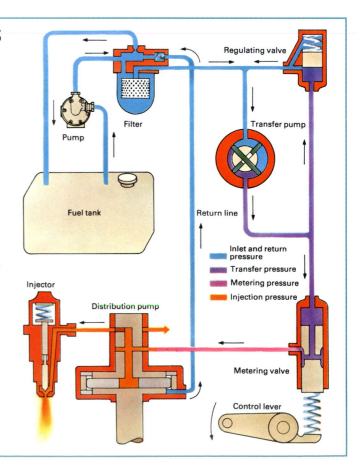

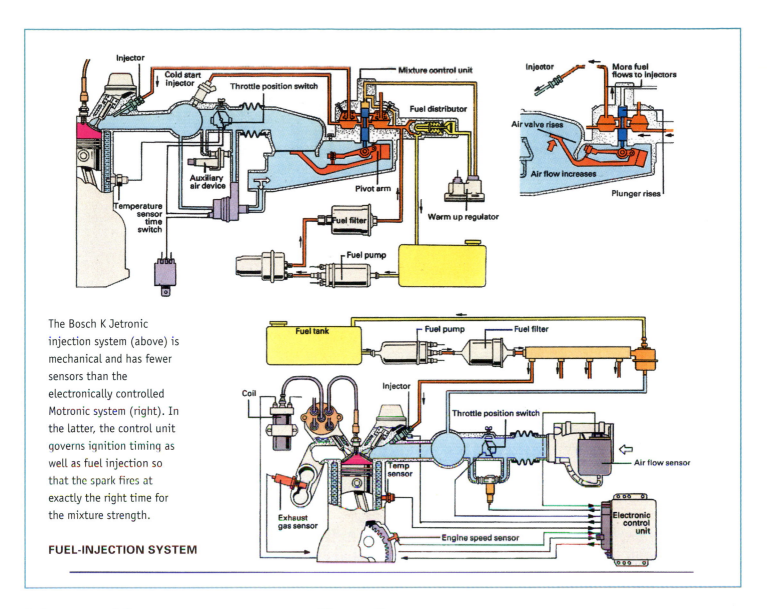

The Bosch K Jetronic injection system (above) is mechanical and has fewer sensors than the electronically controlled Motronic system (right). In the latter, the control unit governs ignition timing as well as fuel injection so that the spark fires at exactly the right time for the mixture strength.

FUEL-INJECTION SYSTEM

Injector positions

Direct-injection (DI) diesel engines have an injector in the head of each cylinder. In the past, this type of injection was used only for large diesel engines with narrow engine-speed ranges, such as heavy-duty truck engines. For smaller engines, inadequate fuel–air mixing caused sooty emissions for at least part of the engine-speed range. In the late 1990s, increased injection pressures and improved nozzle designs helped improve the fuel–air mixing characteristics for small engines.

Indirect injection (IDI) improves fuel–air mixing by spraying fuel into a chamber just above the cylinder head. There, fuel and hot compressed air swirl together to mix and ignite before passing through a throat into the cylinder to burn. These engines are around 15 percent less efficient than DI engines, since the burning fuel mixture loses extra heat energy in the swirl chamber and mechanical energy as it passes through the throat.

Gasoline injectors are usually placed near the intake ports of cylinders. Less commonly, a single injector sprays fuel into the intake manifold.

Electronic systems

A typical electronic injection system takes fuel from a common fuel rail at around 30 psi (210 kPa) for a gasoline engine. An electrically actuated valve admits fuel to the injector, so less pressure is required than in systems where the fuel pressure opens a spring-loaded valve.

An electronic control unit determines the timing and duration of injection in synchrony with the ignition (in the case of gasoline engines). The ECU also calculates the optimum amount of fuel per injection according to factors such as the speed and load on the engine as well as ambient temperature and pressure. A secondary injector is often used to introduce more fuel for cold starts. More sophisticated systems use profiled injection rates, rather than a fixed rate, to improve fuel ignition and combustion characteristics and reduce emissions still further.

SEE ALSO: AUTOMOBILE ELECTRONICS SYSTEM • IGNITION SYSTEM, AUTOMOBILE • INTERNAL COMBUSTION ENGINE

Furnace

A furnace is a closed structure in which heat is applied to a load or charge; the term is derived from the Latin word *fornus*, meaning an oven. Inside the furnace, the charge may be only melted or may undergo permanent physical, chemical, and mechanical changes.

As early as 3000 B.C.E., the Sumerians of Mesopotamia were using closed furnaces (kilns) with controlled draft for firing fine pottery at temperatures up to 2200°F (1200°C). For metal extraction, the pot furnace, which was buried in the ground, replaced the primitive stone- or clay-lined hollow. During the Bronze Age, a more advanced type evolved—the shaft furnace. It was used for smelting and probably derived from the pottery kiln.

Today, the industries using furnaces are those producing iron and steel with blast furnaces, electric arc furnaces, and induction furnaces; cement manufacturers using rotary kilns; glass manufacturers with their tank and pot furnaces; the ceramic industries with their many types of kilns, which are particular types of furnaces; and the numerous nonferrous metal producers. Airtight ovens, which are used for the production of coke, smokeless fuel, and to a lesser extent, town gas (illuminating gas), can also be considered as a type of furnace.

Furnaces are designed for either intermittent (batch) operation or continuous use. In a batch operation, the charge, or load, is placed in the furnace when cold, fired to the required temperature, cooled, and unloaded. The simplest is a box type but there are many variations. A continuous furnace generally consists of a number of zones, preheating, firing, and cooling, and the charge is pushed through the zones on cars using a hydraulic ram that operates from the entrance.

Construction

The type of brick used in furnace construction depends on various factors, such as the maximum firing temperature, the atmospheric conditions, and the reaction of the molten metal, slags, and combustion gases with the refractory (heat resistant) lining. The furnace structure must remain stable under the prevailing heating and cooling conditions, so expansion and contraction must be accounted for. Processes involving rapid changes in temperature require refractories that are resistant to thermal shock. Construction design is very important, the provision of expansion joints, tie bars, and rods being essential to maintain the brickwork's stability. Much use is now being made of cementlike linings that can be sprayed on

▼ A German glass furnace of 1750 (left), one of the earliest types of furnace. In the open-hearth furnace (right), a gas–air mixture is burned over the surface of pig and scrap iron.

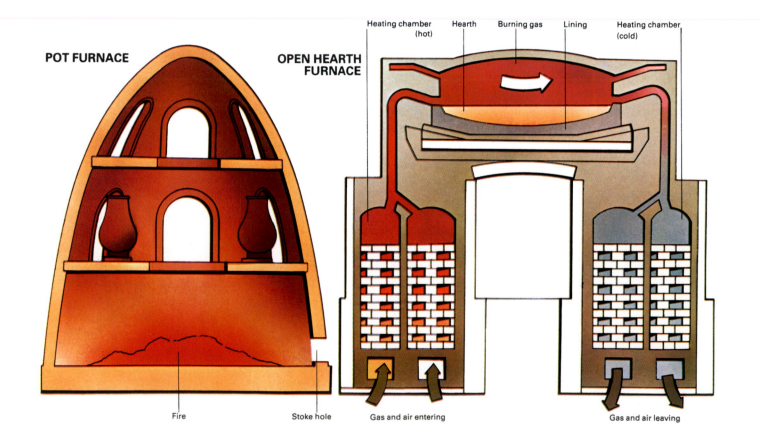

POT FURNACE

Fire

Stoke hole

OPEN HEARTH FURNACE

Heating chamber (hot) Hearth Burning gas Lining Heating chamber (cold)

Gas and air entering

Gas and air leaving

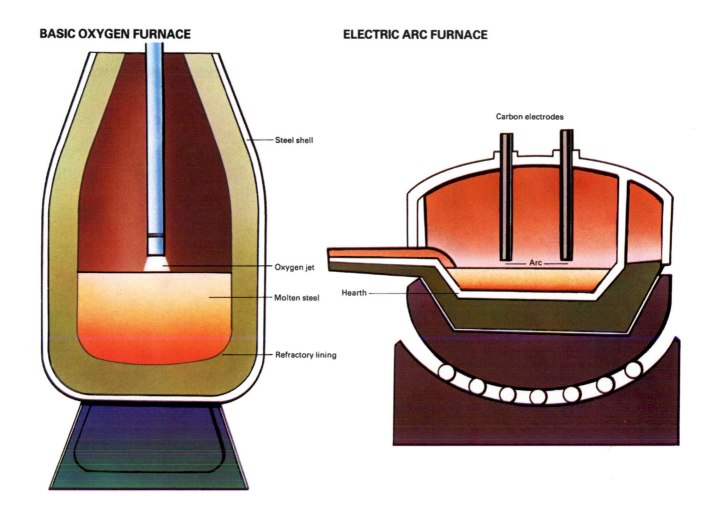

BASIC OXYGEN FURNACE

- Steel shell
- Oxygen jet
- Molten steel
- Refractory lining

ELECTRIC ARC FURNACE

- Carbon electrodes
- Arc
- Hearth

to give a monolithic layer and ceramic-fiber blankets, which are pinned onto the supporting brickwork. China clay, ball clay, and fireclay are extremely good refractories, fusing at more than 3100°F (1700°C). Other materials used include silica, magnesite, dolomite, and alumina.

Fuels

The traditional fuels were coal and coke, but increasing concern for pollution has accelerated changes in methods of firing. Shoveling solid fuel onto fire grates was replaced by mechanical stokers, but there were still problems of handling ash and the harmful effects of oxides of sulfur, which, among other things, can corrode metal ducting and fan blades. Many power plants now use pulverized, or powdered, coal, and expensive precautions are taken to minimize the grit and noxious gases that are released to the atmosphere.

Furnaces have, in many cases, been converted from solid fuel to oil and gas, and the use of these fuels has resulted in improved furnace and burner design. Burner design depends on mixing fuel and air in the correct ratio. It is much easier to mix two gases (as in the combustion of methane with air) than a solid and a gas (coal and air). Some fuel burners have now been designed that will handle both gas and oil with very little adjustment. In the

▲ A basic oxygen furnace (left) uses oxygen from a water-cooled lance, which combines with and eliminates impurities from the molten steel. In the electric arc furnace (right), two carbon electrodes create a highly charged arc of electricity to melt the steel.

past 50 years, the same furnace may have been fired by coal, fuel oil, and gas—and there is a possibility that there will be a return to solid-fuel firing by more refined means in the future.

The combustion process for coal, gas, or oil is one in which the fuel, consisting mainly of carbon and hydrogen, burns to give heat, which is passed to the charge by conduction, convection, and radiation. Conduction occurs when heat passes through solids, as when the handle of a poker becomes hot. Convection occurs, for example, when the hot gases swirling around the furnace load give up their heat to the cooler charge, and in radiation, the heat is transferred in a similar way to that of a conventional electric space heater.

The products of combustion are carbon dioxide and water vapor mixed with the original nitrogen of the combustion air. Control of the furnace is maintained by adjusting the fuel input through a burner, together with the air supply, so that the fuel–air ratio is sufficient to give good combustion conditions. Depending on the type of combustion process involved, the atmospheric conditions prevailing in the furnace may be oxidizing, when surplus air is present, or reducing, when there is a lack of air and unburned gases are present, or neutral, when air-to-fuel ratios are perfectly proportioned.

By measuring the percentage of oxygen or carbon dioxide content of the combustion gases, the furnace operator is able to control the furnace to give maximum efficiency.

Electric furnaces

Electric furnaces do not depend on a combustion process, electric energy from the main grid system being converted directly into heat energy. There are three main types of electric furnace: resistance, electric arc, and induction. The commonest type is the resistance furnace, which consists of a box with wire-wound elements that heat up when an electric current is passed through. The heat generated is proportional to the electric resistance of the element and the square of the current. The element can be set into the refractory brickwork that supports them. The maximum operating temperature depends on the wire used for the elements. Nonmetallic ele-

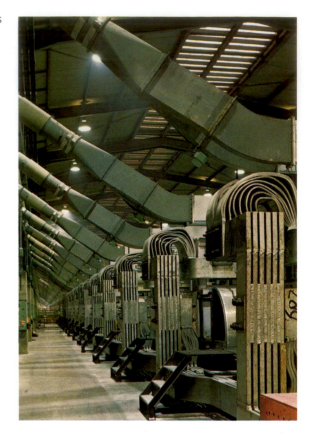

▶ A line of pots—furnaces where metal is purified. The curved strips carry current to the anode blocks. Waste gases are extracted through the large flue pipes at the top and scrubbed before they are vented to the atmosphere.

ments, such as silicon carbide (2650°F, 1450°C) and molybdenum disilicide (3100°F, 1700°C), can also be used. Such furnaces lend themselves to automatic control.

In the electric arc furnace, the lining is made of a high-quality refractory material, and generally the electrodes, made of carbon or graphite, are located in the roof and extend into the furnace chamber and the charge. As the electrodes become consumed, they are lowered into the furnace. An arc is struck, and the heating effect is used to melt metals that can then be removed through tapholes.

In the electric induction furnace, which is used for melting metals and for heat treatment, there is no electric connection between supply and charge. It works on the principle of a transformer with the coil as the primary and the metal charge as the secondary winding. The crucible is surrounded by a water-cooled coil, and the space between is filled with insulating material. A high-frequency power source is applied to the coil, and energy induced in the charge appears in the form of heat capable of producing high temperatures.

Solar furnaces use a series of mirrors to focus sunlight into an intense beam up to 50,000 times its normal intensity. One such furnace in France can reach temperatures of over 7000°F (3800°C).

FACT FILE

- In the early 14th century, cast iron was first produced in what were the earliest blast furnaces in the Liège region of Belgium. By using large furnaces up to 15 ft. (4.6 m) high with a great fuel capacity, the iron became more carbonated and flowed and could be poured more easily. Hydraulically operated bellows were used to achieve the necessary high temperatures.

- By the 18th century, the growth of iron smelting and processing had caused a fuel crisis. It was estimated that in France, for example, for every pound of cast iron produced in a blast furnace, 1¾ lbs. of charcoal were burned. By the end of the century, France was using 770 million cu. ft.(21 million m³) of wood per annum in the iron industry. Because Britain needed so much of its own wood for ships, 60 percent of its iron was imported.

- The Oita Works of the Nippon Steel Corporation contains one of the world's largest and most efficient blast furnaces. The furnace, which is lined with 6,000 tons (5,400 tonnes) of refractory blocks, can produce 10,000 tons (9,000 tonnes) of steel a day and has a projected total production of over 20 million tons (18 million tonnes).

SEE ALSO: CERAMICS • CHINA AND PORCELAIN • GLASS • INDUCTION • IRON AND STEEL • KILN

Fuse and Circuit Breaker

Fuses and circuit breakers are devices for preventing excessive voltage and currents from overloading and damaging an electric circuit. Fuses are suitable only for light industrial and domestic applications, whereas circuit breakers are designed mainly to cope with heavy industrial power requirements, such as in power plant switch gear. Miniature circuit breakers are, however, installed in light industrial and domestic circuits for protection and control.

Fuses

A fuse is essentially a piece of wire of controlled dimensions and composition that is designed to melt when the current flowing through it reaches a certain value. The principle employed here is that a current flowing through a conductor generates heat proportional to the square of the current—that is, doubling the current quadruples the heat generated. The wire is chosen to suit the maximum overload current that the circuit can take, at which point the heat can no longer be dissipated quickly enough, and the wire melts. Once the wire has melted, the circuit is broken and protection is ensured. Fuses are classified by the maximum continuous current they will take without blowing.

Rewirable fuses, which are the simplest type available, can cope only with general overloads. Furthermore, replacement after blowing a fuse entails threading a new piece of wire between the fuse terminals. Not only is this process cumbersome, but also the wire must be strong enough to withstand the handling.

Cartridge fuses provide a solution to such problems because they are manufactured and sealed at the factory. They consist of a hollow, nonconductive body (made of glass or porcelain) containing a fuse element, the ends of which are connected to metal caps forming the fuse terminals. The main disadvantage of the cartridge fuse is that it is not possible to tell by external inspection whether the fuse element has blown.

Domestic cartridge fuses use plain wire elements that are relatively slow to melt, but where a fast response is required, especially in heavy-duty applications, the element is shaped. The ends attached to the cartridge caps are relatively large to act as heat sinks, removing unwanted heat generated by normal usage. Between these large sections, there are one or more narrow sections that will melt first in the event of a current surge. The narrower and shorter these sections are, the faster the response to a current overload. There is,

however, a drawback to making this section too short because once it has melted, the current may simply jump the gap in a process called arcing.

One technique for overcoming arcing is to include several narrow sections separated by thick sections. In the event of an overload, more than one section will blow. Another technique is to surround the element with a powder—usually silica (silicon dioxide, SiO_2, such as quartz). When the wire melts, metal vapor is produced and an arc is struck through this vapor. The heat generated

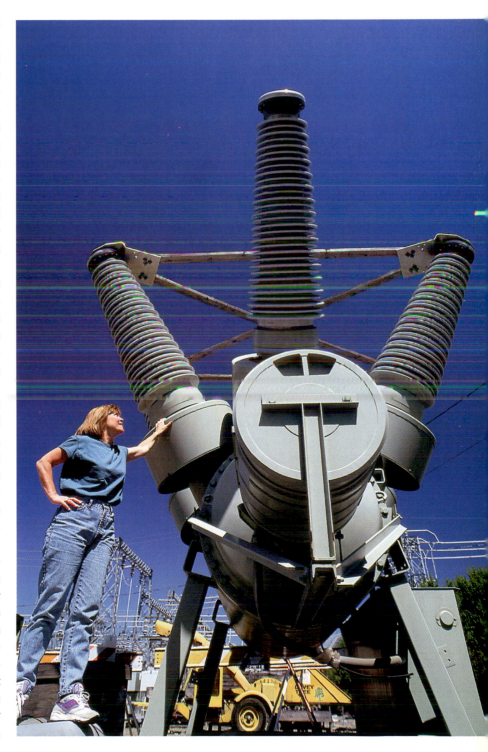

▼ A seismologist stands next to a large circuit breaker in California. This particular circuit breaker is not in use. It is being kept in reserve as a replacement in case of a large earthquake.

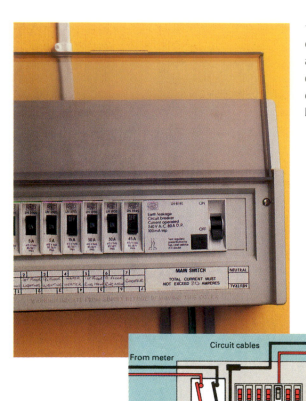

◀ Left and below: The consumer unit is the point at which the supply is distributed to the various circuits, each protected by a circuit breaker.

The speed with which the circuit can be completely broken ultimately depends on the speed of separation of the contacts, the number of pairs of contacts involved, the relationship between current and voltage (this depends on the type of loads being fed from such a supply), and the type of arc-control device employed. Circuit breakers are usually described by the method used to extinguish the arc and include air, oil, air-blast, sulfur hexafluoride, and vacuum circuit breakers.

Air-break CBs have their contacts mounted horizontally, and they are opened rapidly by a precharged spring. The arc formed across the separating contacts is forced to expand upward, thus increasing the arc length until it can no longer be sustained by the voltage across the contacts. In some systems, the arc is forced upward by its interaction with the magnetic field created by an electromagnet. Typically, these CBs are used in the 415 V to 3.3 kV range.

Oil CBs use oil as an aid to arc extinguishing and as an insulating medium. The contacts are mounted in a small oil-filled chamber. When the contacts are broken, the resulting arc—which generates intense heat—breaks down the oil in its path and liberates gases at high temperature. As the AC supply goes through a zero current point during one of its cycles, this gaseous arc path is replaced by oil, which insulates the contacts from further arcing. Because the gases liberated are highly flammable, the oil must be kept pure and free from oxygen, and oil CBs are restricted to voltages between 3.3 kV and 330 kV.

In air-blast CBs, compressed air at high pressure is used to extinguish the arc formed as the contacts separate. This blast of air has the effect of blowing out the arc in a confined space

in this process, however, creates a chemical reaction between the vapor and the powder, fusing them together and producing a high-resistance (insulating) substance that extinguishes the arc.

Circuit breakers (CBs)

A critical consideration in the design of circuit breakers is the necessity to extinguish the highly conductive arc that is drawn between the circuit breaker contacts as they separate. Extinguishing is necessary because while the arc continues, the circuit is not properly disconnected and current still flows and also because the arc damages the contact surfaces.

Alternating current (AC) circuit breakers are the most common type found because the main electricity supply is AC. In AC circuit breakers, use is made of the fact that twice every cycle (that is, 100 times a second where the frequency is 50 Hz) the current is zero. Interruption at or near these points will help prevent arcing, but interruption is complete only when the resistance of the arc gap is high enough to keep the voltage between the contacts from reestablishing an arcing current.

The fault that initiates the circuit breaker action is detected by protection relays. They react to the fault condition extremely rapidly—usually within half a cycle of the AC supply, activating the circuit breaker, which for high-voltage systems, must break the circuit within two or three cycles.

▶ A bulk oil circuit breaker—now commonly replaced by air-blast types. Devices like these are used to interrupt the supply in power plants and substations.

and preventing it from forming by rapid separation of the contacts. By making the moving parts small and light, rapid separation can be achieved. The voltage range of air-blast CBs is typically 11 kV to 750 kV.

Sulfur hexafluoride (SF$_6$) is an inert gas that possesses extremely high insulating properties. The contacts separate inside a tank containing the gas under high pressure. The design of the arc-control device surrounding the contacts subjects the arc to a cross-flow blast of SF$_6$ that extinguishes the arc. The typical voltage range of SF$_6$ circuit breakers is 33 kV to 400 kV.

With vacuum CBs, a number of identical units are connected in a series according to the operating voltage required. The basic unit consists of moving contacts mounted inside a highly evacuated bellows chamber; separation is achieved by an external force applied to the bellows. Because of the vacuum, virtually no arc is formed. The typical voltage range of vacuum CBs is 11 kV to 132 kV.

Miniature circuit breakers (MCBs)

MCBs are used primarily for the control of small industrial motors and domestic circuits. They may also be used for short circuit and overload protection for small substations, industrial and commercial lighting and air conditioning, and underground and overhead cable networks.

The AC supply is never purely sinusoidal, and spikes and other harmless transient overload conditions occur frequently. MCBs must be designed not to respond to them. Slight but continuous overloads must, however, activate the MCB, and dramatic surges of current must initiate a fast response. To decrease sensitivity to transient overloads, a time delay can be incorporated by using a bimetallic strip. Fast response to high surges is achieved by using an electromagnet to break the contacts.

Residual current circuit breakers

Residual current circuit breakers (RCCBs) are sensitive to much smaller currents than other circuit breakers and are designed to reduce the risk of serious electric shock. Also known as ground fault interrupters, RCCBs are used to detect fault currents by comparing the currents flowing down the two conductors of an AC power line and breaking the circuit if the difference exceeds a preset value (often 30 mA). In cases where human contact is less common, RCCBs may be installed with lower sensitivities from 100 to 375 mA, which should give protection from electrical fires.

The ground fault is the current that is diverted from an electrical device into the ground. If, for example, a person were to touch a live part of an

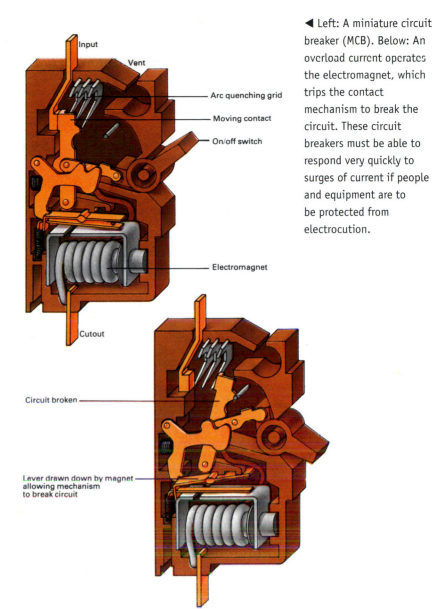

Input
Vent
Arc quenching grid
Moving contact
On/off switch
Electromagnet
Cutout

Circuit broken
Lever drawn down by magnet allowing mechanism to break circuit

◄ Left: A miniature circuit breaker (MCB). Below: An overload current operates the electromagnet, which trips the contact mechanism to break the circuit. These circuit breakers must be able to respond very quickly to surges of current if people and equipment are to be protected from electrocution.

appliance such as a steam iron, the current would pass through their body and into the ground. This would cause a change in the difference between the currents in the live and grounded wire and the RCCB would immediately stop the current. RCCBs fitted to standard domestic electric circuits are made to break within 30 milliseconds; they normally remove the possibility of electrocution if live parts are touched although the victims may get a bad shock.

These circuit breakers are commonly used on small machinery and household electrical appliances. A tester button is provided on RCCBs, and when depressed, it should cut off the current immediately. If the current does not shut off, it is a sign there is something wrong with the circuit breaker, and it should be checked.

SEE ALSO: Conduction, electrical • Electricity • Power plant • Power supply

Fusion

Nuclear fusion is the joining together of two nuclei of light atoms to form the nucleus of a heavier atom. Because of the difference in binding energies required to hold together the particles in the different nuclei, the process can release large amounts of energy.

The most important fusion reactions involve the welding together of the lightest of all the nuclei—those of the hydrogen atom—to make a helium nucleus. In its normal form, the hydrogen nucleus contains a single particle, the proton, but there are variants, or isotopes, where the proton is joined by one or two neutrons. The nuclei of these variants are called, respectively, the deuteron and the triton.

▼ Green light from the Omega Laser at the University of Rochester. The lasers are used to implode a tiny pellet of fuel. This technique may someday lead to a usable source of nuclear fusion energy.

In terms of energy release, the most productive fusion is that of deuteron and triton. It produces a helium nucleus, a neutron, and 17.6 million electron volts (or MeV) of energy. The energy liberated can be calculated by applying mathematics to the masses of the nuclei; the helium and neutron have less mass than the deuteron and triton, and because mass and energy are interchangeable, this difference in mass has been converted into energy. Compared with normal chemical reactions, where only tiny amounts of mass are converted, the quantities of energy released are enormous. If the hydrogen nuclei in a gallon of water could be combined in fusion reactions, they would yield more energy than the burning of a million gallons of oil.

Since the supply of hydrogen is almost limitless (in combination with oxygen in water), nuclear fusion offers the prospect of a limitless source of energy. Fusion reactions, however, are difficult to bring about. The proton in each hydrogen nucleus carries a positive electric charge and, just as like poles of magnets repel one another, so these positive charges repel one another, and the repulsion becomes stronger the closer they come together. To achieve fusion, they have to unite in a tiny volume about a millionth of a millionth of an inch across, and they must fly at one another very fast to get close enough to overcome the repulsive effect of their electric charges. Two factors influence whether productive fusion reactions occur—the closeness with which the nuclei are packed together (the density of the hydrogen) and the velocity with which they are moving (the temperature). Typically, temperatures of many millions of degrees Fahrenheit are needed.

Thus, the problem is to establish a dense volume of hydrogen at a temperature of millions of degrees. To reach break-even point, where the reactions produce more energy than is put in, temperatures in excess of 100 million degrees are required for the densities so far achieved in laboratories. Research centers in many countries are working to achieve controlled fusion mainly by trying various methods to contain a dense hot plasma—a volume of the hydrogen consisting of nuclei and electrons, which are torn off the atoms at high temperatures. Because plasma is a mixture of charged particles, it can therefore be manipulated by using strong magnetic fields that compress the plasma to produce the necessary densities and keep the plasma away from the walls of a containing vessel that would otherwise melt.

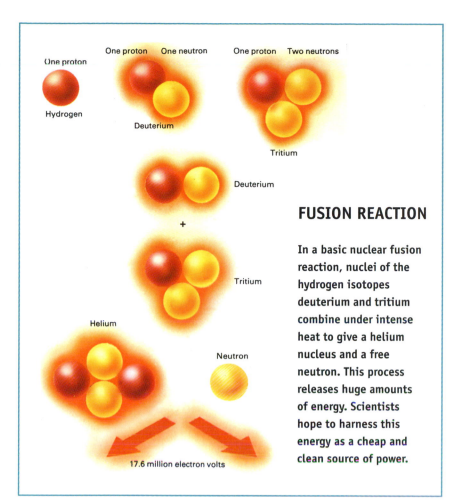

FUSION REACTION

In a basic nuclear fusion reaction, nuclei of the hydrogen isotopes deuterium and tritium combine under intense heat to give a helium nucleus and a free neutron. This process releases huge amounts of energy. Scientists hope to harness this energy as a cheap and clean source of power.

A serious difficulty yet to be overcome by researchers arises from neutrons liberated in the fusion reaction. They are not charged and so can break free of the confining magnetic field to strike the walls of the reactor vessel, seriously weakening it and making it radioactive. Thus, the walls of the vessel must be periodically dismantled and disposed of, a task that is both expensive and a hazard to health.

Another technique is to fire high-power laser beams at pellets of solid deuterium. However, a considerable amount of work is still to be done before fusion can be used in power plants.

Fusion reactions have been created in short intense bursts in hydrogen bombs, using other explosives to create the necessary temperature and density conditions. Energies equivalent to many millions of tons of TNT are produced.

Despite the difficulty of bringing about fusion, it is, in fact, a very common process in nature—for example, the fusion of the Sun and all the other stars. In this case it is the gravitational effect of large masses that pulls the hydrogen nuclei together. At the center of our Sun, for example, the density of nuclei is about 5½ lbs. per cu. in. (150 g/cm³), and the temperature is about 57 million°F (14 million°C). Even then, only one in ten thousand, million, million, million collisions

▶ A neon plasma in a nuclear fusion experiment. The high temperatures involved cause the plasma to be incandescent.

between nuclei results in a fusion. At this extremely slow rate, fusion is converting the hydrogen of the Sun into helium.

Fusion reactors

Scientists working on the Joint European Torus (JET) project at Culham, Oxfordshire, are trying to find ways of producing temperatures of around a hundred million degrees and of releasing the energy locked up in the nuclei in a way that they can use to generate power.

Research in many countries has concentrated on various shapes of magnetic field to find the one most effective at containing and compressing the plasma. The most promising shape tried out is the tokamak, a name derived from the Russian word for "toroidal magnetic chamber." The magnetic fields grip the plasma in a doughnut-shaped vacuum vessel, a torus. The plasma is kept in the center of the torus away from the walls (which would otherwise quench the plasma) by the combined effect of magnetic fields that are produced by external coils around the torus and a current that is passed through the plasma to heat it.

In the JET experiment, which is itself the largest tokamak in the world, the main magnetic field is provided by 32 D-shaped coils, each 18.7 ft. (5.7 m) tall and weighing 12 tons (8.4 tonnes), which surround the vacuum vessel giving a toroidal field that runs parallel to the walls. Additional coils around the outside of the vessel are used to shape and position the plasma. They, together with the coils of the transformer producing the current in the plasma, are the so-called poloidal coils. Together, magnetic fields grip the

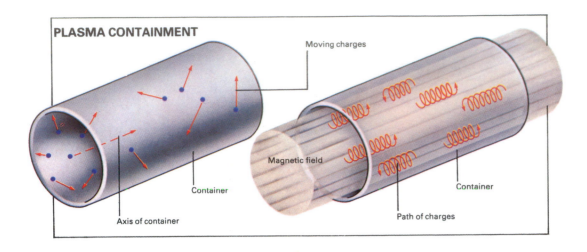

PLASMA CONTAINMENT

Moving charges

Magnetic field

Container

Axis of container

Path of charges

Container

◀ Without a magnetic field, electrically charged particles would move about randomly, colliding with the walls of the vessel containing them. In a magnetic field, their motions become helical, like a spring.

plasma and hold it stable long enough to extract energy from the particles produced when the fusion reaction occurs.

By using a series of heating techniques, JET is able to get within the temperature range required to produce fusion reactions. However, if useful amounts of power by fusion are to be produced, these reactions must take place within the plasma both often enough and long enough so that the energy produced is greater than the amount needed to run the system. There comes a time then when the plasma "ignites" and the temperature is held at the 100-million-degree level without external heating.

JET is not designed to use the fusion energy produced to generate electricity. For that, some means of trapping the energy-carrying neutrons that stream out of the magnetic "bottle" is needed. One possible method is to use lithium, the lightest of all metals, to trap these fast neutrons. By stopping them in a "blanket" of lithium oxide, say, surrounding the vacuum vessel, the neutrons give up their kinetic energy in the form of heat. This heat is transported to a heat exchanger where water is boiled, producing steam to drive a conventional turbogenerator.

In 1991, JET achieved fusion power and produced between 1,500,000 and 2,000,000 watts of power. This was the first time a fusion reactor had produced large amounts of energy. The performance of this reactor has steadily improved, but since the end of 1999, its facilities have been used jointly by the members of the European Fusion Development Agreement for the planned International Thermonuclear Experimental Reactor (ITER). Funding problems have made it necessary for this project to be scaled down. Originally, it was intended to produce 1,500 megawatts, but now, if it is built, it is planned to produce only 500 megawatts. The aim of this project is to create a reactor that will produce far more energy than it consumes.

Fusion using lasers

At the Laboratory for Laser Energetics at Rochester University, the Omega Laser has been successful in creating fusion. A stream of pelleted fusion materials is fed into a spherical reactor, and the pellets are imploded by the intense heat of several laser beams. Originally, this laser was capable of pointing 24 beams at the pellets of fuel. In 1995, however, this facility was improved so that it now has a 60-beam laser capable of producing more than 40 kilojoules of energy from a target area less than 1 millimeter in diameter. A soon-to-be-completed laser at the Lawrence Livermore National Laboratory will produce even higher energies—1.8 megajoules from 192 beams.

◀ One of the D-shaped coils used in JET to produce the toroidal field, positioned upright.

SEE ALSO: ATOMIC STRUCTURE • ENERGY RESOURCES • FISSION • HYDROGEN • NUCLEAR REACTOR • PARTICLE ACCELERATOR • PLASMA PHYSICS

Games Machine

A games machine is a device intended to provide amusement for the people who use it and sometimes to generate profit for its owner. With some types of machines, a player wins or loses purely by chance; such machines include slot machines. With other machines, players can achieve high scores by using various skills—general knowledge or hand-to-eye coordination, for example.

The rewards for winning or achieving high scores vary from credits or tokens for free games to hundreds of thousands of dollars. Often, a good score is rewarded by a position in a ranking of highest-scoring players based on the results of a particular machine or a network of machines.

The earliest games machines were purely mechanical; modern machines are electromechanical or electronic. The sizes of modern gaming machines cover an enormous range, from palm-top devices to large-screen dual-simulator motor-racing games, where two players each have a simulated driver's seat and controls.

Slot machines

Of all the games machines in amusement centers, slot machines—also called one-armed bandits or fruit machines—have the longest history. Their earliest direct predecessor was the 1890s' wheel of chance, which consisted of a spinning indicator mounted in front of a circular display. Segments of the display corresponded to different outcomes: win or lose. The indicator was set in motion by pulling a lever after inserting a coin to release its mechanism. When the wheel came to a halt, its position determined whether or not coins were issued to the player.

By the early 20th century, slot machines had developed the still-current display format of multiple reels, each with numerous facets on which a variety of symbols appear. Typical symbols include different types of fruits—hence the name "fruit machine"—numbers, and images of gold coins. Combinations of these symbols appear in a viewing slot, and some combinations correspond

▲ This game uses a high-speed graphics processor to produce a realistic simulation of the track view of a motorcycle racer.

display combination, but certain combinations are given more output numbers than others, so they have a proportionally better chance of being chosen by the random-number generator.

The player starts the machine by pulling a lever or pressing a button. The microprocessor then calls for a random number to be generated, matches it to a display combination, and instructs the motors that turn the reels to display the appropriate combination of symbols. Since winning combinations are chosen on a random basis, an individual machine might reach its programmed rate of payback only after it has been played many hundreds or even thousands of times.

Many slot machines have features beyond the simple random game. Such features include "hold" buttons for each reel that light up occasionally to offer the choice of freezing one or more reels for the subsequent game. Another feature is the "nudge" function, which allows a player to move reels back or forth by a few positions to adjust the outcome of a game, sometimes resulting in a win. Some enhanced features are completely separate from the reel display. These include games where prize money increases or decreases depending on the timing with which a player hits a flashing "gamble" button.

Coin handling

In addition to the gaming mechanism, slot machines have ancillary devices for checking the coins and tokens fed into the slot and for dispensing prizes. The coin-receiving mechanism checks coins or tokens for their validity and identifies their values by checking characteristics such as size, weight, and electromagnetic properties. This system informs the gaming mechanism of the total value inserted as a basis for calculating the number of game credits, and that number then appears in some form of digital display, usually an LED (light-emitting diode) display. Invalid coins are rejected, and some machines have detectors that sound alarms if a player attempts to withdraw a coin on a string, for example.

After validation, coins are stacked in the cylindrical cartridges of a coin dispenser. If the machine accepts and dispenses various values of coins, different values are stacked in separate columns. One type of coin-dispensing mechanism consists of a ratchet wheel that rotates under a disk with circular openings. Coins drop through these holes into the gaps between the teeth of the ratchet wheel. When prize money is dispensed, the ratchet wheel turns and ejects the appropriate number of coins through a slot at its circumference. The coins then fall into a hopper or tray, from which the player can collect them.

to wins of various values. Winning combinations and their associated prizes appear in bright displays that are intended to attract attention. When a winning combination appears in the display, a coin-release mechanism issues a prize.

For a three-reel machine with 22 facets, there are 22 x 22 x 22 = 10,468 possible display combinations. In early slot machines, which were mechanical, each display combination had an equal chance of appearing. Electromechanical machines use weighted probabilities, so they can be programmed to return a known proportion of their takings as winnings. The weighting system can be used to generate such payout proportions as required by law or stipulated by the person or organization that owns or leases the machine.

The weighting system consists of a random-number generator and a microprocessor. The random-number generator is set to produce integer values from a range that is greater than the total number of possible display combinations. Each value within that range corresponds to one

▲ This "one-armed bandit" typifies a type of slot machine that has changed little since the early 20th century. The lever on the right-hand side of the machine sets the reels in motion, and a random-number generator and microprocessor determine the display when they stop. Illustrations on the front panel indicate the prize values for winning combinations of symbols.

Pinball machines

The classic pinball machine is an amusement device in which a player scores points by causing a steel ball to travel around a playing surface. The object of the game is to achieve as high a score as possible rather than to win money.

The playing surface is a board mounted in a horizontal rectangular cabinet that slopes gently so that a ball tends to fall toward the player. A typical pinball machine has an arch-shaped board that measures approximately 36 in. (91 cm) from the base to the apex of the arch and approximately 38 in. (96 cm) from side to side.

The machine is readied for a game by pushing coins through a slot. A device similar to those in slot machines checks the validity and registers the value of the coins. The number of game credits that correspond to the value of the inserted coins then appears in a display mounted in a vertical board at the far end of the table from the player. The combination of a gaudy display panels, a matching playing surface, flashing lights, and sound effects attracts attention to the machine.

A player starts a game by pressing a button that delivers a steel ball to a channel along the right-hand side of the playing board, causes the machine to light up, and removes a credit from the display. Next, the player pulls a spring-loaded plunger at the right-hand corner of the table, then releases it to send the ball up to the high end of the sloping board. The ball then rolls back down the board, scoring points and penalties as it

▶ Pinball tables such as this reached the peak of their popularity in the 1970s. To give an idea of the size of such a machine, the table top would be around waist height to an adult of average stature.

interacts with obstacles in its path, then eventually falls through a hole in the bottom of the table. At that point, the game is over.

Some of the obstacles on the board are passive bumpers whose rubber surfaces give rebound to the ball; other obstacles are steel-framed runways that guide the ball from one part of the board to another; the third type are active obstacles that propel the ball. When the ball strikes an active object, it closes an electrical contact that often lights the obstacle, adds points to the score, and energizes a solenoid that moves the obstacle in such a way as to accelerate the ball. Mushroom-shaped obstacles have solenoids that pull them closer to the surface, squeezing the ball out as they do. Holes in the surface have solenoids that eject the ball onto the surface, and bumpers have solenoids that simply push the ball away.

The player controls the game to some extent by modifying the initial kick of the plunger, by activating button-operated flippers in the side of the table, and by lifting and moving the table. Motion sensors trigger a "tilt" sign and terminate the game if the table is moved with excessive force or beyond a certain angle. The score depends on how many times the ball hits point-scoring obstacles and other triggers in the board's surface. As such, the longer the ball is kept in play by skillful tilting and flipper action, the higher the final score tends to be. High scores are rewarded by free balls or free "plays" (sets of five balls).

◀ This view of a pinball table has at its center three mushroom-shaped obstacles that kick the ball and add to the score when struck. The ball is currently in a hole near top right, from which it will be propelled across the board by a solenoid-driven rod.

◀ A close-up view of the pair of flippers closest to the exit hole. A well-timed stroke of the flipper can send the ball racing up the table and prolong the game. If the ball slips through the gap between the flippers, it runs off the table and the game is over.

◀ Drop-in program cartridges have made it possible to update arcade machines easily so that players can take advantage of the latest advances in computer-generated graphics. Players are increasingly able to interact with the game environment, a development that will be taken even further with the advent of virtual reality programs.

Electronic arcade games

While sophisticated slot and pinball machines depend to some extent on electronic systems, the term *electronic game* is generally reserved for games that rely on a microprocessor, a memory device, and a video display. The display is usually mounted in an upright cabinet, which also carries display panels that advertize the game. The player controls the game using buttons, joysticks, trackballs, and levers that are usually mounted in a flat or sloping panel below the display screen; some machines have pedal controls mounted in the base of the cabinet. Two-player games often have sets of controls at either side of a reinforced-glass table above a horizontal screen.

The first electronic games were launched in the early 1970s, right at the heyday of the pinball arcade. One of the earliest games was *Pong*, a two-player game based on table tennis. The monochrome display showed a wide rectangle, divided in two by a vertical line, that represented a ping-pong table and net. A white dot drifted from one side of the screen to the other, and each player had a control that moved a "bat" along opposite vertical edges of the rectangle. If the ball struck the bat, the processor used a relatively simple program to calculate the return angle and create the corresponding display. The ball moved faster with each shot until one player failed to intercept it, thereby conceding a point to the other player.

By the end of the 1970s, advances in programming and hardware had revolutionized video games. *Space Invaders*, launched in 1979, was the first game in which the player took on opponents generated by the computer program: the player had to shoot at rows of space invaders to prevent them from landing. A degree of unpredictability was introduced in the form of ships that traveled across the top of the screen. If destroyed, these ships would give the player a mystery bonus.

Space Invaders became immensely popular in the 1980s as a consequence of its absorbing combination of unpredictability and a fantasy setting. Since then, advances in processing power have enabled programmers to devise ever more complex games, just as advanced sound and video cards have enhanced the sensory aspect of game playing. A player can now drive through realistic street scenes—true-to-life or imaginary—play golf in the setting of a world-famous green, or shoot dinosaurs in captivating fantasy landscapes.

Game consoles

From the outset, arcade video games were designed to establish their presence alongside pinball tables. The size of their cabinets was far greater than needed to house the computing hardware for the game. By the mid-1970s, electronic-games companies were starting to respond to the popularity of video games by marketing game consoles that used TV screens as monitors.

The first example of a computer-game console was launched by Atari in 1975; it played a version of *Pong* using a simple microprocessor and a graphics chip that produced a video-compatible signal. Two years later, the same company launched the first console that could accept cartridges for a variety of games. The Atari 2600 had a meager 128 bytes of RAM (random access memory) and each cartridge had 4 kilobytes of ROM (read only memory).

The limited hardware of the 2600 and similar systems soon started to show their weaknesses, as arcade games started to be equipped with more powerful processors and larger memories. The specifications of arcade machines permitted more complex games and better graphics than were possible with home consoles.

Then in 1985, Nintendo launched the NES (Nintendo Entertainments System), which set a marketing trend that would also be followed by companies such as Sega and Sony. The NES was a game console that was equipped to a high specification and sold cheap so that profits would be made in the sale of compatible game cartridges.

At the start of the 21st century, typical game consoles have processors with clock speeds of hundreds of megahertz that run with 3-D video chips, tens of megabytes of RAM, and 4.7 gigabyte DVD-ROMs instead of cartridges. These systems are also equipped with high-speed modems that allow groups to play multiplayer games in real time via telephone and Internet connections.

SEE ALSO: ▷ COMPUTER GRAPHICS • ELECTRONICS • INTERNET

Gas and Dust Mask

Gas and dust masks offer their users protection against hazardous airborne substances, such as gases, fumes, and dusts that are toxic, irritants, or otherwise harmful. Some masks protect against airborne radioactive or biological hazards. Protective masks are often used in industrial environments and construction sites, where routine activities can liberate harmful substances, and they form part of the kit of military and security personnel, who can be exposed to deliberate nuclear, biological, or chemical (NBC) attacks.

Invention and early developments

The first gas mask was a breathing device patented in 1914 by Garrett A. Morgan, the U.S. inventor of the stoplight and numerous grooming products for African-American hair. Morgan's gas mask consisted of a canvas hood with plain eyeglasses. Twin canvas hoses passed from the bottom of the hood under the wearer's arms and merged into a single tube at the back. A water-soaked sponge in the tube filtered and cooled incoming air, making it easier to breathe in smoke-filled environments. Morgan's device gained fame in 1916, when the inventor himself, his two brothers, and two volunteers rescued 20 suffocating construction workers from a smoke-filled tunnel under Lake Erie.

In World War I, a short time after Morgan's invention, a different type of gas mask was used as a defense against chemical weapons that German forces used first against Russian soldiers, then against the Allied forces of Britain and France. These early gas masks had a canister that was worn behind the user's back. The canister contained granules of activated charcoal, which served to absorb airborne chemicals, including poisonous gases. A tube led from one end of the canister to the user's mouth, and a clip prevented accidental inhalation through the nose.

Apart from providing air that was fit to breathe, the device had an airtight face mask with eyeglasses that formed a barrier against poison gases. Eye protection was important, since gases such as phosgene ($COCl_2$) and mustard gas react with moisture to form hydrochloric acid, which can irritate and cause permanent damage to the delicate tissues of the eyes if exposed.

In 1918, the original military gas masks were improved by the inclusion of hopcalite, a catalyst that eliminates carbon monoxide—a suffocating poisonous gas. Hopcalite functions by promoting a reaction between carbon monoxide and oxygen in the air to produce carbon dioxide.

▲ Gas masks are part of the equipment that protects these workers from contamination by toxic industrial waste.

▼ This construction worker wears a mask to prevent the inhalation of dust, which in certain cases may contain asbestos, a material that can cause chronic lung diseases.

Chemical filters

The principal method by which modern gas masks remove harmful chemicals from air is absorption, just as it was with World War I gas masks. Activated charcoal is still used in many modern filters, others use porous minerals called zeolites, which are particularly effective absorbers of moisture and acid gases. Such materials allow smaller molecules, such as oxygen and nitrogen, to pass through them with relative ease; larger molecules become trapped in their pores. After a while, the pores become saturated and the filter canister or cartridge has to be changed.

The useful life of absorption filters depends on the concentration of absorbable materials in the air: the greater their concentration, the quicker the pores become full. The rate at which a filter reaches saturation also depends on the wearer's level of activity, since a running soldier or firefighter will draw more breaths in a given period of time than will a calm, seated person.

Absorbent filters are of little use against harmful materials that are either too small to be trapped in their pores or too large to even enter them. Ammonia, carbon monoxide, formaldehyde, and certain acidic gases can be destroyed only by filters containing substances that react with such compounds and make them harmless. Acid gases can be neutralized by basic compounds, for example, while ammonia and simple amines can be eliminated by metal salts that bind them in stable compounds.

Particle filters

Substances that present biological or radiological hazards tend to be particulate mists or aerosols rather than molecular vapors. Biohazardous materials travel through the atmosphere as spores or waterborne mists, for example, while radioactive fallout can take the form of a mist or a dust cloud. As such, these types of substances call for filters that physically block their passage into a gas mask and the lungs of its wearer.

Developed in the 1940s, HEPA (high-efficiency particulate air) filters block at least 99.97 percent of particles with diameters of 0.12 thousandths of an inch (0.3 µm) or more. Such filters are sufficient to exclude particulate and aerosol contaminants, including spores, bacteria, viruses, and radioactive dust.

Industrial gas masks

The appropriate choice of protective mask for an industrial environment depends greatly on the type or types of hazards likely to be encountered there. People who work in stone renovation should wear particle-filter masks to exclude the harmful silica dust caused by sand blasting, for example, while chemical workers might need to use absorbent masks to avoid the inhalation of potentially harmful chemical vapors.

Self-contained breathing apparatuses are sometimes the only effective protection for people who encounter high concentrations of noxious substances, such as rescue workers. Under such circumstances, absorbent filters can become saturated—and therefore useless—in a short time. Breathing apparatuses supply pure air through a mask from compressed-air cylinders, thereby avoiding the need for air filtration.

Positive-pressure devices

Both absorbent filters and particle filters cause some resistance to the passage of air. Positive-pressure gas masks use a battery-driven fan to blow air through their filtration systems, thereby reducing the effort of breathing.

Military masks

Modern military gas masks are intended to help soldiers survive and fight in an environment polluted by nuclear, biological, or chemical (NBC) weapons. They generally combine a close-fitting rubber face mask with detachable filtration cartridges that are easily replaced when exhausted or when a different type of filter is required.

The exact configuration of the mask and filter units varies to accommodate the activities of different types of soldiers. Masks for infantry personnel have cheek-mounted filters that interfere

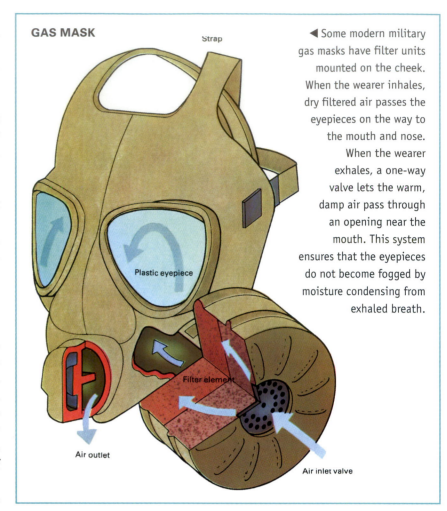

GAS MASK

Strap

Plastic eyepiece

Filter element

Air outlet

Air inlet valve

◄ Some modern military gas masks have filter units mounted on the cheek. When the wearer inhales, dry filtered air passes the eyepieces on the way to the mouth and nose. When the wearer exhales, a one-way valve lets the warm, damp air pass through an opening near the mouth. This system ensures that the eyepieces do not become fogged by moisture condensing from exhaled breath.

little with the use of firearms, for example, while masks for tank personnel are attached to their filter units by hoses to avoid crowding in the limited headroom of a tank or armored vehicle.

Good vision and ability to communicate are vital if fighting ability is not to be impaired. Thus, the Canadian CML-BIO C3 apparatus has large, flat, shatterproof lenses that fit close to each eye so that gun sights and binoculars can be used. Incoming air passes over the inside surfaces of these lenses to keep them from fogging, and an internal nose cap ensures that expelled air is passed through an outlet valve.

The mouthpieces of many military gas masks have some form of device to aid clear vocal communication. Some have a diaphragm that vibrates to transmit speech, while others have an internal microphone that can be connected to the intercom system of a tank, for example. Since an NBC environment would require soldiers to wear protective clothing for long periods, some apparatuses permit the wearer to take uncontaminated drinks without having to remove the mask.

SEE ALSO: BREATHING APPARATUS • CHEMICAL AND BIOLOGICAL WARFARE

Gas Industry

The gas industry has its origins in the late 18th-century development of gas lighting, but the use of gas for heating and cooking did not become widespread until the second half of the 19th century.

The first company to manufacture and supply equipment for using coal gas on a commercial basis was Boulton and Watt of Birmingham, Britain. This company, founded by Matthew Boulton and James Watt, employed William Murdock as a steam engine erector, and it was the experimental work of Murdock that led to their early involvement with the gas industry.

The development of the industry was continued by the Gas Light and Coke Company in London. Their chief engineer was Samuel Clegg, whose expertise helped the Gas Light and Coke Company to develop the system of distributing gas by pipeline from a central gasworks.

The American gas industry started in Baltimore, Maryland, in 1816 when the city council authorized Rembrandt Peale to manufacture gas and distribute it by pipes laid under the streets. The modern use of natural, rather than manufactured, gas began in the middle of the 19th century, when the Fredonia Gas Light and Water Works Company was formed in 1858, and there are now over 100,000 natural gas wells in the United States alone.

The three major types of gas in use are coal gas, oil gas, and natural gas, which is now by far the most important of the three. Liquefied petroleum gases (LPGs), such as butane and propane, are also distributed in some areas.

Natural gas

Natural gas, of which the main constituent is methane (CH_4), is usually found in the same type of geological strata as oil and is often found in association with oil deposits, the oil being driven to the surface by the pressure of the gas. In the early days of oil production, the gas was regarded as a nuisance and was just piped clear of the oil lines and burned off. The Chinese were using natural gas to evaporate brine for salt production as long ago as the first millennium B.C.E.

Natural gas became the major source of gas in the United States in the 1930s, following the discovery of extensive deposits and improvements in

▼ An underground storage project for natural gas. A gas-tight cavity is hollowed out in a layer of rock salt by washing out the salt with seawater (left). When a large cavity has been made, the pumping system is removed and replaced by gas equipment. Gas comes from a drilling rig and is pumped into the cavity and stored under pressure (right).

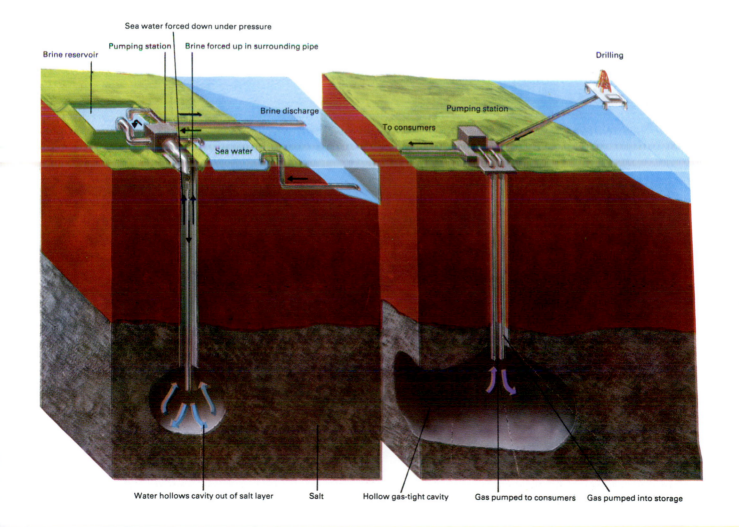

Sea water forced down under pressure
Pumping station
Brine forced up in surrounding pipe
Brine reservoir
Drilling
Brine discharge
Pumping station
To consumers
Sea water
Water hollows cavity out of salt layer
Salt
Hollow gas-tight cavity
Gas pumped to consumers
Gas pumped into storage

pipeline technology. In Europe, one of the most significant finds was made at Gröningen, northern Holland, strengthening the opinions of many geologists who believed that there was gas, and possibly oil, in vast quantities under the North Sea between Britain and the Netherlands.

The first commercial find in the North Sea was in 1965, and it was soon being piped ashore for use in Britain. There was a problem, however—the calorific value of natural gas is about twice that of manufactured gas. The calorific value is the amount of heat available from a given volume, the figure for manufactured gas in Britain being 500 Btu per cu. ft. (14.94 kJ/m^3). Thus, appliances designed to burn manufactured gas could not burn natural gas safely or efficiently.

There were two solutions to this problem: to use natural gas as a feedstock for the manufacture of gas by an adaptation of the oil gasification methods available (reforming) or, and this was the solution chosen, to convert the whole gas supply system of the country to handle natural gas. This decision was made mainly for economic reasons, as it was estimated that the cost of conversion would be $960 million, spread over 10 years, but over a period of 30 years the total cost of reforming the gas would be $3.36 billion more.

North Sea gas is brought by pipeline from offshore drilling rigs to coastal reception terminals and distributed by a 2,000 mile (3,219 km) high pressure pipeline network, operating at up to 1,000 psi (68.95 bar). The gas is taken from the main grid and distributed locally at lower pressures.

Natural gases vary in content, and some contain amounts of heavier hydrocarbons, which are removed to produce liquefied petroleum gases. Other gases must be treated to remove unwanted sulfur compounds and carbon dioxide. A typical treated natural gas contains over 80 percent methane (CH_4), together with ethane (C_2H_6) and about one percent nitrogen (N_2). Natural gas has no appreciable smell of its own, so to prevent accidents, a small amount of a liquid odorant—usually hydrogen sulfide, which smells like rotten eggs—is added to the basic gas so that it can be smelled when leakage occurs.

Natural gas provides one-fifth of all the energy used in the United States and supplies nearly half of all the energy used for cooking, heating, and fueling home appliances. It is trans-

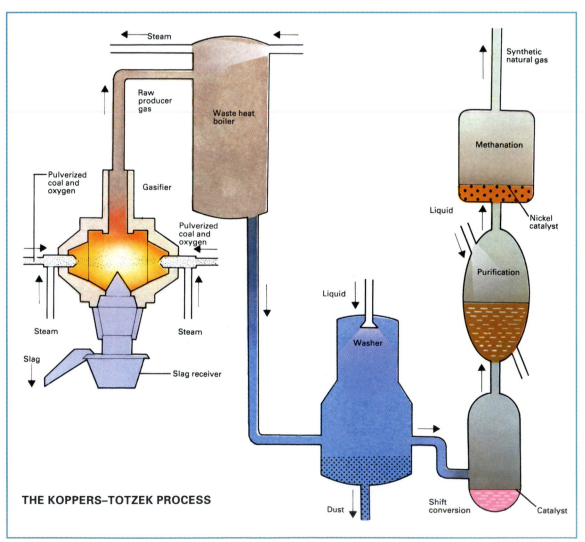

THE KOPPERS–TOTZEK PROCESS

◄ The Koppers–Totzek process makes producer gas. Powdered coal is mixed with oxygen and steam and heated. After cooling, dust is removed. It can then be converted to synthetic natural gas by using catalysts.

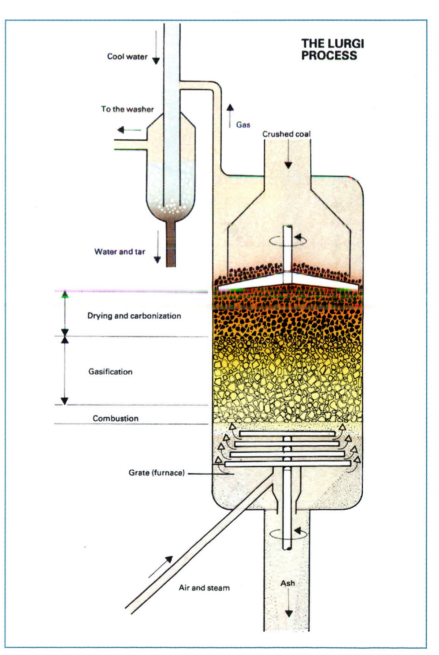

◀ A plant for reforming low-sulfur-content feedstocks into town gas (illuminating gas). The feedstock is heated under pressure in the presence of a nickel catalyst.

▼ The Lurgi process. When the coal passes down through the gasifier, it is transformed into coke, and a gas is produced.

more difficult gas so that it can be relied on increasingly in the future.

For example, large quantities of gas remain untapped in Alaska's North Slope region because of the difficulties and costs of transporting it by conventional pipelines. Deep offshore deposits, such as those in the Gulf of Mexico, are untapped for similar reasons. One way to overcome these problems would be to convert the gas chemically into a stable liquid that could be tankered to where it is needed or, alternatively, used as a vehicle fuel. Contaminated resources could also be used if new production technologies are developed to make the product usable.

Coal gas

Coal gas is made by the carbonization of coal, a process that involves heating the coal in the absence of air to drive off the gas and that also

ported through a network of over 1.3 million miles (2.1 million km) and can deliver 75 billion cu. ft. (1.5 billion m^3) per day when demand is heaviest. To ensure that the supply can meet the demand for gas, vast quantities are stored at sites around the United States, chiefly in the east and midwest regions. These sites are usually underground in depleted oil reservoirs, aquifers, mines, and salt caverns.

The United States has vast natural gas reserves, sufficient to last for at least another 60 years and in reality probably considerably longer. Canada also has massive gas reserves, and there are a number of gas pipelines that run from Canada into the United States.

The United States is looking for more ways to use gas, largely because it is easy to pipe from one location to another and because it burns very cleanly. Natural gas is increasingly being used in power plants to generate electricity. Factories are also using more natural gas, both as a fuel and as an ingredient for a variety of chemicals.

While natural gas is plentiful, there is still some uncertainty about how much it will cost to get it out of the ground in the future. As with oil, there is "easy" gas, which can be abstracted reasonably simply from underground formations, and there are reserves that are more difficult to tap. Much research is being undertaken to find better and more cost-effective ways of reaching larger quantities of the easy gas and some of the

THE LURGI PROCESS

Cool water

To the washer

Gas

Crushed coal

Water and tar

Drying and carbonization

Gasification

Combustion

Grate (furnace)

Air and steam

Ash

yields several useful by-products. The most important constituent elements of coal are carbon, hydrogen, oxygen, nitrogen, and sulfur, and it is the hydrogen and carbon that form the basis of coal gas.

There are many factors affecting the exact composition of coal gas, including the type of coal used, the manufacturing temperature, and the type of retort in which the coal is carbonized. The crude gas obtained from the coal is passed through several purification stages to remove unwanted constituents, such as ammonia, hydrogen sulfide, hydrogen cyanide, tars, and various hydrocarbons, before it is suitable for use.

A typical purified coal gas may contain approximately 50 percent hydrogen (H_2), 25 percent methane (CH_4), and 10 percent nitrogen (N_2), together with, for example, carbon monoxide (CO), carbon dioxide (CO_2), ethylene (C_2H_4), benzene (C_6H_6) and oxygen (O_2).

The earliest retorts were cast iron pots heated by burning coal underneath them. These retorts had a short working life, and because the temperature of distillation was low, the yield of gas was comparatively small. Firebrick retorts were soon developed, and they allowed carbonization temperatures to be raised to about 1742°F (950°C).

In the United States coal gas ceased to be of major importance in the 1930s, as natural gas exploitation increased, but the prospect of natural gas supplies eventually giving out has led to a renewed interest in its production.

Carbonization

Coal was usually brought from the mines to the gasworks, where it was first broken down to a size suitable for distilling in the particular system of carbonization employed. From the breaker, the coal was conveyed to the overhead storage hoppers of the retort house in which the retorts were situated and subsequently fed into the retorts. The retorts, either horizontal or vertical, were surrounded by a chamber heated by producer gas,

▲ Storage tanks for liquefied natural gas. In liquid form, the gas is greatly reduced in volume.

a cheap low-grade gas used in many industrial processes. Producer gas, also known as Siemens's gas, can be made in several ways, all of which involve blowing air or air and steam through a bed of heated fuel such as coal, coke, or lignite.

The retorts, made of a refractory material, heated the coal to a temperature of around 2462°F (1350°C). On being subjected to heat, the coal gave off gases, steam, and tarry vapors and passed through a plastic stage during which the evolution of gas through the plastic layers of coal formed the porous structure of the solid residue, the coke.

From the retorts, the gas, steam, and tarry vapors passed into a collecting main, where a considerable quantity of the tarry vapors was deposited. From the collecting main, the gas and impurities went into a condenser, where the temperature was reduced and where the tar and ammoniacal liquor condensed and ran off into a well. The ammoniacal liquor was formed by the condensing steam dissolving most of the ammonia and other impurities in the gas and consisted of ammonia, phenols, and various sulfur and hydrogen compounds. The tar contained pitch, creosote, carbolic and other oils, naphtha, and a small amount of water.

The gas was then pulled forward by an exhauster, which fed it through the rest of the washing and purifying plant and into a gasholder. In the first washer, the gas was bubbled through weak ammoniacal liquor to remove any residual tar and some of the remaining ammonia, which was completely removed in a second washer.

The next purification stage removed the hydrogen sulfide (H_2S) from the gas by passing it over grids covered with hydrated iron oxide. The iron oxide absorbed the hydrogen sulfide and was converted to iron sulfide. The final stage involved washing the gas with oil to remove naphthalene and benzole, and it was then treated in a drying plant to extract any remaining moisture so as to minimize corrosion in the distribution pipes.

Oil gas

The first uses of petroleum oil for the manufacture of gas were those in which crude oil was thermally "cracked" with steam at atmospheric pressure and at temperatures of between 1832 and 2012°F (1000–1100°C). This process was known as the noncatalytic process.

Subsequently, the range of process materials was extended to include most liquid hydrocarbon feedstocks, but this purely thermal cracking process was superseded by a more efficient cyclic catalytic process and, eventually by a whole range of cyclic and continuous processes (reformers).

Oil gas processes lent themselves more readily to full mechanization and automatic control than did coal gas procedures. The purification process is simpler, because oil gas contains no ammonia or hydrocyanic acid, and the overall result of changing to oil gas was a relatively lower capital cost and lower operating labor costs. The introduction of oil gas was the first large-scale revolution in gas-making technology since the first commercial applications of coal gas manufacture.

The objectives of catalytic processes are twofold: first, to produce gas from hydrocarbon feedstocks with a reduced yield of by-products and, second, to obtain higher gas yields compared with those that can be achieved by unaided thermal cracking in steam.

Large-scale cyclic and continuous reformers do not differ greatly in terms of capital cost and thermal efficiency, but the pressures achieved in continuous reformers are very much higher, resulting in a greater gas yield. This improved yield represents the greatest single advantage of the continuous process.

Other processes

There are several other important gas-making processes. The water gas process involves blowing first steam then air through a bed of heated coke. The gas produced is often called "blue water gas" because it burns with a characteristic blue flame. Carbureted water gas is produced by using the hot gases from the water gas generator to crack oil, producing an oil gas that is mixed with water gas to enrich it.

The Lurgi process, introduced in Germany in 1945, uses steam and oxygen under pressure to make gas from lignite or low-grade coals. Liquefied petroleum gases, chiefly butane (C_4H_{10}) and propane (C_3H_8), are by-products of oil refinery processes and natural gas treatment. Coke oven gas is a by-product of industrial coke making. Another type of gas, known as blast furnace gas, is produced during the process of smelting iron and is used at the iron works for steam raising, power generation, and preheating the blast air for the furnace.

Future uses

In future, new ways of producing gas may ease shortage problems. For instance, biomass gasification, which converts solid plant material into a rich gaseous fuel, allows it to be used in high-efficiency gas turbine plant and fuel cells. Commercial applications are being actively pursued.

Liquid propane gas is also increasingly being used as a fuel for vehicles—it is the most widely used alternative fuel in the United States today, powering nearly 300,000 vehicles.

Propane's popularity is partly due to its effect on vehicle maintenance: propane vehicles suffer less internal carbon buildup than gasoline vehicles. This means their spark plugs often last longer, and their oil changes are less frequent. Propane is also less sensitive to cold than gasoline, so vehicles start more readily and emit fewer pollutants during cold starts.

One of the major benefits of propane vehicles is their greatly reduced carbon monoxide (CO) emissions. They generate 40 to 60 percent less carbon monoxide than gasoline and up to 80 percent less during coldstarts. Their particulate emissions are generally lower than gasoline vehicles, and much lower than diesel vehicles.

◀ A section of the Trans-Mediterranean pipeline, which transfers gas over a distance of 1,500 miles (2,500 km) from Algeria to northern Italy.

SEE ALSO: CARBON • GAS LAWS • GASOLINE, SYNTHETIC • HYDROCARBON • METER, GAS • OIL REFINING • PIPELINE

Gas Laws

The gas laws describe the relationship between pressure, temperature, and volume of an ideal or perfect gas. An ideal gas is a hypothetical gas whose molecules are considered to be tiny hard spheres that, apart from collision, do not interact with each other. Although in reality gases are not ideal (there will always be some attraction between molecules and this fact becomes increasingly important at high pressures, when the molecules are squeezed close together), their behavior closely approximates that of an ideal gas at low pressures. In such conditions, their behavior is well described by the gas laws.

Boyle's law

The Anglo-Irish chemist Robert Boyle announced the discovery of the relationship between a gas's pressure and its volume in 1662. Boyle's law states that the pressure and volume of a gas kept at constant temperature are inversely propor-

tional. This means that when a gas is allowed to expand without any temperature change to twice (or three times, and so on) its initial volume, its pressure drops to a half (or a third, and so on) of its initial value. The more a gas expands in such conditions, the lower its pressure falls.

This law is easily explained in principle by the kinetic theory of gases. According to this view, the pressure force exerted by the gas on the walls of the containing vessel is the cumulative effect of the millions of elastic collisions that take place every second between the moving gas molecules and the containing walls. In an elastic collision, a molecule rebounds off a wall without any loss of kinetic energy; the component of its velocity normal to the wall is simply reversed. An increase in volume—whereby the gas molecules have farther to travel before they can collide with the walls—should therefore result in fewer such collisions per second. Decreasing the containing volume,

▼ Illustration of the general laws of Boyle and Charles (left). At right, another law discovered by Gay-Lussac shows that the volumes in which gases combine bear a simple relationship to one another. For example, one volume of chlorine (Cl) plus one volume of hydrogen (H) produces two volumes of hydrogen chloride (HCl).

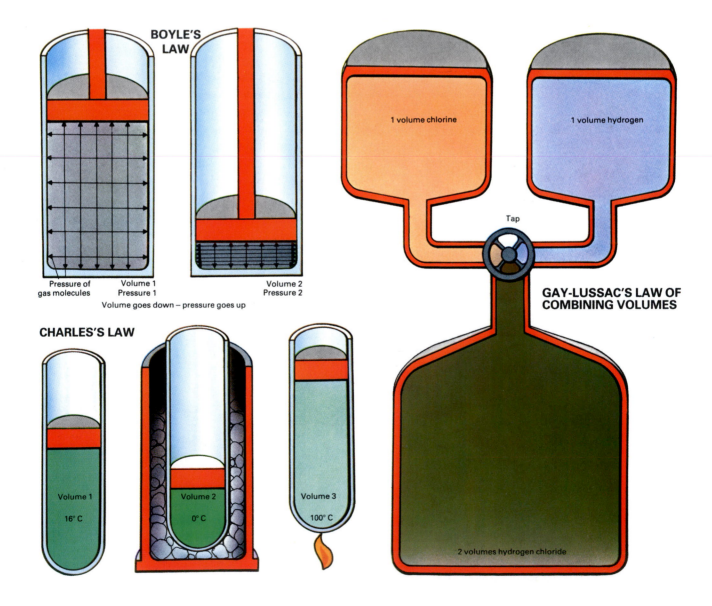

BOYLE'S LAW

Pressure of gas molecules | Volume 1 Pressure 1 | Volume 2 Pressure 2

Volume goes down – pressure goes up

CHARLES'S LAW

Volume 1 — 16° C | Volume 2 — 0° C | Volume 3 — 100° C

1 volume chlorine | 1 volume hydrogen

Tap

GAY-LUSSAC'S LAW OF COMBINING VOLUMES

2 volumes hydrogen chloride

on the other hand, means that the molecules have less far to travel between the walls, and so more collisions will take place every second. Reducing the volume, therefore, brings about a greater total pressure thrust on the walls.

Charles's law

Just over a century later, the French physicist Jacques-Alexandre-César Charles discovered the relationship between a gas's temperature and its pressure. He determined experimentally that the pressure of a gas that is kept at constant volume is directly proportional to its temperature, provided that the temperature is measured with respect to an absolute zero of –459°F (–273°C). When an enclosed mass of gas is heated, its pressure rises in proportion to the amount of heat and the corresponding temperature increase. When the gas is cooled, its pressure drops in proportion to the fall in temperature.

According to the kinetic theory, heat energy imparted to a gas causes the gas molecules to move more rapidly. Obviously, the speeds at which the molecules are traveling determine how great an impact they will have on the containing walls when they collide with them. The pressure the gas exerts is therefore increased when its temperature is raised and decreased when it is cooled.

Gay-Lussac's law

In the early 1800s the French physicist and chemist Joseph-Louis Gay-Lussac published his finding that the volume and temperature of a gas are directly proportional to each other if the pressure of the gas is held constant. This law again is only strictly true for an ideal gas, for it requires that the volume of the gas should become zero when the temperature reaches absolute zero—the temperature at which a substance contains zero heat energy, about –459°F (–273°C). In reality, gases liquefy before absolute zero is reached.

The general gas law

The laws of Boyle, Charles, and Gay-Lussac are summed up in what is known as the general gas law, which states that the product of the pressure (p) and volume (V) of a gas will be proportional to its temperature (T). This law can be written mathematically as $pV = RT$, where R is a proportionality constant called the gas constant. Many other isolated relationships between the various physical and chemical properties of gases were found before the appearance of the general gas theory, which placed them in a broader context. For example, Dalton's Law of Partial Pressure states that when different gases are mixed, the total pressure exerted by the mixture is simply the sum of the individual pressures and not some complicated interaction of the individual pressures. This law may not appear so surprising at first sight. What it means, however, is that all gas molecules, whatever their atomic and molecular structures, must behave physically in a very similar fashion. The kinetic theory includes this idea as one of its basic assumptions; it considers that the collisions of gas molecules are all of the elastic type. In this model, a gas is pictured as a furiously moving assembly of tiny but hard billiard balls. The only essential physical difference between all gas molecules is simply the size of the ball. This implication of a sort of qualitative similarity between gases was developed by the Italian chemist Amadeo Avogadro in 1811 in what is now known as Avogadro's Law: equal volumes of different gases at the same temperature and pressure contain equal numbers of molecules.

The operation of the gas laws is also apparent in unmanned gas-filled balloons, where the size of the envelope must always allow for expansion of the enclosed gas as the balloon ascends. The reason for this calculation is that the pressure of the atmosphere decreases as the height above the ground increases. Thus, in accordance with the gas laws, the volume of the gas in the balloon envelope at ground level will be much less than it is at the operating height of the balloon, which can be as much as 90,000 ft. (27,000 m).

◄ Balloons fly because they are filled with a gas that is lighter than air. Hot air balloons work because the heat from a burner forces the gas molecules that make up air farther apart, expanding the volume of gas in the envelope and creating lift.

SEE ALSO: AIR • BALLOON • KINETICS • PRESSURE • TEMPERATURE

Gasoline, Synthetic

Although present proven reserves of oil and natural gas, together with probable future discoveries, will be sufficient to meet the demands for liquid fuels for some time yet—probably into the first or second decade of the 21st century—it is clear that this is a declining resource. Liquid fuels have significant advantages for applications such as transportation, offering a high energy density and easy refuelling along with safety (so long as appropriate precautions are taken). So although alternative energy sources are being developed, there will be a sustained demand for liquid fuels, and to ensure that this demand can continue to be met, synthetic fuels have been and will continue to be developed.

▲ Sugarcane stalks being crushed prior to their being turned into alcohol. Brazil makes great use of alcohol as a fuel for cars and trucks because it is cheap and reduces the country's dependence on oil imports.

A further factor influencing the development of synthetic fuels is the security and cost of supply of oil-based products. Some countries may find it difficult to satisfy their fuel requirements with imports even though the oil is still available somewhere else in the world. It is the balance between security of supply and cost that determines the extent to which substitution processes are adopted, with present economics still tending to favor mineral oils for general use, while the technologies for producing synthetic fuels are developed to meet anticipated future requirements for clean-emission fuels.

There are two main approaches to the production of synthetic fuels, though in some areas these approaches tend to merge, with the most appropriate approach depending to a large extent on the raw material available. The direct approach is to produce a synthetic gasoline (or kerosene or fuel oil) by the chemical treatment of coal or organic material, while the alternative involves the replacement of some or all of the gasoline with alcohol-based products.

Alcohol-based fuels seem set to be the major source of synthetic gasoline, as they can be manufactured from readily available feedstocks. These biofuels, as they are called, are derived from cellulosic biomass, which include agricultural and forestry wastes, specially grown herbaceous crops, and even municipal wastes. The most widely used biofuel today is ethanol. Over 1.5 billion gallons (5.7 billion l) are added to gasoline in the United States every year to increase the octane level and improve exhaust emissions. Amendments to the Clean Air Act in 1990 mandated the sale of oxygenated fuels in states suffering from high levels of carbon monoxide. The usual blend is 10 percent ethanol to 90 percent gasoline, but concentrations of 85 percent, or pure ethanol are permitted for all vehicles.

Alcohols can be used directly as a liquid fuel provided that the engine is modified to take account of the fact that alcohols have a lower energy density, and thus, a larger volume of alcohol has to be used. Problems can also arise with cold starting since alcohols are harder to vaporize at low temperatures, but solutions to these difficulties are available.

Conversion processes

Four processes for converting biomass to ethanol are under development in the United States. Three of them use hydrolysis reactions to turn the biomass into sugars that can then be fer-

mented. The fourth process follows a different route, thermally converting biomass to gaseous hydrogen and carbon dioxide before fermentation. Acid hydrolysis, using concentrated or dilute sulfuric acid, is used to break down hard, woody fibers into cellulosic sugars. A key development in the process has been the removal of hemicelluloses before hydrolysis begins, as the resulting 5-carbon sugars are unfermentable. After hydrolysis, the sugars are separated from the acid by chromatography or membrane separation, which allows the acid to be recycled for further processing. Any cellulose or lignin left in solids from the reaction can be used to fuel a boiler to produce steam or electricity.

The fermentation reaction that follows uses enzymes that have been specially selected for the type of biomass being used. *Saccharomyces cerevisiae* is frequently used to convert wood-derived sugars, whereas a strain of *Zymomonas mobilis* has been developed for one project that is experimenting with rice straw.

Enzymatic hydrolysis dispenses with an acid hydrolysis step and simply employs a cellulase enzyme to break down the wood structure after pretreatment by thermal or chemical means. An important development in this type of process is the combining of cellulase enzyme with fermenting microbes in a simultaneous saccharification and fermentation reaction. As the sugars are produced they are converted to ethanol, eliminating the need for separate reaction steps.

One of the most established ethanol production programs is the Brazilian National Alcohol Program, which uses sugar molasses, but other materials such as grain and agricultural wastes can also be used. In this case, the polysaccharides in the material (such as starch and cellulose) are first converted to sugars by the use of enzymes—for example, amylase for starch—and then they are fermented to give the alcohol.

▶ A laboratory experiment to extract hydrocarbons from *Euphorbia lathyris*. There is a considerable amount of interest in developing technologies that can extract the maximum amount of fermentable sugars from plant material.

Biodiesel

Another type of fuel obtainable from renewable sources is biodiesel. Vegetable oils produced from oilseed crops, such as sunflowers, rape, and soy, can be transformed into biodiesel together with waste cooking oils and animal fats. Oils and fats are composed of fatty compounds called triglycerides that can be converted in the presence of alcohol into esters. These esters can then be blended with conventional diesel to form biodiesel or used as a neat fuel.

Production of biodiesel in the United States currently stands at 30 million gallons (115 million l) per year, mainly used as a 20 percent blend with ordinary diesel. Most is made from soybeans to fuel-grade quality standards. Like ethanol, it can be used safely in diesel engines without any modifications or retrofits being necessary. There is growing interest in using it in areas where workers are exposed to high levels of diesel emissions, such as airports, railroads, and marinas.

SEE ALSO: ALCOHOL • BIOFUEL • ENZYME • FERMENTATION • HYDROCARBON • OIL REFINING

Gas Turbine

The gas turbine and its variant, the jet engine, are the latest developments of old ideas. The word *turbine* comes from the Latin *turbo*, which means a "whirl, or top," and was originally used for the description of totally immersed waterwheels. One of the first gas turbines was the smokejack, a device for turning meat above a fire by using the rising heat from the fire to turn sails.

In 1791, the gas turbine as we know it was described in a patent by the English inventor John Barber. His drawing showed the essential parts of the gas turbine engine: a compressor, from which air is passed to a continuous-flow combustion chamber in which the fuel is burned and a turbine, through which pass the resultant hot gases. The hot gases turn the blades of the turbine, and this motion is used to drive the compressor. There is a surplus of power over that needed to drive the compressor, because it is a feature of the behavior of gases that the work that is made available from the expansion of a hot medium is greater than the work that is required to compress the same medium when it is cold.

Other internal combustion engines (the spark-ignited gasoline engine and the compression-ignited diesel engine) work on an intermittent cycle. Any single part of the engine is exposed to combustion gases for only a short time and is then washed by the relatively cool charge of the next cycle. Practically the whole of the oxygen in the air can be utilized, giving temperatures of more than 2500 K (4040°F, or 2230°C) in the combustion products, while few parts of the engine exceed 500 K (440°F, or 230°C).

By contrast, the blades of a turbine, which experience a continuous flow of combustion gases through them, can withstand a temperature of only about 1100 K (1520°F, or 827°C) if they are to be reliable over a useful period of time, even when they are made of complex modern alloys of nickel and cobalt. Only part of the oxygen in the air can be used if the temperatures of critical parts are not to exceed this figure. This fact seriously limits the output and efficiency of the gas turbine and proved a stumbling block for many years.

The patent for the first steam turbine, designed in 1844 by the English inventor Charles Parsons, included a reference to the use of a reversed turbine as an axial compressor for a gas turbine. There were a number of other proposals for gas turbines, but there were no practical developments until the beginning of the 20th century.

Turbochargers

The turbocharger was the first successful use of the principles of the gas turbine. A variant of the gas turbine, it produces no power in itself but increases the power output of the engine to which it is attached. A turbine is operated by the flow of hot exhaust gases from the engine; the turbine operates a compressor, which raises the density, and hence the mass flow rate, of the air charge to the combustion chamber of the engine. The first turbocharger was designed by Alfred Büchi and built by the Swiss corporation of Brown–Boveri in 1911. In 1916, turbochargers were first used in aircraft, and they were subsequently used in the most successful airplanes that operated in World War II.

Just before World War II, gas turbine engines were built by Brown–Boveri and installed for standby electric generation and electric generation in oil refineries. These have multistage axial-flow compressors, which have rotating blades and stationary blades arranged so that pressure is built up in stages. More efficiency and higher pressure ratios are available from this type of compressor.

Jet engines

The first person to envisage the use of gas turbines for aircraft propulsion was Frank Whittle, a pilot officer in the British Royal Air Force, who was later knighted for his achievement. In 1930, he patented the combination of a simple gas turbine and a nozzle to provide a jet-propulsion device, or turbojet. In 1936, he formed a com-

pany, Power Jets Limited, to develop it, and in 1939 the company received a contract for a flight engine. The same year, a German design, the Heinkel He 178, made a short flight; the Gloster–Whittle E 28/39 was more successful in 1941 with further developments of the engine, resulting in the W2B, which went into production as the Rolls Royce Welland powering the Gloster Meteor. A W2B engine was flown to the United States, and the General Electric Company used the design for development into the General Electric 1A that powered the Bell XP59 airplane that was launched in October 1942.

Since then, the main thrust of gas turbine development has been for airplane use, with the main advantage being that the gas turbine can provide a greater propulsive thrust with reduced weight and bulk. Another important advantage is that the efficiency of the engine increases with increased speed and height. As a result, the gas turbine has now effectively replaced the combination of piston engine and propeller for aircraft propulsion, with the exception of light airplanes.

Engine efficiency

The early engines all had centrifugal compressors, with the first axial design being tested by General Electric in the United States in 1944.

Axial-flow compressors offered higher efficiency and resulted in a greatly reduced engine frontal area compared with centrifugal designs, thus allowing better aircraft aerodynamics. In jet engines, the specific power output (the power

▶ The DA5 is a German development aircraft that employs the technique of afterburning to increase thrust.

obtained divided by the air-mass flow rate, a size criterion) and the thermal efficiency (the power obtained divided by the fuel energy rate, a running-cost criterion) both increase with turbine inlet temperature, compressor pressure ratio (up to a point), and the efficiencies of compressor and turbine. Efficiency is determined by comparing the power of the actual machine with that of a theoretical machine having no frictional or other heat losses. Efficiencies of both compressors and turbines can be as high as 90 percent today, but they were very much lower at the beginning of their development.

In modern jet aircraft that fly below the speed of sound, modifications to the engine are made. The efficiency of the engine is high only if the pressure ratio and turbine inlet temperature are high; this high jet velocity is wasteful at lower forward speeds. This problem is aggravated by the use of air cooling for the turbine blades, which allows inlet temperature to go still higher. Accordingly, an additional turbine stage is used to extract more power from the gases, with this power being used to drive a fan mounted in front of the compressor. This fan blows air back between the core engine and an outer casing to join the turbine jet, so giving a greater mass flow at a lower jet velocity. The fan drive passes through the core engine and in some designs—such as the Pratt and Whitney JT9D—is also used to drive the LP compressor stage. If the core engine is a two-spool type—as in the Rolls Royce RB211—the result is a three-spool engine.

An advantage of this type of engine, called a turbofan or fanjet, is that it is quieter because the jet velocity is lower. The ratio of the airflow through the outer duct to that going through the turbine is the bypass ratio. Fanjets with high bypass ratios propel large modern airliners.

Thrust augmentation

For supersonic flight, the simple jet engine is entirely suitable, as the high speeds match more closely the high forward speed of the aircraft. Jet speeds are sometimes increased by burning extra fuel between the turbine and the propelling nozzle, using surplus oxygen left in the turbine gases. This process is called afterburning and increases thrust considerably. During takeoff, fuel consumption increases faster than thrust, but at cruising speeds afterburning can be quite economical.

Another technique used to obtain increased thrust for takeoff is coolant injection, where a coolant such as water is injected into the compressor or combustion chamber to cool the air.

Other types of jets

The turboprop engine, like the fanjet, makes use of the extra turbine energy to save fuel but uses it to turn a conventional propeller rather than a fan inside the engine cowling. During the 1950s, turboprops were used on large jetliners, but cruising speeds have increased since then with development of the jet engine, and turboprops are used today only on small aircraft. However, considerable development effort is being applied to new turboprop designs, with one arrangement using multiblade fans mounted on the rear of the engine and directly driven from low-pressure turbines. Engines of this type are intended for

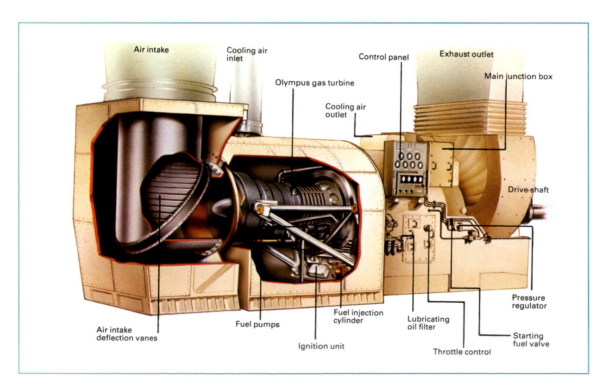

◀ A compact Rolls Royce TM3B marine gas turbine engine is designed for easy repair; it can be replaced in just a couple of days, even at sea. A spare engine is carried on board for use in emergencies.

Air intake

Cooling air inlet

Control panel

Exhaust outlet

Olympus gas turbine

Main junction box

Cooling air outlet

Drive shaft

Air intake deflection vanes

Fuel pumps

Fuel injection cylinder

Ignition unit

Lubricating oil filter

Throttle control

Pressure regulator

Starting fuel valve

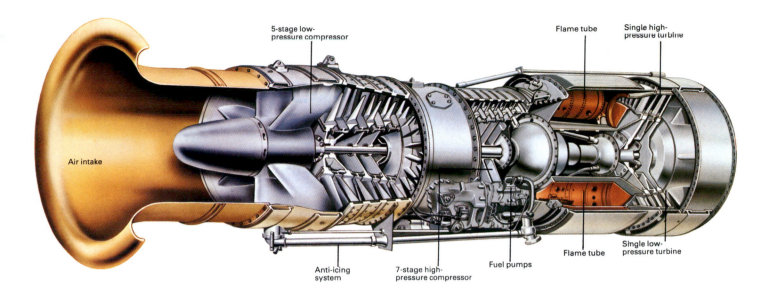

5-stage low-pressure compressor

Flame tube

Single high-pressure turbine

Air intake

Anti-icing system

7-stage high-pressure compressor

Fuel pumps

Flame tube

Single low-pressure turbine

mounting at the rear of the aircraft, with the fans acting as pusher propellers.

An engine similar to a turboprop, but used to drive a transmission shaft rather than a propeller shaft, is called a turboshaft engine. Such engines have been used to drive helicopter rotors, notably by the Bell Aircraft company, on several models, beginning with the XH-13F of 1955.

In the ramjet, incoming air is compressed by a specially shaped inlet nozzle, which slows its velocity and raises its temperature. After combustion, the hot gases are allowed to expand and leave the rear nozzle at a velocity greater than that of the aircraft, resulting in thrust. The ramjet operates only at forward speed, so a takeoff assist is necessary. The ramjet has been used to power guided missiles, which do not fly outside the atmosphere, and target drones. Ramjets are most efficient in the 1,500 to 2,500 mph (2,400–4,000 km/h) range.

The pulse jet, as its name implies, operates intermittently. The air enters through a valve that then closes. Combustion takes place and thrust is produced until the pressure in the combustion chamber drops, when the valve opens and the cycle begins again. Pulse jets were used during World War II in the German V-1 flying bomb.

The turboramjet is a hybrid jet engine in which the turbojet section is closed off from the airflow when speed is attained, and the bypassed air is used in a large afterburner.

Other turbine applications

The highly developed gas turbine engine is used to provide a versatile shaft-power (turboshaft) engine for peak-load and emergency electric power generation, to provide power at oil fields and refineries, for gas pipeline pumping, for warship propulsion, for hovercraft, and for other applications where the low weight and fast response are valuable in spite of increased fuel consumption over conventional power plants.

These engines are specifically designed for industrial purposes. In some cases, their combustion chambers are modified so that, like the early jet engines, they can burn a variety of fuels including industrial fuel gases and natural gas. In some installations, the heat energy remaining in the turbine exhaust is used to generate steam, which can be used for electricity generation or for industrial processes. This is the total energy concept. Normally, industrial gas turbines run on an open cycle using air as the working medium, but closed-circuit designs are also used, with the working fluid being heated externally, and coolers are used to remove excess heat from the exhaust fluid.

Of the next 1,000 power plants to be built in the United States, as many as 900 may use natural gas-powered gas turbines. In the past, it has not been cost effective to use gas turbines in power plants. For these systems to become more efficient, they must be able to have higher inlet temperatures than were previously possible. To achieve this goal, new materials and designs have been developed. One turbine, invented by General Electric, uses a steam cooling system and single-crystal turbine blades. Single-crystal materials are much stronger and resistant to the corrosive effects of high temperatures than polycrystalline materials. Another design developed by Siemens-Westinghouse has a thermal coating on the blades to allow higher operating temperatures.

▲ Cross section of a TM3B engine showing the low- and high-pressure compressors and turbines.

SEE ALSO: AIRCRAFT DESIGN • AIRLINER • COMPRESSOR AND PUMP • GAS INDUSTRY • POWER PLANT • ROCKET AND SPACE PROPULSION • SUPERSONIC FLIGHT • TURBINE

Gear

Gears are toothed wheels used to transmit power between components of a machine. Cars, clocks, machine tools, adding machines, cameras, and many other devices essential to our modern way of life contain various kinds of gears. The invention of the toothed wheel is second in technological importance only to that of the wheel itself.

The most important single use of gears is to transmit motion from a power source, such as an internal combustion engine or an electric motor, to a shaft that can do useful work, such as the propeller shaft in a car or the spindle of a machine tool. The power must be transmitted at a usable speed. When two gears are running together, the larger one is called the wheel and the smaller is called a pinion. If the pinion drives the wheel, the unit is a speed reducer; if the wheel drives the pinion, it is a speed increaser. Gears are more commonly used as speed reducers, because the speed of an electric motor, for example, is normally far too high to be used by a machine without reduction.

The second major function of gears is to provide a usable range of gear ratios in a machine: three or four forward gears in a car, for example, or a wide range of cutting speeds in a lathe. The gear ratio, the ratio of the number of teeth on one gear to the number of teeth on the other, determines the amount of speed reduction or increase that takes place. For example, if a pinion has 20 teeth and the wheel has 60, the ratio is 1:3, and the wheel will make one revolution for every three of the pinion. Since the teeth on a pinion each do more work than the teeth on the wheel, the pinion is sometimes made of harder material in order to prevent the pinion from wearing out before the wheel.

When one gear drives another, they turn in opposite directions (unless one of them is an internally toothed gear). If they must turn in the same direction, a third gear called an idler gear is interposed. Idler gears are sometimes used in transmission designs to provide the reverse gear.

Spur gears

Spur gears, the most common gears, have straight teeth and are used to transmit power between two parallel shafts or two shafts in the same axis. Their efficiency can be more than 95 percent.

The sides of the teeth, in profile, describe an involute curve. (If a piece of string is wrapped

▼ Gears are designed to suit many purposes. (1) Spur gear section, (2) spur gear teeth, (3) worm and gear, (4) spur gears in mesh, (5) helical gears meshing, (6) bevel gears connecting two shafts.

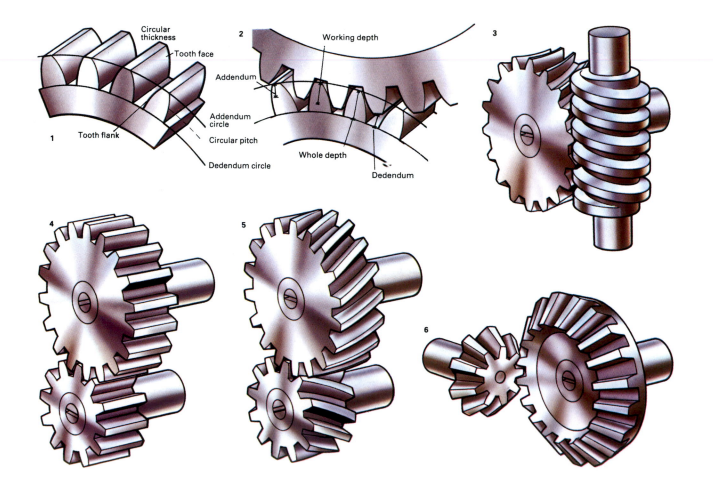

1 — Circular thickness, Tooth face, Addendum, Addendum circle, Circular pitch, Dedendum circle, Tooth flank

2 — Working depth, Whole depth, Dedendum

around a cylinder, a point on the piece of string will describe an involute curve as the string is held tautly and unwound.) The sides of the teeth must be curved or the operation of the gears would be noisy, wear would be excessive, and a great deal of vibration would be generated.

An arrangement of spur gears in which one or more small planet gears travel around the outside of a sun gear, while at the same time running around the inside of an enclosing annulus gear, is called a planetary, or epicyclic, system. (An annulus is an internal spur gear, that is, it has teeth on the inside instead of the outside.) An epicyclic arrangement allows more than one gear ratio to be selected, without moving gears in and out of mesh, by locking various components or combinations of components of the system. It is used in bicycle gears, automatic transmissions, and other applications where complexity and absorption of power must be avoided.

A flat piece of material, oblong in cross section, with involute teeth cut on one side of it is called a rack. A rack and pinion gear system, in which a spur gear runs back and forth on a rack, is used in the steering mechanism of some cars, in hydraulic door closers, and for reciprocating motion of tables or workheads of machines.

Bevel gears

Bevel gears are shaped like sections of cones. They are used to transmit power between shafts whose axes intersect. The teeth on an ordinary bevel gear are straight but tapered in length and depth; if extended in length, they would meet at a point ahead of the gear on the axis of the shaft called the pitch cone apex.

Hypoid bevel gears have teeth that are straight but cut on the face of the gear at an angle to the axis of the shaft. They can be used to transmit power between two shafts whose axes cross each other, but not in the same plane.

Helical gears

Gears that are shaped like sections of cones, such as bevel gears, or like sections of cylinders, such as spur gears, can have spiral teeth, enabling them to be designed to transmit power between shafts at any angle to each other, according to the spiral of the teeth. They are called helical gears. The curved teeth enter the mating teeth while the previously meshing teeth are still in contact; thus, some sliding of the teeth against each other takes place, and power is transmitted with relative smoothness and silence. Helical gears, like hypoid bevel gears, can transmit power between shafts that are not in the same plane; their combination of running characteristics and design possibilities makes them ideal

for pinion and crown gears in the differential of an automobile.

Worm gears

When a pair of gears with helical teeth is used to transmit power between two shafts whose axes intersect, but not in the same plane, very high gear ratios are possible. In such a case, the gear ratio is commonly as high as 1:100; the pinion may have multiple threads, or just one, curving all the way around it and resembling a screw thread. Such a pinion is called a worm. The speed reduction of a worm and gear unit is very great and is used between an electric motor and a slowly moving conveyor, for example. If, for instance, the worm and gear ratio were 18:1 and the worm speed 360 rpm, the speed reduction to the gear would effectively be to 20 rpm.

Nonmetallic gears

Where quiet operation at high speeds is desired and if the operating load or torque is not too high, one or both gears may be made out of plastic or a fibrous composition material. The timing gear in an automobile, which drives the camshaft from the crankshaft by means of a chain, is frequently nonmetallic. The speed of the timing gear is high; while the timing is important, the load carried is relatively small.

Gear cutting

The machines used for cutting gear teeth are of three general types. For cutting spur gears, a cutter blade conforms to the size of the space between the teeth. The second type generates the teeth either by a pinion-shaped cutter, which rotates in unison with the blank and in reciprocation cuts the teeth or, alternatively, uses a cutter shaped like a section of a rack and planes the teeth as it moves across the face. The third type is a hob, which is a worm with gashed and relieved threads to give a cutting action.

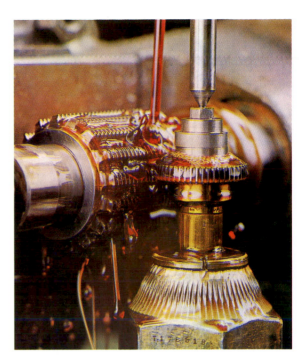

▲ A machine tool, lubricated and cooled with a medium-viscosity cutting oil, cuts a spur gear.

SEE ALSO: Automobile • Clutch • Flywheel • Internal combustion engine • Lubrication • Machine tool • Transmission, automobile

Geiger–Müller Tube

The Geiger–Müller tube is a device for detecting a charged particle. It was invented by two German physicists, Hans Geiger and Walther Müller, in 1928, and though it has now generally been replaced by much more sophisticated detectors, in the early days, it was a vital instrument for investigating the nature of the nucleus of the atom and the behavior of the minute particles of which the atom is built.

Basic construction

In its usual form the counter consists of a glass tube about ¾ in. (20 mm) in diameter enclosing a metal cylinder, often of copper, about 4 in. (10 cm) long with a thin tungsten wire running along its axis. The cylinder and wire are connected through the end wall of the glass tube to a source of electric voltage. The tube is filled with a gas, usually argon, at a low pressure, equivalent to a pressure of a few inches of mercury. A voltage is set up between the cylinder (the negative electrode, or cathode) and the wire (the positive electrode, or anode) that is just a little less than that needed to create an electric discharge between the two electrodes. This voltage is typically 500 volts.

Operating principles

When a charged particle with high energy flies through the glass tube, it knocks electrons out of the atoms of the gas. These electrons, being negatively charged, are attracted to the wire anode, and the damaged atoms (which are positively charged argon ions) make for the cathode.

Since there are 500 volts between the wire and cylinder, the electrons are affected by a high-voltage gradient—rolling, as it were, down a very steep electrical hill. They pick up enough energy to knock further electrons out of atoms, and they in turn roll down the electrical hill picking up more energy and liberating further electrons. This chain reaction is known as an electron avalanche. At the same time, the positive ions hit the cylinder with enough energy to release still more electrons. An avalanche of electrons therefore descends on the wire and is detected as a pulse of electric current, indicating that a charged particle has passed through the tube.

Before a discharge, the Geiger–Müller tube is charged rather like a capacitor, but when a discharge occurs, both the stored charge and the corresponding voltage between the cylinder and wire are reduced, thus "killing" the discharge in the tube that would otherwise go on indefi-nitely—an important feature, because while the discharge continues, the device is insensitive to further charged particles arriving at the detector.

Another way of stopping the avalanche is to put about 10 percent ethyl alcohol into the argon. Because of the way the atoms bump around, it tends to be alcohol ions rather than the argon ions that reach the cylinder, and there they prefer to break up rather than release more electrons. The alcohol vapor also smothers electron production within the gas mixture. It takes about a ten thousandth of a second to snuff out an avalanche, and the voltage then builds up again so that the device is ready to record another charged particle. This period is known as the detector's dead time, since the detector is effectively dead to incoming particles for this interval.

With the coming of electronic amplifiers, the pulse of electric current could be made audible through a small loudspeaker. When a Geiger–Müller tube is switched on, irregular clicks will always be heard, originating in cosmic rays (very-high-energy particles that shower onto Earth from outer space) or in natural radioactivity (spontaneous emission of particles from some forms of chemical element that make up the natural environment). Uranium is a prolific source of natural radioactivity, disintegrating into other types of atom by emitting charged particles from its nucleus.

Limitations

The Geiger–Müller tube has limitations in pinning down charged particles as regards both their position in space and their time of arrival. Furthermore, it is unable to distinguish between the various ionizing particles: alpha and beta particles and gamma rays. The counter can only say that a particle has passed through the volume enclosed by the glass tube but cannot show its exact position.

▼ Prospecting for radioactive materials with a Geiger–Müller tube. A high-energy particle ionizes some argon gas atoms and this creates a discharge.

SEE ALSO: ATOMIC STRUCTURE • ELECTROMAGNETIC RADIATION • ELEMENTARY PARTICLE • PARTICLE DETECTOR • RADIOACTIVITY

Generator

A generator is a rotating machine that converts mechanical energy into electrical energy. Alternating-current (AC) generators are called alternators, and direct-current (DC) generators, are referred to as dynamos. Generators make use of a phenomenon discovered by the British chemist and physicist Michael Faraday. In general terms, when an electrical conductor is moved in the vicinity of a magnet, a voltage is created, or induced, in the conductor. If the ends of the conductor are connected in any kind of closed electrical circuit, this induced voltage (electrical pressure) causes a current to flow in the circuit. The result is that mechanical energy has been converted into electrical energy.

For a more detailed explanation it is necessary to consider the principles of electromagnetism. In an electrical circuit it is voltage that causes the current to flow. The voltage, or electromotive force (emf), is the cause, and current the effect. By analogy, in a magnetic circuit, the driving "pressure" is called the magnetomotive force (mmf). This is the cause and magnetic flux is the result, or effect. Between the north and south poles of a magnet can be envisaged a set of flux lines spreading out from the magnet—the closer these lines are together, the greater the flux density. Flux density is determined by the mmf of the magnet and the permeability of the surrounding medium.

The emf induced in an electrical conductor moving in a magnetic field is determined by the rate at which the conductor "cuts" the lines of flux. The induced emf is therefore related to the speed of the conductor and the flux density. It is also related to the length of the conductor.

A simple alternator

When a closed rectangular loop of wire is mounted on a rotating axis (the rotor) and rotated between the north and south poles of a horseshoe magnet (the stator), the following occurs. When the two sides of the loop parallel to the axis of the rotor (these are the conductors) form a line between the north and south poles, the rate at which these two conductors cut the lines of flux is at a maximum. The induced emf in the conductors is therefore also at a maximum and the current flowing around the loop at its largest value.

When the rotor has turned through 90 degrees, the instantaneous direction of motion of the conductors is along the lines of flux. No lines of flux are therefore cut, no emf is induced in them, and the loop current is zero.

When it has rotated by a further 90 degrees, the rate of flux cutting is again at a maximum with maximum emf and loop current. The loop is now, however, upside down compared with its position 180 degrees ago, and the induced emf and current

▲ The turbine hall of a power plant. The turbochargers each have an output of 500 MW. In the United States, the electric frequency is 60 Hz, so alternators run as high as 3,600 rpm. Some countries have a frequency of 50 Hz, and the alternators run at 3,000 rpm.

CAR DYNAMO

This typical car dynamo provides DC power through the arrangement of brushes and a commutator. The windings of the revolving armature cut across the flux of the magnetic field provided by the field windings and induces an electric current in the armature windings that can then be used to power the electrical components of the car. The fins on the back of the pulley act as a cooling fan, blowing air through the dynamo to cool the windings.

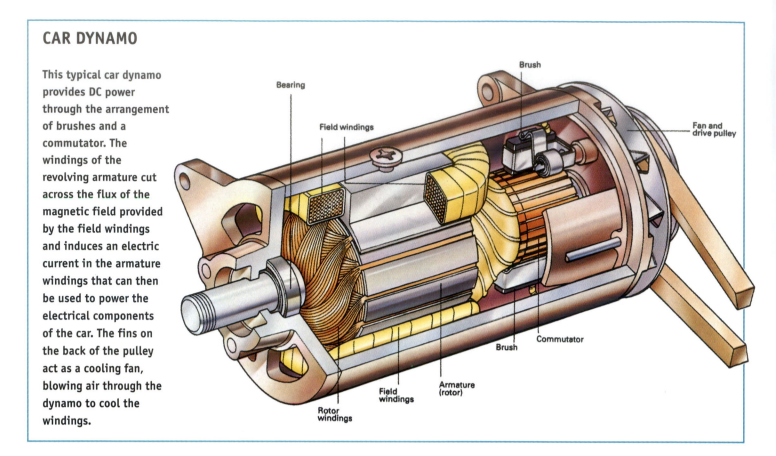

Bearing

Brush

Field windings

Fan and drive pulley

Brush

Commutator

Armature (rotor)

Field windings

Rotor windings

are at a maximum in the opposite direction. A further 90-degree rotation and the current is again zero. By breaking the loop at one end near the axis and connecting the ends to two slip rings on the shaft, this alternating emf can be tapped using brushes touching the rings to drive a circuit.

Most large-scale alternators do not use permanent magnets because they give no degree of control of the magnetic field generating the voltage. Instead, the field is provided by electromagnets consisting of coils of wire fed with direct current (DC). The amount of power required by the field-producing magnets is of the order of around 20 megawatts. The power generated in a large power plant alternator, however, may be 550 megawatts. It would be impractical to collect so much power through slip rings and brushes, and accordingly, alternators are built so that the electromagnets are made to rotate and the coils that receive the induced voltage remain stationary. The DC current for the electromagnets is fed via slip rings and brushes.

From alternators to dynamos

To construct a dynamo, several loops are positioned in sequence around the rotor. This time, instead of taking the loop ends to slip rings, they are connected in the same sequence to individual segments of a commutator (a divided rotating contact). Two brushes are mounted on opposite sides of the commutator such that, as the rotor

rotates, the brushes form an electrical contact with the two ends of just one loop at a time.

By positioning the brushes so that they tap that loop which is in the position of maximum flux cutting, they will tap each loop as it comes into that position during rotation. The induced emf is therefore always in the same direction (that is, a DC voltage) and always with the maximum value.

Increasing the speed of rotation will, to a certain extent, increase the DC voltage available at the brushes. One other way to improve the dynamo performance is to increase the number of turns in each loop, because, as already stated, the length of the conductor also determines the emf that can be induced. Finally, the performance can be further improved by increasing the flux density, and several methods are available. First, stronger magnets or electromagnets can be employed, and second, the magnetic poles can be shaped to concentrate the lines of flux.

When electromagnets are used to provide the magnetic field, they draw some of the current generated by the machine. When starting from rest, the current to start the electromagnets working is derived from what little residual magnetism exists in the electromagnets and magnetic circuit.

SEE ALSO: Automobile • Electricity • Electromagnetism • Magnetism • Power plant

Genetic Engineering

Genetic engineering is the manipulation and study of genes, which are complex subunits of DNA that pass from one generation of a species to the next. Genes carry with them the instructions that determine how the cells of an organism develop and function. Because genes are so fundamental to life processes, understanding how they function—and malfunction—creates the opportunity to cause radical changes in the traits of an organism by changing its genes.

Genetic engineering has had many achievements to date: genetically modified crop plants give greater yields of fruit and vegetables than their "natural" relatives, for example, while genetically modified animals produce human insulin for the control of diabetes. Genetic engineering has made possible the mass production of various vaccines and of interferon, which attacks viruses and is a possible cure for some cancers.

DNA

Deoxyribonucleic acid—DNA—was discovered in 1869 in Germany by a Swiss doctor, Friedrich Miescher, who was investigating a substance found in the nuclei of white blood cells in pus from surgical wounds. Richard Altman, a student of Miescher, called the substance nucleic acid.

Miescher noted that nucleic acid consists of sequences composed using a few relatively simple chemical subunits and recognized the potential of such sequences to harbor messages about heredity, "just as the words and concepts of all languages can find expression in 24 to 30 letters of the alphabet." Miescher, however, mistakenly thought proteins were the agents of heredity.

By the 1920s, it was established that nucleic acid exists in two varieties. The two variants were called deoxyribonucleic acid and ribonucleic acid—DNA and RNA. These names refer to the two pentose sugars, deoxyribose ($C_5H_{10}O_4$) and ribose ($C_5H_{10}O_5$), that are characteristic structural elements of the two types of nucleic acid. Then in the early 1940s, DNA was finally confirmed by experiments in the United States to be the carrier of hereditary information.

The structure of DNA

The structure of DNA eluded detection for many years. Then in 1953, a British molecular biologist, Francis Crick, and a U.S. biologist, James Watson, proposed a structure that explained the results of X-ray diffraction studies of DNA performed by British crystallographer Rosalind Franklin and British physicist Maurice Wilkins.

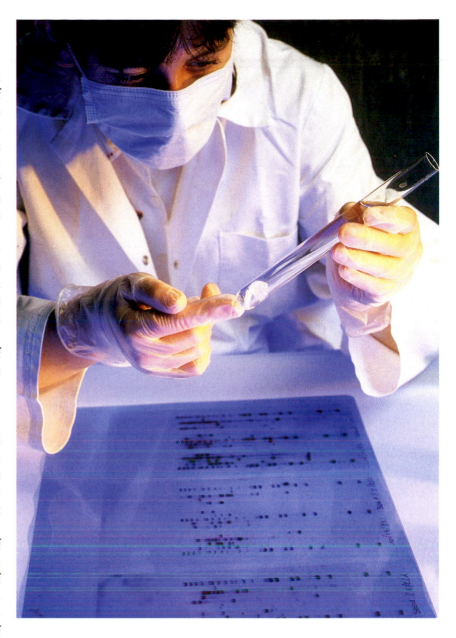

The Watson–Crick model of the structure of DNA resembles a ladder twisted into a spiral: it has two helical molecular strands wrapped around each other and linked together at regular intervals along its length. Watson and Crick calculated the molecule to be around 20 angstroms (2 nm) across, and 0.04 in. (1 mm), or more, long.

Each strand of DNA consists of a string of chemical subunits called nucleotides, of which there are four types. Each nucleotide involves a phosphate group (PO_4) bonded to a deoxyribose molecule, which in turn is bonded to a purine or a pyrimidine base. In DNA the phosphate of each nucleotide has formed an additional bond to the deoxyribose part of its neighbor, and the two strands of the DNA double helix are bound to each other by somewhat weaker hydrogen bonds. The four nucleotides are distinguished by the four possible base groups—adenine, cytosine, guanine, and thymine—which are represented by letters A, C, G, and T.

▲ The white mass in the tube is a sample of DNA; the trace on the table is an autoradiogram. When DNA is treated with agents that cause it to fragment, the resulting mixture can be split into a series of bands by a technique called gel electrophoresis. To make an autoradiogram, the fragments are modified to make them radioactive and then separated by electrophoresis. The radioactive bands expose photographic film through lightproof paper. After developing, the pattern on the film gives information about the composition of DNA.

Structure and base pairing

Adenine, cytosine, guanine, and thymine are compounds of carbon, hydrogen, nitrogen, and in the cases of cytosine, guanine, and thymine, oxygen. They are called bases because they contain amine groups, which form salts with acids. Two of the bases—adenine and guanine—have at their core a purine structure: two rings of carbon and nitrogen atoms joined along one edge. The other bases—cytosine and thymine—have a pyrimidine core, a single six-membered ring of carbon and nitrogen atoms. The two purine bases have different chemical groups attached to their cores, as do the two pyrimidine bases.

The different structures of the four bases have profound consequences for genetics, since an A in one strand is always paired with a T in the other, while a C is always paired with a G. The two strands of DNA are therefore complementary, since the sequence of bases in one strand is matched by the appropriate sequence of matching bases in the other. In this way, the two strands are more like a photographic positive negative pair rather than straightforward mirror images.

The reasons for the specific pairings of bases in DNA are twofold. First, a purine base always forms a pair with a pyrimidine base, so the length of the bridge between the two strands is fairly constant (the purine system is larger than the pyrimidine system). Second, the types and positions of the functional groups on the different bases favor the formation of hydrogen bonds between A-T pairs and C-G pairs. Hydrogen bonds, which form bridges between the strands of DNA, are weak compared with covalent bonds.

Protein synthesis

The principal function of DNA is to direct the manufacture of proteins in living organisms. Proteins play vital roles in the life of organisms: some are building materials in the composition of cells; others, called enzymes, are remarkably efficient catalysts for the processes in cells.

Like some types of nylon polymers, proteins are polyamides that form by reactions between amino acids—molecules that have an acid group and an amine group each. A protein may be formed from 50 to 500 amino acid residues that are held in a chain by amide linkages, which are called peptide linkages in biochemistry.

The sequences of amino acids in proteins determines both their form and function. There are 20 natural amino acids that participate in protein formation, and DNA holds the recipes that dictate how sequences of those amino acids line up to be joined together as functional proteins.

In the first stage of protein synthesis, the two strands of DNA separate, and one strand acts as a template for the formation of a molecule of mRNA—messenger RNA. Messenger RNA is ribonucleic acid that contains the sequence of bases that match those in a stretch of DNA that is responsible for the formation of a specific protein. Such a section of DNA is called a gene.

The nucleotides in RNA differ from those in DNA in that they are based on ribose rather than deoxyribose, and a uracil-based nucleotide, represented by U, takes the place of T in pairings with A nucleotides, Once the mRNA is complete, it drifts away from the DNA, allowing the two strands of DNA to join up again.

▼ The polymerase chain reaction is a vital process in genetic engineering. The reaction, which results from the introduction of an enzyme known as DNA polymerase, is a cyclical process. In the first stage, the DNA is heated to separate the two strands, and extra DNA segments called primers are attached. In the second stage, the temperature is lowered, and as the enzyme takes effect, each strand of DNA splits into two. The temperature is then raised again, causing each new strand to split into two. This cycle is repeated as many as 25 to 30 times until the desired number of copied DNA strands is reached.

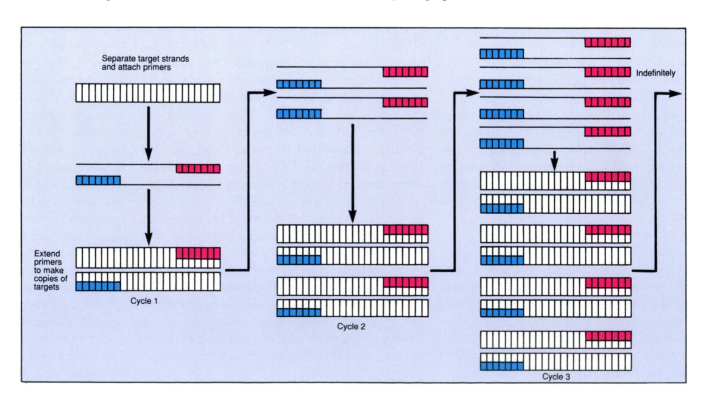

Separate target strands and attach primers

Extend primers to make copies of targets

Cycle 1

Cycle 2

Cycle 3

Indefinitely

In another part of the cell, amino acids assemble in an order dictated by the sequence of bases in the mRNA. An enzyme then catalyzes the formation of peptide linkages. When a protein molecule is complete, it separates from the mRNA that has acted as the template for its formation.

Codons: genetic words

While it is clear that a strand of DNA acts as a template for mRNA by attracting bases similar to those that it interacts with in its complementary strand, it is less clear how mRNA organizes amino acids into the correct sequence for a protein. In 1961, Francis Crick solved this puzzle with the South African-born British molecular biologist Sydney Brenner.

Crick and Brenner identified the basic features of a genetic code, whereby triplets of nucleotides in mRNA, called codons, correspond to specific amino acids. Since there are 64 possible combinations of three nucleotides and only 20 amino acids, most amino acids are represented by more than one codon. For example, the amino acid glycine, formula $CH_2(NH_2)COOH$, can be represented by any of four codons in mRNA: GGA, GGC, GGG, or GGU. These correspond to CCT, CCG, CCC, and CCA triplets in DNA. Crick and Brenner also noted that mRNA consists of a straightforward sequence of codons, without gaps or overlaps between adjacent codons. This means that nucleotides are "read" in groups of three from a defined starting point.

If the bases A, C, G, T, and U are the letters of the genetic alphabet, then codons are the words of the genetic language. This language is read when amino acids assemble on mRNA according to its codon sequence. The process is selective because the functional groups of the three bases of a given codon have an orientation in space and a pattern of electrical polarity that attracts one amino acid more strongly than any of the others. The codon AUG forms part of the sequence that initiates protein formation (it also codes for the amino acid methionine within a chain). Any of the codons UAA, UAG, and UGA can indicate the point at which the protein chain ends.

Replication

Each cell of an organism requires DNA for it to function properly. Consequently, when cells divide as an organism grows, each fragment of an old cell must possess DNA as it forms a cell in its own right. The process by which new copies of DNA form is called replication.

Many stages of replication are similar to the formation of mRNA from DNA. First, the two strands "unzip" from one end of the DNA. As

they do, nucleotides attach to each strand according to the standard base-pairing pattern for DNA: A with T, and C with G. Enzymes join the nucleotides to form new strands of DNA. At the end of the process, each strand of the original DNA has acquired a new complementary strand identical to its partner in the original DNA.

Sequencing: restriction enzymes

When genetic engineers want to break down DNA to study its nucleotide sequence, they use substances called restriction endonucleases. These are enzymes, produced by bacteria, that catalyze the cleavage of peptide linkages. They are named using three letters from the name of the originating bacterium and, when necessary, a letter to identify the specific strain of the bacterium and a roman numeral to differentiate between enzymes derived from the same strain. By this system, *Eco*RI is the first enzyme derived from the R strain of *Escherichia coli*.

Restriction enzymes are useful because they act where specific sequences of nucleotides occur in DNA. There are now many hundreds of restriction enzymes that recognize different sites.

There are three subgroups of restriction enzymes, classified according to how they act at their characteristic sites. A class I restriction enzyme recognizes a sequence of nucleotides in DNA and can cleave a peptide link anywhere within that sequence. Much more selective—and therefore much more useful as tools—are class II restriction enzymes. These not only recognize a specific sequence in DNA, they also cleave at a particular point within that sequence.

The third group of restriction enzymes is usually called class III, but sometimes treated as a subgroup of class II. Restrictions in this class recognize a sequence within DNA and cleave a set number of nucleotides from that sequence.

▲ Injecting messenger ribonucleic acid (mRNA) into a frog's eggs, where it will organize the formation of protein molecules from natural amino acids.

HUMAN GENOME PROJECTS

A genome is the complete set of genetic instructions contained in a single cell of an organism. These instructions are encoded in genes, which are segments of DNA. In most cases, all the cells of a given organism contain identical DNA.

The principal goal of a Human Genome Project, or HGP, is to establish the whole sequence of nucleotide bases in human DNA. From that sequence, scientists hope to identify the estimated 40,000 to 100,000 genes that determine how human cells develop, function, and finally die.

Human DNA varies slightly from one individual to another, as do the genes encoded in it. These variations account for the unique appearances of individual humans, for example. Genes determine the relative susceptibilities of individuals to certain diseases, such as cancer, diabetes, and osteoporosis, as well as the nature and strength of an individual's response to compounds used to treat disease.

In the United States, the Department of Energy and the National Institutes of Health started independent preliminary plans for human genome projects in the mid-1980s. By 1988, the two bodies had signed an agreement to work together on the project; in 1990, they published a plan for the first five years of work in what was planned to be a 15-year project.

From its early years, the U.S. Human Genome Project benefited greatly from unforeseen advances in the technologies used to fragment and sequence the base pairs in DNA (there are estimated to be some 3 billion such pairs in human DNA). These advances, such as the introduction of robotics to automate sequencing, increased the rate of sequencing and

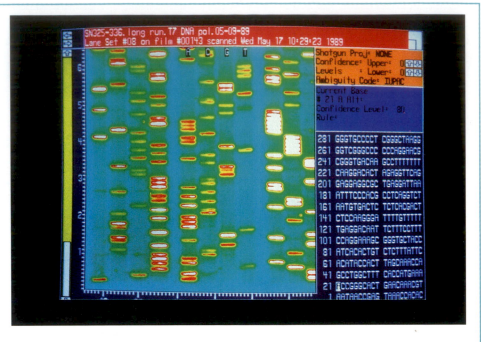

reduced its cost from $10 per base pair to around 50 cents per pair. The U.S. project also benefited from cooperation with HGPs based in other countries, notably those in Australia, Britain, France, and Japan.

The U.S. HGP uses a technique called shotgun sequencing, whereby a reaction promoted by enzymes cuts whole DNA chains into fragments around 500 bases long. This is the fragment length best suited to cheap, fast, robotic sequencing.

Individual fragmentation reactions of identical DNA molecules produce different sets of fragments, corresponding to the DNA chain breaking at different points. These fragments help piece together the overall DNA sequence, since a fragment from one reaction may contain sequences that occur in the ends of two fragments from another reaction. A computer can recognize those two end sequences in the fragment from the first reaction and so identify the positions in a DNA chain of the fragments produced by the second reaction.

▲ DNA sequencing of the human genome. This computer is displaying the results of an automated method of decoding the sequence of base pairs in fragments of DNA extracted from human chromosomes. Mapping and sequencing are two phases of the human genome project, an ambitious plan to reveal all of the information encoded in the 23 pairs of human chromosomes. Mapping refers to a physical survey of each chromosome to determine the exact location of genes or other genetic markers. Sequencing of all the DNA in the human genome would involve manipulating 3 billion base pairs.

The rapid progress of the HGP allowed its coordinators to publish a revised schedule in 1998. A "working draft" of the gene map was delivered in February 2001, and included the positions of many genes important for the study of diseases. The full gene map is expected to be available before the end of 2003—two years ahead of the original schedule.

Sequencing: chemical methods

Some chemical procedures reliably cleave open DNA next to a specific type of nucleotide. These can be used to cause further degradation of the fragments released by restriction enzymes.

One such procedure breaks the chain on one particular side of cytosine nucleotides. It can be used in sequencing by labeling a specific type of fragment at one end using phosphate groups with radioactive phosphorus (^{32}P). The procedure is then applied, cleaving the DNA wherever there

are cytosine residues, so ^{32}P-GCAATACGCTC forms ^{32}P-GCAATACGCT, ^{32}P-GCAATACG, ^{32}P-GCAATA, and ^{32}P-G, for example.

The mixture is then separated by gel electrophoresis, whereby an electric field drags the negatively charged fragments through a viscous gel on a plate. The fragments move at different rates, and when the field is switched off, their positions in the gel help identify them. The positions of labeled fragments are revealed by using their radioactivity to expose a photographic plate.

Recombinant DNA

Once the genetic code was cracked in the 1960s, scientists became keen to make use of the newly acquired information. One of their goals was to introduce donor genes into the DNA of an organism in order to introduce favorable traits of the donor organism. Another was to harness harmless, fast-multiplying bacteria for the production of useful proteins for medicine and industry.

In the early 1970s, the U.S. molecular biologist Paul Berg developed a reliable technique for splicing together DNA from different sources to produce so-called recombinant DNA. His first experiment used homopolymer tails—stretches of DNA based on single repeated nucleotides—to bring the DNA together for splicing.

Starting with a purified sample of the DNA of SV40 (simian virus 40), Berg prepared one part of the recombinant DNA by first using *Eco*RI to cleave the DNA at a specific site. He then used another enzyme, exonuclase, to strip away certain bases from the end of the strand before mixing the resulting fragment into a solution of adenine-based nucleotide with terminal transferase. Terminal transferase is an enzyme that adds nucleotides to the ends of DNA strands, so the SV40 DNA strands acquired tails of adenine-based homopolymer in this stage.

Separately, Berg treated a variety of DNA called lambda DNA in the same way that he had treated the SV40 DNA. In the final stage, though, he used terminal transferase with a solution of thymine-based nucleotide to add thymine-based homopolymeric tails to the lambda DNA. Since adenine and thymine form base pairs in DNA, the two types of homopolymer tails held the two DNA fragments together when they were mixed, thus preparing them for the final stage in the preparation of recombinant DNA.

Berg spliced the two types of DNA together using two enzymes: DNA ligase and DNA polymerase. DNA ligase cleaved the DNA fragments from their respective homopolymer tails, and DNA polymerase united the two fragments as continuous strands of recombinant DNA. In later experiments, Berg found that the homopolymer tails were unnecessary: cleaving two types of DNA with *Eco*RI produces fragments that can be directly spliced together using DNA polymerase.

Plasmid vectors

Berg's choice of lambda DNA as a partner for splicing with SV40 was not random: lambda DNA is an example of a plasmid, a type of circular DNA molecule found in bacteria that contains genes for its own replication within the cells of the bacteria. Berg's technique opened up the circle using *Eco*RI and then spliced the fragment of SV40 between the free ends. The result was a larger plasmid that combined the SV40 genes with a mechanism for self replication.

Plasmids are examples of vectors—substances whose function is to carry genes from one situation to another. Berg's original intention was to use lambda DNA to carry fragments of SV40 DNA into *Escherichia coli* cells. This bacterium—usually referred to as *E. coli*—whose strains are mostly harmless, is an inhabitant of the human gut. It is widely used in biochemical research, and its function in genetic engineering is to provide an environment that contains the nutrients necessary for recombinant DNA to replicate.

E. coli cells are made "competent"—ready to accept plasmids—by treating them so as to weaken the walls that contain them. A sample of plasmids is then mixed with the competent cells, some of which take in plasmid and cater for its replication. Berg stopped his experimental work short of performing this procedure as a response to growing concern about the potential danger of introducing SV40—a tumor virus—into an organism that can thrive in the human gut.

Phage vectors

Bacteriophages are viruses that invade bacteria; they consist of DNA wrapped in a coat of protein. Phage vectors are bacteriophages whose DNA has been modified to include genes from another organism using the techniques used to modify plasmid DNA. Like plasmids, phage vectors are used to carry donor genetic material into bacterial cells where they can replicate. However, the DNA of a bacteriophage can accept much more donor genetic material than can a plasmid.

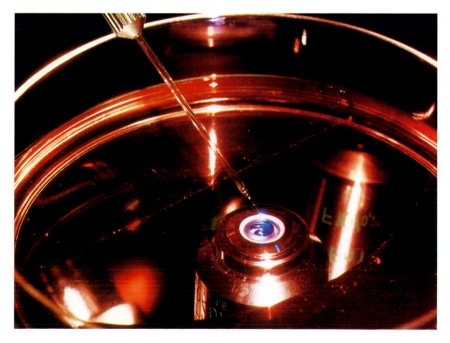

▼ Microinjection being used to introduce foreign genes to a cell during research on cancer-inducing genes. Genetic research of this sort led to the development of the anticancer drug interferon. A suction probe holds the cell still, while a finer probe penetrates the nucleus and manipulates the genetic material.

Protein manufacture

Vectors are used to introduce strands of a donor organism's genetic material into host cells, where they can replicate and initiate the synthesis of proteins usually found in the donor. In general, the convenient and rapid manufacture of these proteins is the goal of such an exercise.

One use of vectors is in the manufacture of antigens for use as vaccines. An antigen is a protein that surrounds a bacterium or virus; it is also the substance that prompts the immune system to produce antibodies that kill such an organism. Genetically engineered vaccines are produced by introducing the gene responsible for synthesizing antigen into harmless organisms. The bacteria then produce antigen protein, which is sufficient to prime the immune system for attack, without introducing all the DNA of the harmful organism. Vaccines against hepatitis, herpes, and influenza are made by inserting the genes for the antigens of those viruses into cowpox virus.

Since 1982, human insulin has been produced using *E. coli* cells into which the gene for human insulin—a hormone, and therefore a protein—has been inserted. The same technique is used to produce hormones that dissolve blood clots and stimulate the formation of red blood cells. Factor VIII—a blood clotting agent absent in the blood of hemophiliacs—has been produced in this way, as has interferon, an antiviral agent.

The use of live organisms to produce useful proteins is not restricted to simple organisms such as *E. coli*—mammals can also be genetically modified to produce such proteins in their milk. The gene for a protein is linked to the genes responsible for milk production and then introduced into eggs of a given mammal. When those eggs develop into a mature female mammal, the donor gene becomes active only in its milk-producing cells. The host mammal then produces the required protein in its milk, from which it is easily collected and, if necessary, isolated. This approach has been used to make therapeutic proteins such as lactoferrin, which is useful in the treatment of bacterial infections.

Gene therapy

Certain human disorders are caused by inherited defective genes failing to synthesize proteins that are necessary for healthy physical function. Examples of these disorders include cystic fibrosis and muscular dystrophy. Researchers hope to find cures for such diseases by inserting genes that compensate for the defective inherited gene, but success has been limited to date. Other disorders might be treated by inserting genes that produce therapeutic proteins within the body.

Genetically modified food

The insertion of donor genes can improve properties such as the milk or meat yield of animals or the yield, shelf life, flavor, or nutritious value of food crops. Before genetic engineering, such changes often required several generations of selective breeding and hybridization.

Genetically modified (GM) food has caused a great deal of controversy. One motive for its concern is that cases have arisen where genes from a donor food organism that can cause allergic reactions, as do certain types of nuts, have conferred those allergenic properties to the host organism. Opponents of GM food also argue that it is impossible to prevent contamination of non-GM crops by cross pollination.

DNA fingerprinting

An autoradiogram of DNA fragmented by enzymes is unique to the organism from which the DNA was taken. As such, this test can be used to identify criminals from minute samples of tissues or body fluids left at crime scenes.

DNA testing depends on a technique called polymerase chain reaction to produce useable samples of DNA from minute forensic samples. The original DNA is first heated to 203°F (95°C) for around 20 seconds in a solution that contains the four nucleotide bases, a small amount of DNA necessary to initiate DNA polymerization, and DNA-polymerase enzyme. The DNA separates into its component strands at this temperature. When the mixture cools, complementary nucleotides attach themselves to the single strands and are connected by the enzyme to form new double helices identical to the original DNA.

By repeating the heating and cooling cycle 20 to 30 times, the sample can be increased to several billions of times its original size. Crucial to the development of this technique, which has been in use since 1988, was the isolation of heat-resistant DNA polymerase from *Thermophilus aquaticus*, a microbe whose natural habitat is in hot springs.

▲ This litter of cloned piglets—named Millie, Christa, Alexis, Carrel, and Dotcom—were born at Virginia Technical University in March 2000. They were produced by substituting the DNA of a fertilized egg with DNA from cells of an adult pig, to which they are genetically identical.

SEE ALSO: Amino acid • Biochemistry • Biotechnology • Cell biology • Chemistry, analytical • Enzyme • Evolution • Hormone • Immunology • Life • Reproduction • Vaccine

Genetics

Genetics is the study of inheritance—how physical features, characteristics, and even behavior are passed from parent to offspring. People have long been intrigued by the subject, especially the way inherited features, known as traits, run in families.

Our modern understanding of genetics dates from 1865, when an Austrian monk, Gregor Mendel, presented the results of his experiments with peas to the Natural Science Society of Brün (now Brno in the Czech Republic). Mendel theorized that hereditary characteristics were transferred through pairs of hereditary units. He observed that heredity followed certain statistical laws and that in sexual reproduction half of the information for creating a new life comes from the female and half from the male. Mendel realized that the reproductive cells must contain alternative arrangements of the paired hereditary information in the parent and that only one gene

from each pair would be found in the reproductive cell. When the male and female reproductive cells come together, the heredity information combines to create new pairs. For many years, Mendel's theories went unnoticed, and it was not until 1900 that his ideas were rediscovered and fully appreciated.

We now know that the gene is the basic unit of inheritance. Genes exist as segments of a very long, twisted, ladderlike chemical molecule called deoxyribonucleic acid, or DNA, found in living cells. DNA forms long strands called chromosomes. In humans, there are 23 pairs of chromosomes consisting of paired genes. A gene is a segment of DNA that contains the instructions, as a chemical code, to produce a specific protein. Proteins are central to the structure and workings of all cells. Both genes in a pair are concerned with the same function, but sometimes only one is

▲ Albinism, seen here in a peacock, is caused by a flawed recessive gene. A pair of these recessive genes must be present on a chromosome for albinism to be expressed. Albino creatures lack pigmentation in their skin or feathers and commonly have pink eyes.

expressed. Genes can be broadly classified into four types. These are dominant, recessive, intermediate, and polygenic. Dominant genes are always expressed. If, for example, a person possesses genes for brown eyes and genes for blue eyes, the person will have brown eyes because these genes are dominant. The genes for blue eyes are said to be recessive because they are only expressed when both the paired sets of genes for eye color are for blue eyes. Two brown-eyed parents, however, may still give birth to a blue-eyed baby if, as well as possessing genes for brown eyes, they both possess genes for blue eyes, which they then pass on to the child.

Most characteristics, however, are not the result of dominant and recessive genes but are the product of combinations of genes, as is the case with intermediate genes, which are partly expressed, and polygenic genes, where a characteristic is the result of a number of different combinations of paired genes.

Genetic disorders

Genetic disorders may be either autosomal or X-linked. In the case of autosomal disorders, the defective gene is not carried on either of the chromosomes responsible for gender—the X and Y chromosomes. Several autosomal genetic diseases and conditions, such as cystic fibrosis, sickle cell anemia, albinism, and Tay-Sachs disease, are transferred through recessive genes and are said to be autosomal recessive. A few others, such as Huntington's chorea, are carried by dominant genes, and are called autosomal dominant. Dominant genes are always expressed, but in the case of Huntington's chorea, the condition begins to manifest itself only when the carrier is in his or her 30s, when the carrier is likely to have had children and passed on the defective gene.

Conditions, such as hemophilia, Christmas disease, and Duchenne's muscular dystrophy, are X-linked and are carried by recessive genes on the X chromosome. Women have a pair of X chromosomes and so if the recessive gene is present it is unlikely to be expressed. Men, however, have one X chromosome paired with a Y chromosome. Therefore, if the recessive gene is present, it will be expressed.

Making gene maps

The entire set of genes in an organism is known as its genome. In the human being, for example, there are between 50,000 and 100,000 genes, packed into 23 pairs of chromosomes. The huge human genome project has succeeded in mapping all genes on the human chromosomes. A technique that helped achieve this enormous task is

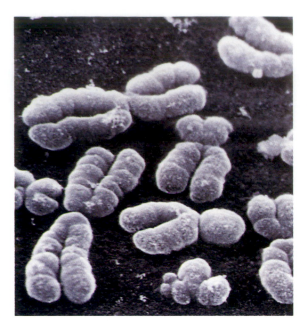

▲ Scanning electron micrograph of human chromosomes. Each one has two strands joined at the center, a region known as the centromere or kentochore, which splits when cell division takes place, thus providing half of each chromosome to the new pair of cells.

chromosome in situ hybridization. This is a technique for getting labeled chromosomes (using a radioactive or fluorescent dye) to match up with other chromosomes in a cell or a laboratory preparation. The degree of matching or hybridization shows how similar or complementary the chromosomes (or the DNA in the chromosomes) are. Very simply, the most similar chromosomes stick together.

Chromosome mapping will help to diagnose inherited or genetic diseases to gain a greater understanding of how genes work and to replace defective genes with normal ones, thereby treating genetic disorders.

Embryo gene testing

In the United States, one baby in 25 has a disorder caused by abnormal genes. Many of these genes can be detected by taking samples at an early stage, when the baby is developing in the mother's uterus, and examining the chromosomes.

When a couple has a very high risk of conceiving a baby with a genetic disorder, it is now possible to carry out the in vitro, or "test tube baby," procedure. At a very early stage, the embryo is just a tiny ball of cells. One cell is removed, and its DNA is extracted and analyzed. If the results of these tests are clear, the ball of cells may then be implanted in the mother's uterus, and pregnancy begins.

▶ Each human has 46 chromosomes, arranged in 23 pairs. These are normal female chromosomes; male chromosomes would have one XY pair instead of one set of XX chromosomes.

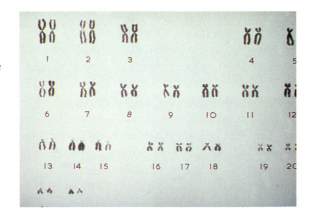

SEE ALSO: BIOTECHNOLOGY • CELL BIOLOGY • GENETIC ENGINEERING • MOLECULAR BIOLOGY

Geochemistry

◄ In Bangladesh, arsenic occurs naturally in certain kinds of rocks and is released into groundwater. People who drink this water over a period of many years may develop serious illnesses, such as various forms of cancer. In response to this problem, the British charity WaterAid has tested all the tube wells it has installed in Bangladesh and painted the safe ones green and the unsafe red.

Geochemistry is the science that applies the principles of geology and chemistry to materials in Earth's crust. Many Earth science studies, from the evolution of the planet to the exploration for oil or precious metals, involve geochemistry. The subject can be broadly divided into low-temperature geochemistry—concerned with soils and sediments—and high-temperature geochemistry, which deals with rocks that have undergone exposure to heat.

Types of rocks

Rocks can be grouped into three types—igneous, sedimentary, and metamorphic. Igneous rocks are those that originated as molten magma and then cooled and solidified. These kinds of rocks are usually compact and nonporous.

Sedimentary rocks, such as sandstone, are formed in a different manner. Various kinds of erosion cause the breakdown of rocks into small pieces that are washed into lakes, rivers, and oceans where they fall to the bottom and are deposited in layers. Eventually, over millions of years, these sediments become compacted and form new deposits of rock.

Metamorphic rocks, such as marble, are formed where the structure of existing rocks—either igneous or sedimentary—is altered by the processes of heat, pressure, and the movement of chemicals. Of these three processes heat has the most influence.

Chemical composition of rocks

Igneous rocks are largely composed of silicates but may also contain oxides of titanium and iron. The exceptions are the carbonatites, which consist of carbonates of magnesium, iron, and calcium. When igneous rocks cool, the chemicals that they contain form crystalline structures. Rocks that contain different chemicals will display different crystal structures. The crystals may be dispersed evenly throughout the rock, or in the case of igneous rocks that have experienced cooling and crystallizing in a subterranean chamber, they may show a layering of different sizes of crystals, because the heavier crystals are able to fall slowly to the bottom of the cooling magma. One common form of igneous rock is granite, in which the silicate is held in quartz, SiO_2, and is combined with feldspar.

Chemical weathering may alter the structure of many rock minerals. Water, for example, is capable of dissolving many different kinds of minerals. These minerals may then recombine to form new chemical structures. The fragments of igneous or metamorphic rocks, from which sedimentary rocks are formed, are altered in this way.

In metamorphic rocks, the processes of heating and cooling causes the chemical structures of the minerals to achieve new states of equilibrium. This process may occur in situations where the rock is buried deep underground or is in proximity to areas of molten magma.

The different chemical structures of the three main types of rock enable geochemists to understand the processes that created them. High-temperature systems can often be more accurately modeled, but it is the low-temperature research that is currently receiving the most attention. In the latter field, many recent advances have been made by taking into account the effects of organic matter (micro and macro, living and dead), in a subdiscipline known as biogeochemistry. In addition, the application of low-temperature geochemistry to current environmental problems (environmental geochemistry) is an important area for research.

Geochemical mapping

The soils and sediments of a region may be sampled and analyzed to reveal the elements present. It is then possible to make geochemical maps of the region. These maps are very useful not just for mineral exploration but also for studies of the relationship between geochemistry and health, as they can highlight areas of pollution or trace element deficiencies. The geochemical map of China provides a dramatic example of the way in which geochemistry and health can be related. It shows that selenium-rich sediment is widespread in the southwestern part of Hubei Province, where both humans and livestock in the area suffer from hair and nail loss caused by an excess of selenium. It has been clearly demonstrated that the selenium contained in soil, drinking water, crops, and vegetables originated directly, or indirectly from seleniferous rocks.

Analytical geochemistry

Geochemistry relies on fast and accurate analytical techniques for its success. One important analytical tool is the ICP-MS (inductively coupled plasma-mass spectrometry). The sample is first vaporized to form a plasma—a hot, highly ionized gas that reaches temperatures of up to 11,000 K. Such a high temperature dissociates the sample into ions; the mass spectrum of the ions is measured using a quadruple mass spectrometer.

Most elements in the periodic table can be determined, though not hydrogen, helium, carbon, nitrogen, neon, or argon. The analysis takes less than one minute for over 90 elements, with concentrations as low as tens of parts per trillion. Isotope ratios are also easily determined. Lasers may also be used to vaporize very small and specific areas from thin sections of rocks, which can then be analyzed by ICP-MS.

From crystals to mountains

High-temperature geochemistry shows how the history of huge mountain belts can be understood from the study of tiny garnet crystals with a diameter no bigger than $\frac{1}{16}$ in. (1.5 mm). It is possible, for example, to obtain precise heating and burial rates for garnets. This constitutes a significant advance in geochemistry, since modern geothermometry and geobarometry, combined with precise dating of garnet, enables scientists to define the pressure–temperature–time history of metamorphic rocks. Once the heating and cooling rates of mountain belts are known, the processes responsible for their origin can be deduced.

▲ A demonstration of the role played by bacteria in the geochemistry of iron. The tube on the right has been sterilized and is uniform in color. The tube on the left has not been sterilized. The actions of microorganisms in different parts of the tube, affecting the iron's mobility and oxidation, has led to the development of different colored regions in the tube.

Bacteria and metals

One important area of biogeochemical research is the sedimentary geochemistry of iron. Iron is a key constituent of Earth materials, being the fourth most abundant element in Earth's crust and vital for the metabolism of plants and animals. Certain bacteria can produce hydrogen disulfide from naturally occurring sulfates. This then converts iron oxyhydroxides into iron sulfides, which play a significant part in the sedimentary cycle of iron. One bacterium, called *Desulfivibrio*, is also able to produce iron directly—and thus may be significant in establishing how deposits of iron were formed.

SEE ALSO: CHEMISTRY, ANALYTICAL • GEOLOGY • GEOPHYSICS • MASS SPECTROMETRY

Geodesic Structures

Geodesic structures are frame structures composed of triangles that together form hexagons (and sometimes pentagons), resulting in a many faceted dome or sphere. The more triangles that are used, the more the dome approximates to a smooth curved surface. These structures are extremely strong and efficient in their use of materials such as steel, concrete, or wood, and they can be used to cover enormous areas without internal supports.

Frame structures

In general, frame structures consist of relatively long thin members interconnected at joints to form an arrangement capable of carrying loads without undue distortion of shape. The way in which the members are arranged and the nature of the joints are critical. If the joints are free to rotate (pin joints), then the shape of the frame can be maintained only by the correct number and arrangement of the members. If there are too few members, the arrangement is called a mechanism, structurally unacceptable although mechanically useful. A sufficient number of members produces a simply stiff structure; any additional members are redundant (though there may be other reasons for including them), and the structure becomes overstiff, being com-

▼ The Takara Beautillion, designed by the Japanese architect Kisho Kurokawa and built in Osaka, Japan, for Expo '70. A prefabricated framing unit—a steel, six-pointed 3-D cross—was repeated over 200 times. Capsule rooms of 24 sq. ft. (2.2 m²) were then plugged into the 3-D grid. Additions or subtractions could be made by the use of open flange plates and high-tension bolts.

monly called a redundant frame. In contrast, a rigid frame retains its shape by the use of stiff joints that do not allow the members to move relative to one another.

The engineering attraction of frame construction is the very economical use it makes of material. In a massive structure, much of the material is used uneconomically because it is not loaded to its full capacity. In an ideal framework, the members are so arranged that they all work to their full strength. It is possible in fact to arrange the members in such a way that the minimum weight of material is used—this is especially the case with a geodesic structure.

In a conventional dome, the construction materials would hold the structure together in compression. In a geodesic dome, however, the structural elements form triangles with members that are mostly in tension. In this way, loads are distributed evenly across the web of the structure. Triangles are inherently strong and rigid structures, so a network of connected triangles produces one of the strongest structures possible. Geodesic domes also require no buttressing and so can be placed directly on the ground.

The first geodesic domes

The first geodesic structure was a planetarium built in Germany in 1922 by Walter Bauersfeld. However, the person most connected with these domes is the American polymath Richard Buckminster Fuller. His system—invented in the 1940s—was derived independently of the German design and has been used and developed extensively throughout the world for a wide variety of building projects.

In 1927, Buckminster Fuller predicted a future housing shortage and felt that geodesic dome houses could be the solution to the problem. The ability to mass-produce these structures as lightweight prefabricated components makes them a potentially cheap means of construction. Buckminster Fuller intended to mass-produce them as homes but was not successful in doing so. He also envisaged domes that were so light and strong they could be lifted in one piece by helicopter and placed on site with minimum damage to the local ecology.

Today many geodesic dome manufacturers around the world offer these structures as kits of parts that can be assembled on site to create relatively inexpensive homes. These domes have also found deployment as temporary military structures, but they first came to a wider public atten-

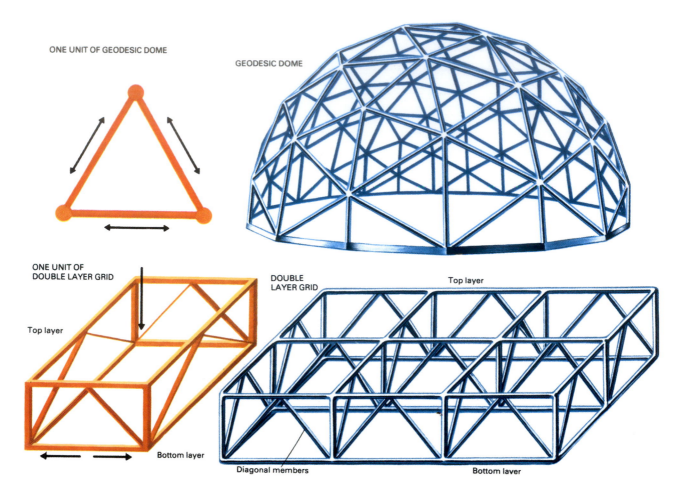

ONE UNIT OF GEODESIC DOME

GEODESIC DOME

ONE UNIT OF
DOUBLE LAYER GRID

Top layer

DOUBLE
LAYER GRID

Top layer

Bottom layer

Diagonal members

Bottom layer

tion with the building of the 1967 U.S. Pavilion at the Montreal World Exposition. Designed by Fuller in conjunction with another architect, Shoji Sadao, this structure stood 200 ft. (60 m) high and was 250 ft. (76 m) in diameter. Its lightweight steel frame produced a lacelike effect and created a memorable and dramatic building. Since then, geodesic domes have been used on a range of large-scale projects. One of the most famous of these is the Spaceship Earth Pavilion at Disney's Epcot. This structure is a full geodesic sphere reaching 180 ft. (55 m) and containing 17 storeys. Its 16 million lb. (7,260 tonne) frame supports 954 triangular panels and contains a volume of 2,200,000 cu. ft. (62,300 m³). The panels themselves are made from two layers of anodized aluminum around a polyethylene core.

Eden Project

In Cornwall in the southwest of England, an innovative project is nearing completion. The Eden Project will contain 80,000 plants under a series of geodesic biomes. This chain of greenhouses will snake around a site that was once a quarry. The largest of the structures—the Humid Tropics Biome—will be 790 ft. (240 m) long and span 360 ft. (110 m) at its widest point with no internal supports and will reach up to 180 ft.

(55 m) high. The project as a whole will create the largest series of greenhouses in the world, with a variety of different types of climates, from tropical rain forest to Mediterranean fruit groves.

These biomes are a development of the geodesic dome idea comprising a two-layer structure. The outer layer is made of hexagons and a few pentagons, while the inner layer is made of a combination of hexagons and triangles, giving the appearance of stars. This kind of structure is called a hex-tri-hex.

Instead of covering this structure with glass, the designers have opted for a material called ETFE (ethyltetrafluoroethylene), which weighs less than 1 percent of the equivalent area of glass, permitting a much lighter structure. The covering of each hexagon will consist of three layers of ETFE welded together at the edges and then inflated to form strong transparent bubbles 6 ft. (1.8 m) deep. In hot weather, it will be possible to partially deflate the bubbles as the hot air expands, while in cold weather, the bubbles will be inflated to maintain the cushion of air between the warm inside and cold outside.

▲ Geodesic domes are constructed from a network of plane triangles built up to form a hemisphere. This frame is extremely strong and can be covered with a lightweight material such as plastic. Double-layer grids are another form of frame construction. Here, diagonal struts connect the top and bottom members of a lattice girder.

| SEE ALSO: | BUILDING TECHNIQUES • TENSILE STRUCTURE • VAULT CONSTRUCTION |

Geography

Traditionally, geography divides into physical geography—the study of the world's natural features and processes—and human geography—the way people cover the world. However, current interest in environmental issues has linked the two, with the realization that the environmental problems we face almost always have both a physical and a human dimension. Technological advances have enabled us to understand this interrelationship and to make sense of the huge amounts of data involved.

Work on tropical deforestation shows how this interrelationship works. Tropical forests differ from temperate forests in that almost all the nutrients are held in the standing stock of trees, with very few being held in the soil. This means that once the trees are removed from a tropical rain forest, usually by logging, most of the nutrients are removed as well. The heavy rains of tropical areas soon wash the remaining nutrients

and topsoil away, taking with them any chance of forest regeneration.

In temperate forests, a much larger proportion of the nutrients are held in the humus-rich soil so that even if the trees are removed, it is usually possible for the forest to regenerate in time. The physical geographer can help predict what will happen when a forest is cleared. On the local scale, deforestation may cause soil erosion and siltation of reservoirs and waterways, while globally, the complex interactions of the climate have to be considered.

On the human level, the geographer needs to study the social and economic pressures that are leading to deforestation in tropical countries. These countries, many of which are termed developing countries on account of their relatively low income per head of population, require more land for development as populations grow and "hard" overseas currency for international

▲ Accurate topographical maps may be linked to information about specific locations.

◄ Geographical information systems allow data to be stored, manipulated, and displayed easily and quickly on screen.

◄ Satellite images are used in conjunction with information gathered at ground level to help interpret what they show. The blue lines in this image of the Brazilian rainforest reveal deforestaion on a huge scale. The farmers burn the trees to release their nutrients into the soil, then move on when the soil is exhausted.

trade. Often the situation is further complicated by the need to pay interest on debts owed to banks in richer countries. Faced with such compelling needs, developing countries in tropical areas often have no alternative but to allow their forest stock to be destroyed.

New techniques in geography

New technological advances mean that geographers can now study more problems than ever before. Improved computer systems allow data, such as soil, topography, and vegetation maps, to be stored, manipulated, and displayed on screen. These are known as geographical information systems and enable maps to be updated very rapidly. They can also combine and analyze information from different sources. For example, soil maps can be integrated with topographic and rainfall maps to find areas where clay soils, steep slopes, and high rainfall combine to create a high risk of landslides.

Geographical information systems can handle efficiently the large amounts of data produced by modern instruments. The work in 1991 on the siting of the U.S. Superconducting Super Collider (SSC) used several different data sets in this way. The SSC was designed to be an advanced particle accelerator housed in an elliptical underground tunnel, 53 miles (85 km) in circumference, for researching into the basic structure of matter. Although the U.S. government finally decided not to fund the completion of this project, much work went into choosing the location for what would have been a very large research facility.

First and foremost, the land had to be suitable for tunneling, so a place with stable geological conditions had to be found from geological maps. Also, to make sure that the extra staff would have nearby housing with good communications, information on regional resources had to be considered. Details of utilities had to be included as well, since the SSC requires ample supplies of electricity, water, and waste disposal facilities. Ecological and other geographical data were added to make sure that the development had the least effect on the local environment.

A geographical information system combined all this information so that various scenarios could be tried out on screen before the best location for the SSC was finally chosen.

Information from space

Remote sensing uses electromagnetic sensors and cameras to observe Earth from aircraft or satellites. Meteorological satellites have been providing images of Earth for use in weather forecasting since the 1960s.

Increasingly sophisticated sensors carried on board modern satellites enable us to learn even more about what is going on in the world. Multispectral scanners sense energy coming up from Earth's surface at different wavelengths. Some sense visible light, some sense invisible reflected solar radiation at infrared wavelengths, and some sense thermal energy being emitted by Earth in the far infrared. All of these forms of energy can be displayed as color pictures that show features on the surface (such as the distribution of types of vegetation) or in the atmosphere (such as cloud distribution).

Often cloud obscures the surface features that the geographer is interested in. However, there are now satellites that carry radar that can "see" through cloud, to collect images in any weather. Radar is particularly useful for remote sensing in tropical low-pressure belts and high-latitude areas, which are frequently cloud covered.

Remote-sensing images are used to map the distribution of surface cover, such as forests, ice caps, deserts, and urban areas. As satellites orbit, they pass over most parts of Earth again and again, collecting a series of images over time. This information allows geographers to monitor changes, such as the shrinking of ice caps or the growth of deserts in response to a warmer climate, providing a new way of measuring the rates of global environmental change.

SEE ALSO: Environmental science • Geology • Geophysics • Mapmaking techniques • Plate tectonics • Surveying

Geology

The purpose of geology is to discover and explain the structure and behavior of Earth's crust. Earth is continuously in a state of change, a fact that has long been known from the observations of such violent earth movements as earthquakes and volcanic eruptions. Most movements, however, are imperceptibly slow, and until the 20th century, scientists were perplexed by the fact that whole mountain chains can be made of rocks raised from the floor of the sea and contain remains of the shells of sea animals. It is now known that the life of a mountain chain, from its formation as sediment in the sea to its gradual wearing down or weathering by the forces of erosion, must be reckoned in terms of hundreds of millions of years.

Modern geology is based on the principle of uniformitarianism, expounded in 1830 by the Scottish geologist Sir Charles Lyell; namely, that the history of Earth can be explained in terms of the natural processes now observed to be still in operation, such as the erosion of a mountain or the deposition of new sediments.

Rocks and minerals

Examination of small specimens of rocks and the minerals they contain, either in the field or in the laboratory, is an essential technique of geology. Specimens may be collected in different ways: from an outcrop of rock with a geological hammer, from boreholes, or from the seafloor with a device known as a coring tube, which works like an apple corer. A vertical, hollow, weighted tube

▲ Sedimentary rocks are created by the deposition of granular material at the bottom of seas or lakes, which gradually becomes compressed as more layers are built up. Although most sedimentary rocks are deposited in horizontal layers, stresses within the crust can cause them to become twisted and folded, as seen in the bottom layer of rock. At some point in time, the bottom layer has suffered erosion and new horizontal layers of rock have been laid down on top. The surface has then been eroded again by glaciation to give the sculpted structure seen today.

is dropped from a ship to the seafloor. The force of the impact rams the tube into the seabed, and the corer is hauled back up to the ship with the rock sample inside it. For obtaining specimens of hard rocks, a hollow drill with a cutting edge made of industrial diamonds is used. This drill produces cylinders of rocks that can be assembled to show the strata.

Identification of the constituent minerals in the sample of rock is the next problem; over 2,000 minerals have been discovered. Some are recognizable by such visible features as color, luster (the way light reflects from the surface of the sample), cleavage (the way in which it splits), or crystal forms. Simple tests may be made to determine the hardness of a mineral. Mineralogists have devised a scale of hardness from talc (1) to diamond (10); a mineral will scratch any other mineral lower on the scale.

A standard laboratory technique for examining rocks is to look at a thin section under a microscope. A slice of rock about a thousandth of an inch thick is put under the microscope with light shining through the specimen from underneath. This arrangement allows the optical properties of the minerals to be studied and also reveals the microscopic structure of the rock, which gives clues about its mode and place of origin. For instance, a rock composed of the shells of minute marine animals began as a characteristic sediment of the deep ocean.

Fossils

When a sea animal dies, its bones or shell sink to the bottom of the sea and become covered by mud, which is later turned by geological processes into rock containing the remains of the animal as a fossil. Fossils may be formed in other ways: a fern leaf buried in a swamp may be preserved as an impression in coal, and rocks formed from intertidal mud flats often contain fossil traces of worm burrows and casts. The fact that animals and plants are continuously changing through the process of evolution has great significance for geologists.

There are two important facts about fossil species, the first of which is that once a species has died out, it never reappears in younger rock. The second is that no two species are identical, and therefore, a new species is never exactly like an extinct one. These two facts have given rise to the principle that like fossil organisms indicate like geological age for the rocks that contain them. The principle coupled with dating methods based

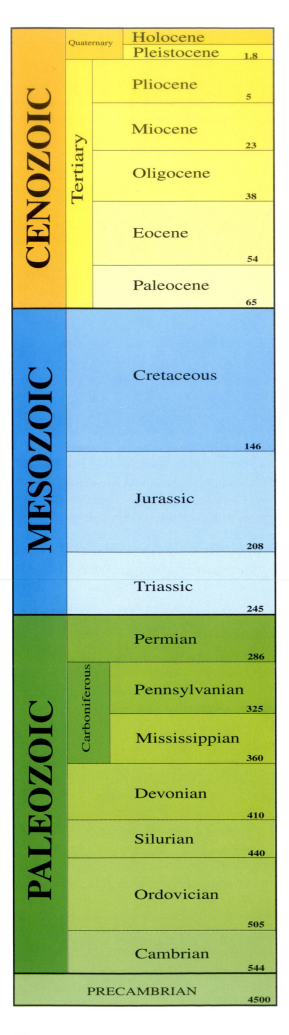

◄ Geologists have used a variety of techniques to determine Earth's history. Key to drawing up a timescale of events have been the use of radioactive dating techniques and discovery of the presence or absence of certain fossils in rock strata. The numbers on the right correspond to when each period started, in millions of years before the present. Mankind is a comparatively late arrival in geological terms, not appearing until the end of the Pliocene period, about 2 million years ago. Our own epoch, the Holocene period began only 10,000 years ago.

on the principle of radioactive decay, has enabled geologists to establish a geological timescale, a chronological chart of the various events in the history of Earth. Key to establishing this timescale is the law of superposition, the principle that the youngest layers of rock are laid down on top of older deposits. Although this sequence can sometimes be interrupted by volcanic intrusions and folding and dislocation processes in Earth's crust, the presence of fossil animals and plants can usually help determine the correct ages of rock strata.

The geologic timescale

By examining rocks and fossils, geologists have been able to discover much about environmental conditions on Earth at the time rocks were forming. Rocks of the Precambrian eon are believed to be the oldest rocks on Earth, dating from 4.5 billion years ago, when Earth was formed, though no rocks have yet been found to confirm this estimate. The oldest minerals discovered so far are zircon grains, found in an Australian sandstone, dating from roughly 4.4 billion years ago.

Fossils began to make their appearance 3.5 billion years ago. Photosynthetic bacteria fossils have been found grouped in colonial structures called stromatolites. These bacteria could tolerate living in an atmosphere of methane, ammonia, and other gases that would be poisonous to most organisms living on Earth today. As a waste product they breathed out oxygen, which began to build up in the atmosphere. Geologists have found beds of red iron oxides that can have formed only in fluctuating low levels of oxygen that confirm this hypothesis. The buildup of oxygen also created an ozone layer that began to shield life from dangerous levels of radiation. About 2.2 billion years ago, the first eukaryotes (cells with a nucleus) evolved. By the end of the Precambrian eon, an oxygen-rich environment had been established, and complex lifeforms, including the first animals had begun to appear.

The Phanerozoic eon, comprising the Paleozoic, Mesozoic, and Cenozoic eras, approximates to only one-eighth of the geological timescale, but this period corresponds to an explosion in the number and diversity of life-forms and significant changes in Earth's crustal features. The Paleozoic era, sometimes called the Age of Fishes, saw the rise of animals with internal and external skeletons. During this period, higher plants began to flourish, and the swamp forests that developed during the Carboniferous period eventually became thick seams of coal. Six major continental landmasses existed, and where these collided, they formed massive mountain ranges.

Extinction of the dinosaurs

The Mesozoic era is generally known as the Age of Dinosaurs, although mammals, reptiles, birds, and insects all began to develop during this era. Flowering plants began to dominate, and large deposits of chalk were laid down in the warm seas of the late Cretaceous period. However, the great geological

mystery of why dinosaurs became extinct at the end of the Cretaceous period may be near a solution, because geologists map the distribution of rocks vertically as well as horizontally.

In 1980, Walter Alvarez and co-workers suggested that an asteroid 6 miles (10 km) in diameter struck Earth and sent up a dust cloud that blanketed Earth in darkness, disrupted the food chain by stopping photosynthesis, and caused an episode of global cooling. This calamity led to the sudden demise of 52 percent of all species on Earth but affected land-based organisms most, with an 81 percent extinction rate, including all the dinosaurs. The clue that led Alvarez to put forward his controversial suggestion was a surprisingly high amount of the element iridium in the layers of rocks that mark the boundary between the Cretaceous and the Tertiary periods—known as the K-T boundary. Iridium is rare on Earth but more common in asteroids and meteors.

In their efforts to prove or disprove the hypothesis, geologists have mapped iridium anomalies in K-T boundary rocks in many parts of the world. They have found several other pieces of evidence pointing to a major impact at that time. Rocks of this age also contain such features as tektites (silicate glass spherules that appear to have spent some time in space), shock-metamorphosed quartz (which forms only under extremely high pressure), and the effects of tsunami (seismic sea waves), which would have followed an impact. A mounting body of evidence in favor of the impact hypothesis was built, but the crucial evidence, the impact crater itself, remained hidden.

Direct evidence of the impact may, however, have been found. The 113 mile (180 km) wide Chicxulub crater (Yucatan Peninsula, Mexico), originally located using magnetic and gravity anomaly maps, was discovered to be the same age as the K-T boundary. This location fits nicely

▲ A fossil of a marine ammonite, which became extinct at the end of the Cretaceous period along with the dinosaurs and half the families of living things. The fossil record can give clues about conditions and events on Earth that caused such mass extinctions.

▶ By taking samples of rocks with a coring tube, the strata at various depths can be determined and a thin slice examined under a microscope. Samples like these are used to find possible oil- or mineral-bearing rocks as well as testing for structural integrity when civil engineering projects are planned.

with tektites of this age found in Haiti, northern Mexico, and Ocean Drilling Project boreholes in the Gulf of Mexico.

However, many geologists still do not fully accept the impact hypothesis. Some suggest that intense volcanic activity played a role, noting that volcanism can put large amounts of ash and dust into the atmosphere and that at the same time as the K-T boundary there was extensive volcanic activity that formed the huge Deccan Trap in India. Work in paleontology shows that many of the extinctions were gradual, not sudden, and were probably related to falling sea level and episodes of oceanic oxygen starvation. They see the impact as a possible coup de grâce, not an underlying cause of the extinction.

Economic geology

Most of the raw materials used by industry are taken from Earth's crust: fossil fuels, such as coal and oil; ores; building stone and cement; and water. It is the task of the economic geologist to locate these natural resources.

The first task is to survey the geological structure of the area, that is, to find out what different rocks are present and how earth movements have influenced their relative position. The traditional technique of geological mapping involves detailed examination of the rocks outcropping at the sur-

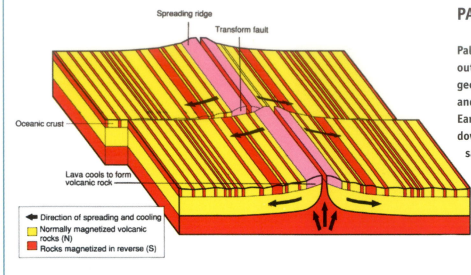

Spreading ridge

Transform fault

Oceanic crust

Lava cools to form volcanic rock

← Direction of spreading and cooling
▢ Normally magnetized volcanic rocks (N)
▢ Rocks magnetized in reverse (S)

PALEOMAGNETISM

Paleomagnetism is a technique used to find out the latitude at which a rock formed in the geological past. Magnetic particles in igneous and sedimentary rocks align themselves with Earth's magnetic field at the time they are laid down. By measuring the magnetic field of rock samples, a picture of how Earth's magnetic field has changed can be created. Studies of the Atlantic floor show a series of stripes that indicate that not only does Earth's magnetic field reverse every 100,000 to 100 million years, but that the Atlantic Ocean is gradually widening.

face and of the rocks recovered from boreholes, but today data gained by the methods of geophysics play a large part. Aerial photographs are used for determining the overall structure of large tracts of unknown country. The photographs are taken in stereoscopic pairs, which when looked at through a stereoscope give the impression of relief, which is itself largely dependent on the underlying geological structure.

Another method for finding the relief of unknown areas of land is to use sideways-looking radar equipment carried on aircraft. At sea, echo-sounding devices using oblique echoes are used to determine the profile of the seabed, while coring and grabbing techniques yield information about its composition. Grabbing is similar to coring except that the grab is lowered as gently as possible to the ocean floor where it is tripped to close on impact. From a knowledge of the structure of an area, the geologist can predict how the rocks at the surface are continued underground.

Oil and gas are often found in association and are known to be able to diffuse through porous rocks until they become trapped in certain rock structures. Oil exploration consists largely of the search for these rock structures; once one has been found, it is tested for oil or gas by a test drilling.

All rocks are divided into blocks of different sizes by structures such as joints and faults, and it is along these structures that ores are often found. Detailed structural mapping is needed to identify the structural setting where ore bodies may be found. Consideration of these structures is also important in the siting of major engineering works, such as dams, bridges, and tunnels. The engineering geologists must judge the geological feasibility of projects, for instance, to predict whether the underlying rock structure is strong enough to support the weight of a dam or canal.

Continental drift

The plate tectonics revolution of the 1960s showed that because Earth's lithosphere (outer shell) is mobile, the continents change their positions and oceans are created and destroyed. It forced geologists to produce a new type of map—paleogeographic maps that show the positions of continents at various times in Earth's history. These use both lithological data found on modern geological maps and paleomagnetic data.

To the human eye, the continents of South America and Africa roughly seem to fit together like pieces in a jigsaw puzzle. Proving that this theory was once the case has been a puzzle for geologists. Similarities in the rock deposits on both continents have been known for nearly 150 years, but it is only with the advent of computer programming, radioactive dating, and mid-Atlantic drilling that the likelihood of their once having been combined into a supercontinent, called Gondwanaland, has become more certain.

The first clues came with a computer program that gave a good fit to the coastlines at submarine contour levels of 3,000 ft. (1,000 m). Study of the direction of glacial deposits also indicated that the two continents underwent a single glaciation event rather than localized glaciation. It was the orientation of magnetic particles in igneous rocks that provided the key evidence for continental drift, however. If the continents had undergone glaciation, they must at some point have been sited near a pole. By plotting the angle of orientation of magnetic rocks, scientists proved not only that the continents were once joined but also that at a later point they moved to their current positions.

SEE ALSO: EARTH • EARTHQUAKE • GEOCHEMISTRY • GEOPHYSICS • PALEONTOLOGY • PLATE TECTONICS • SEISMOLOGY

Geophysics

Geophysics is the science and study of Earth's interior. As it is concerned with the whole planet, it incorporates many other fields of study, such as geology (the study of Earth's crust), mineralogy, and oceanography. As well as giving purely scientific information about the structure of Earth, such as the formation of volcanoes and the existence of continental drift, the techniques of geophysics are used in the search for minerals, in oil exploration, and in civil engineering. With the advent of space exploration, the same techniques are being used to study the interiors of the Moon and planets, thus, helping to show how Earth fits in as a member of the Solar System and why it alone supports life. Satellite technology is also making a significant contribution to our knowledge of Earth's geological processes.

It is 3,940 miles (6,371 km) to Earth's center, and our deepest borehole reaches only 7½ miles (12 km) into the surface. Nevertheless, geophysicists have explored the interior of our planet very effectively. They have discovered the structure and composition of Earth by remote-sensing techniques, that is, by observing the passage of seismic waves through it and by measuring its electrical, magnetic, thermal, and gravitational properties.

Seismology

The most important technique in geophysics is seismology. To study Earth's interior, geophysicists use sound waves of low frequency (below about 100 Hz), either in the form of explosions or as vibrations. These sound waves can travel through solid rock and are reflected from different layers of rock to be picked up at the surface.

Such methods can give information only about the top few percent of Earth's interior. But much more intense seismic shocks are produced by earthquakes, and these natural waves can travel completely around Earth in some cases. By studying the records obtained at widely separated stations, clues about the nature of the deep interior of Earth are provided.

Once the nature of subsurface rocks has been decided by seismic methods, better information can come from well logging, which consists of drilling boreholes as deep as 15,000 ft. (4.5 km). A sensitive microphone or geophone is lowered down the well, and by firing seismic shots at the surface, it is possible to find the velocity of sound in the various rock layers. In addition, such details as radioactivity and electrical conductivity of the rocks can be found.

▼ A relief map of the Atlantic Ocean. The central ridge is the source of upwelling material from beneath the crust spreading outward. Magnetic field reversals lie in strips (brown) with ages in millions of years. At the edge of the Caribbean Sea, the seafloor dives below the plate that originated in the Pacific Ocean; this subduction zone forms the Puerto Rico Trench. Orange dots mark earthquake epicenters.

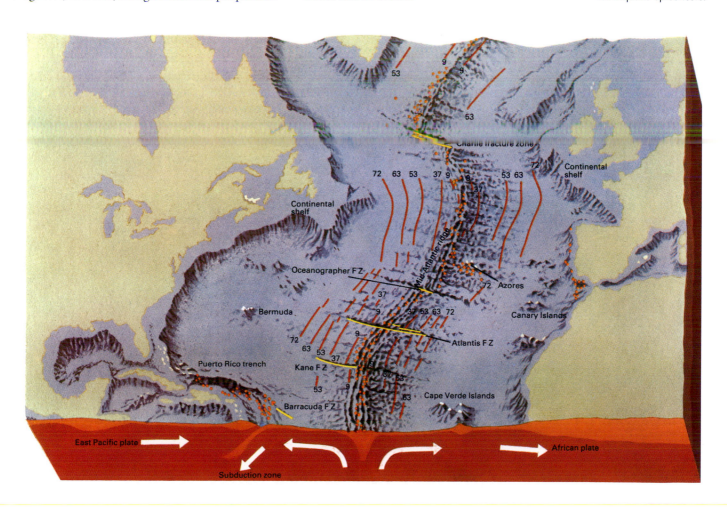

Gravimeters

Different rocks have different densities, and a region of high-density rocks will have a stronger gravitational pull than one of low-density rocks. The effect of these gravity anomalies is very small and is measured in units that are about one-millionth of the overall pull of gravity. The small variations are measured on a gravimeter, which works on the same principle as a spring balance. A weight is attached to a very sensitive hairspring made of fine wire or quartz, and a pointer indicates the deflection of the weight caused by gravitational attraction. Despite its sensitivity, very robust gravimeters have been made that are generally used in one of two ways. For a quick look at the gravity characteristics of an area, the device is flown in an aircraft over the area in a pattern of intersecting lines. This shows the general structure of a region a few hundred miles in size and can yield valuable information about the mineral value of an area (such as the Arctic Slope of Alaska, whose crude-oil production is second only to Texas) as well as purely scientific details.

Alternatively, portable gravimeters may be taken, usually mounted in rucksack-style carriers, to many points in the area of interest. This technique can still be used at sea, but in a limited way. Recent advances in satellite gravimetry will probably make this approach outdated except where expense is a vital consideration.

Magnetic anomalies

Just as regions of unusually high or low gravity are of interest, so magnetic anomalies are equally worth studying. The magnetometers used have a compass-like needle that is held away from the north–south line by a fine spring. The tension in the spring gives a direct measure of the magnetic field strength. In more modern proton magnetometers, the magnetic field in a crystal bar alters the energy of the protons in it, which in turn affect the electrical properties of the crystal.

Magnetometers, like gravimeters, can either be carried by hand in ground-based surveys or flown in an aircraft, where a quicker and not much less detailed picture is obtained. The magnetic anomaly method has the advantage that metal-bearing areas, such as the vast ore fields in the Australian outback, show up very strongly.

From the geological technique of taking core samples of near-surface rocks, more detailed magnetic studies can be carried out using more specialized magnetometers. They, for example, may spin the core sample and detect the small current induced in coils by the oscillating magnetic field. When molten rock containing iron minerals solidifies to form a new stratum—after volcanic activity, for instance—it is affected by Earth's magnetic field so that solid rock is weakly magnetized. In many core samples, it is found that different layers of rock are magnetized in different directions. The upper layers will be magnetized in the same sense as Earth's present field direction, but deeper layers may have reversed magnetism, with south and north interchanged.

Deeper still, the magnetic rocks may have the same magnetism as surface rocks. This fossil magnetism, or paleomagnetism, indicates that Earth's magnetic field must have reversed direction several times over the period when the rocks were being laid down, each change lasting many hundred thousands of years. The causes of these

▼ An example of four-dimensional seismic surveying from the North Sea, off the eastern coast of the United Kingdom. These pictures show the changes—owing to oil production—of a gas cap, which has been tapped by a deviated (nonvertical) well from 1989 to 1991. The difference, in seconds, between the locations of the gas cap indicates that by 1991 the cap was 145 ft. (44 m) deeper than it was in 1989.

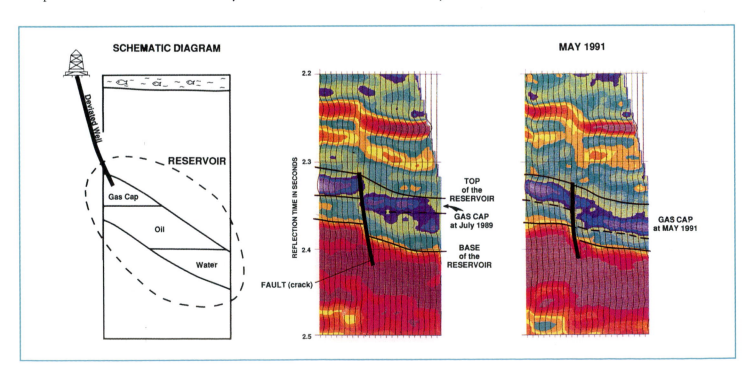

reversals are still largely a mystery, but the fact of their existence can be used to trace geophysical changes in Earth's crust.

Airborne surveys and, in particular, deep drilling at sea by research vessels have shown that just as successive depths of core samples may have reversed magnetism, on the seabed, adjacent strips of rock can show the same effect.

Oil and gas exploration

At the moment we have inexpensive energy from plentiful oil and gas supplies. Unfortunately, the population of the world is rising very rapidly, with a consequent increase in demand for energy from these fuels. At the present rate of world consumption, it has been estimated that all the known reserves will be exhausted by the year 2025. Exploration geophysicists are under great pressure to find new oil reservoirs, and they are searching for the remaining smaller reserves in increasingly hostile environments.

Geophysicists have been very successful in finding these smaller oil fields, and the proportion of successful discoveries to every 100 boreholes drilled has doubled since the 1980s, owing to constant improvement in the techniques used to explore for oil and gas reservoirs.

Oil and gas are fossil fuels—they originated millions of years ago as decaying organic remains. As the ground surface was buried under an increasing thickness of sediments, the combined effect of high temperature and high pressure turned the sediments into rock and the organic remains into oil and gas. They found their way upwards until they were trapped in porous sandstones beneath an impermeable cap-rock. Oil and gas sandstone reservoirs occur at depths from the surface down to 3 miles (5 km). Unfortunately, there are no geophysical techniques that will detect oil and gas directly at great depths, but from experience, geophysicists know that the sandstone reservoir rocks often have a characteristic structure or shape that can be detected using seismic waves. The geophysicist's role is to use these waves to map the subsurface rocks as accurately as possible.

The basic idea of the method is simple. A source sends seismic waves (which are similar to sound waves) into Earth's interior. The seismic waves are reflected from the boundaries, or interfaces, between the different types of rocks, such as sandstone, shale, and limestone. The reflected energy returns to Earth's surface, where it is detected by receivers and recorded by a computer on a magnetic tape or disk. The time of travel of the wave from the surface to the interface reveals the depth of the structure. By moving the shot

▶ This satellite picture of the Hayward Fault in California (marked by the thin red line) was taken using radar interferometry to show movements in the fault over a period of five years. The color changes from orange to blue across the fault show that the southwestern side has moved by about 1.1 in. (3 cm) between the time the two pictures were taken, suggesting that the potential for an earthquake at this site, which experienced its last major tremor in 1868, might be less than was previously thought. The blue area near the center on the southwest side of the fault is thought to be due to rising groundwater levels pushing the surface in this area upward.

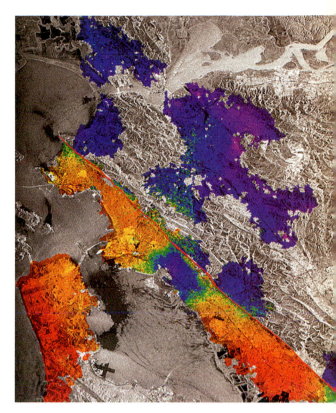

and receivers from one position to another across the ground surface, scientists can map the variation in the depth of the interface in detail.

Originally, massive charges of explosives were used as the sources of seismic energy both at sea and on land. However, not only were the explosives dangerous to handle, but they also caused severe damage to fish and to property. The modern source at sea uses a high-pressure pulse of air from a tube or gun, which safely produces a large-energy seismic wave. On land, mechanical vibrators mounted on trucks are used to shake the ground surface, again producing a high-energy seismic wave. Until recently, geophysicists carried out the subsurface investigation at sea by towing the seismic source and receivers in a straight line behind the ship. After processing the data, the result was a seismic section, a flat picture of the geology beneath that particular surface line down to a depth of about 3 miles (5 km).

You can get a good idea of what a seismic section looks like by imagining a picture of an enormous cliff; you see the beds of sedimentary rock running across the cliff face, giving the geology in that plane in very great detail. However, from this display you have no idea how the beds change behind the cliff face, and geophysicists have realized that it is necessary to obtain a complete image of the subsurface geology by "shooting" in many different directions, not just in straight lines. The difference between the two surveying methods is that of trying to decide on the shape and structure of an object by viewing it from one

◄ Subsurface radar equipment. The radar is capable of reading both very shallow and very great depths, making it extremely useful for environmental protection and engineering work, where it is important to know what lies immediately beneath the surface.

position compared with lifting it up and rotating it around in front of our eyes to pick up the subtle variations in form and shape.

Three-dimensional seismology

The new way of acquiring seismic data is called three-dimensional reflection seismology. The three-dimensional survey requires the geophysicist to transmit and receive at many different points, so powerful computers are required to plan the survey, to keep track of the positions of all the shots and receiver points, and to process the seismic data to produce the three-dimensional image of the subsurface geology.

Two factors have greatly helped geophysicists to carry out these surveys—the growth in the power of computers and the recent availability of satellite navigation systems. Since the 1980s, the processing power of supercomputers has been increased from an ability to carry out 200 million arithmetic calculations each second, to 10 billion such calculations. Computer experts believe that computers will soon be able to carry out 100 billion calculations each second. These astronomical numbers are difficult to comprehend, yet such power is needed to handle the enormous amount of seismic data that are continuously collected in the three-dimensional surveys.

The growth of satellite navigation systems during the past decade has greatly helped marine surveys. The system of satellites circling Earth means that the geographical position of the survey vessel, each shot point, and each seismic

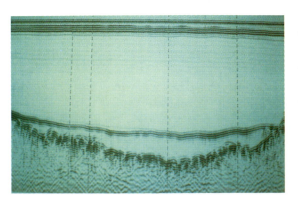

◄ This cross section from subsurface radar equipment shows not only the profile of a lake bed but also the structure of the bedrock beneath it.

detector can be determined every few seconds throughout the survey, with an accuracy of less than 10 ft. (3 m), by means of a radio receiver no bigger than a pocket calculator.

Geophysicists store the three-dimensional seismic image of Earth's subsurface structure in a computer memory. The computer can be used to display the results in any form, in a series of cross sections as with the cliff face or as maps of the sediments at any depth below the surface.

Four-dimensional seismology

Perhaps even more clever than three-dimensional seismology is the four-dimensional version, in which the seismic survey is repeated at regular intervals to observe the changes in the subsurface over time—the fourth dimension. Using this technique, geophysicists can tell oil reservoir engineers what is happening in the reservoir during production. All oil reservoirs have several wells drilled through them so that the oil or gas can flow out of the reservoir and up to the surface.

Geophysicists place seismic sources in one well and seismic receivers in a separate one so they can measure the speed of the seismic waves through the reservoir. By combining the results from all the sources and all the receivers, the computer can create a seismic image of the reservoir as a large-scale version of the medical scans of the inside of a human being using ultrasound. They allow reservoir engineers to see exactly what is going on inside the reservoir and to judge the effectiveness of such techniques as using steam piped in to increase the temperature and thus the "runniness" of the oil. Geophysicists are able to undertake and interpret these complex surveys because of the continuing growth in the power of computers and the miniaturization of electronics, which enables the sources and receivers to be sent down a 6 in. (15 cm) borehole.

The traditional role of geophysicists has been to make images of Earth at great depths. During the last twenty years, geophysicists have become increasingly involved with undertaking very detailed shallow surveys in connection with environmental problems.

For instance, in the case where hazardous waste is buried at shallow depths, it may be dangerous to disturb the soil, and engineers call on the remote sensing techniques of geophysicists. In many such cases the hazardous waste is present within the groundwater, and causes a change in the electrical properties of the water.

Geophysicists then use ground-penetrating radar, a system exactly like radar used on ships and aircraft but with the antenna pointing into the ground. The microwave electromagnetic pulse can penetrate to 160 ft. (50 m) in dry soil and sand but is rapidly absorbed by electrically conducting groundwater.

The technique used pulls the antenna across the ground region to be investigated; the equipment produces an image of the rock interfaces. From the image, the geophysicist can interpret the change from poorly conducting uncontaminated groundwater to highly conducting contaminated groundwater and thus plot the position of the contaminated zone.

Alternative energy sources

There is a finite amount of oil and gas and eventually this fruitful source of energy will run out. Geophysicists are looking at other sources of energy that exist within Earth and that may be able to make a contribution toward the total requirements of mankind. Igneous rocks contain significant amounts of the radioactive elements uranium, thorium, and potassium. The natural decay of these elements generates heat.

By drilling boreholes several miles into the granite, fracturing it, and then pumping water through the borehole/fracture system, boiling water can be obtained in large quantities. The system acts like a very low level, very safe, nuclear reactor with no hazardous by-products. Geophysicists have discovered that the important factor in the efficient heating of the water is the fracturing of the rock between the boreholes. Fracturing allows the water to flow freely and gives a large surface area for transferring heat from the hot rock to the water.

Earth's moving surface

Until recently, theories that the continents were once part of one land mass that broke up, with the pieces drifting apart, were regarded as unlikely if not absurd. Modern geophysics has changed this view and the new science of plate tectonics has been introduced to deal with the new concepts.

New portions of Earth's crust are continually being brought up from Earth's interior along ocean ridges, and as they move away from the ridges, the seabed spreads wider. So instead of the older rocks being deeper, they are farther away from the ocean ridges. The picture is complicated because, as well as the continents drifting apart as the seafloor spreads, some have twisted out of alignment. The fossil magnetism of the rock strips shows just how much movement of the continents has occurred.

To counterbalance the production of new seafloor at the ocean ridges, crust is also destroyed in the ocean deep at the edges of some oceans, such as the western Pacific Ocean around Japan.

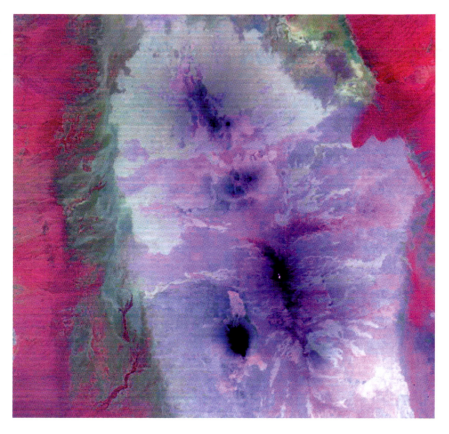

There, the ocean crust dives under the thicker continental crust and is eventually consumed in the molten interior. This powerful geophysical process is the cause of the earthquakes for which the region around Japan is notorious.

The crust of Earth is now pictured as a series of relatively rigid plates that float on a more fluid, plastic layer, the mantle. This model explains the mobility of the continents over many millions of years. Further evidence for the theories of seafloor spreading comes from studies of the heat flow inside Earth, particularly below the oceans. Temperature measurements of the sea floor indicate that the heat flow near the ocean ridges is indeed higher than normal, suggesting that the theories are correct.

Geophysicists also use techniques that are more common in other sciences. The archaeological techniques of thermoluminescence and radioisotope dating reveal the ages of rocks. Thermoluminescence applies in the case of igneous materials—those that were once molten but which have since solidified. By heating the sample, accumulated electrons, caused by the decay of radioactive materials, release energy in the form of light, which when detected gives a measure of the time that has elapsed since solidification.

▲ Mapping areas of chemically similar rock can be a time-consuming process, but it may be speeded up in the future by the use of thermal-infrared imaging cameras mounted on satellites. This picture of the Rift Valley in Ethiopia was taken by the *Terra* satellite and shows the distribution of different rocks containing varying amounts of silicon dioxide. The grayish color indicates a large area of basalt rock, whereas the purple area in the center contains large amounts of the mineral andesite.

SEE ALSO:

EARTH • EARTHQUAKE • GEOLOGY • GRAVITY • OCEANOGRAPHY • OIL EXPLORATION AND PRODUCTION • PLATE TECTONICS • SEISMOLOGY

Gerontology

It may be an unpalatable fact, but we are all aging. From age 12 or 13, we decline slowly and steadily until we die, with no sudden increase in the rate of deterioration at the age of 60 or 65. Gerontology is the study of how aging takes place and how to overcome its more distressing effects.

The ultimate biological marker of aging is an increase in the risk of death. As we age, we are less able to adapt to changes in our environment, whether they are external or internal to the body. A younger person is almost certainly better able to dodge a flying missile or a car that is out of control; his or her body can deal more effectively with a clot in an artery. Older people have slower reactions and less strength in their muscles. They are less able to survive assaults on their internal well-being, such as exposure to an extreme environment or to thirst.

Research has shown that the age at which the aging process starts is constant in all populations in which it has been studied. So is the maximum life span, at about 110 years. Claims that people in some mountain ranges live to 140 appear to be myths, generated largely because of a lack of documentary evidence.

Genetic influences

Such consistency suggests that the onset of aging and maximum life span are under genetic control. Recent studies have shown that there are indeed genes that help to control aging, probably by determining the accuracy with which the organism repairs damage to its cell constituents. Such repair is essential to correct the constant assaults by cosmic radiation, ultraviolet radiation, and the myriad chemical reactions that go on in every cell of the body. How long we live may therefore be determined by how efficiently our bodies can repair this kind of damage.

Until recently, all the genes that had been found to be involved with aging, in both humans and animals, had functions that accelerated the process. Then, a few years ago, scientists discovered a gene in the humble nematode worm, *Caenorhabditis elegans*, that prolongs its life span. Although most nematodes live for about two weeks, the lifespan of worms with this gene was increased by 60 percent. It is not yet known if an equivalent gene exists in humans nor what the gene's function is. It is possible that it assists the cellular repair processes.

No one would want a gene transplant that would allow them to live for another 10 years if it meant suffering longer with an unpleasant condi-

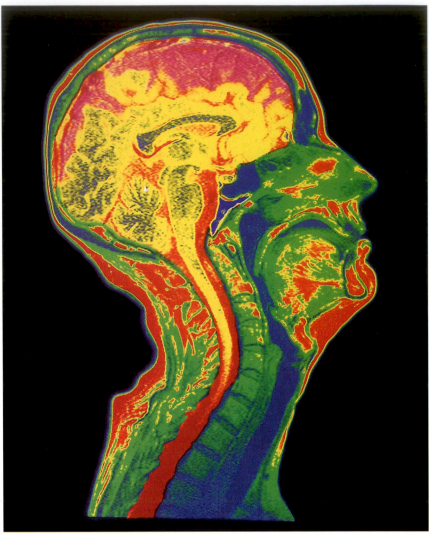

tion, such as the side effects from a stroke or Alzheimer's disease. Yet the prospects for preventing many of the diseases of old age are good. Although it was once thought that diseases were genetically determined and that therefore nothing could be done to avoid them, it is now known that environmental factors are largely to blame.

For example, many studies conducted over the past couple of decades have shown that some components of the diet in excess, such as saturated fat, carcinogens, salt, and alcohol, are linked to problems such as heart disease, cancer, high blood pressure, and strokes.

This is in fact good news, as it is much easier to change one's lifestyle than it is to modify one's genes. Healthier lifestyles will allow more people to achieve their genetic maximum life span, barring accidents. Population statistics show that since the 1870s, the average life span has gone up significantly, whereas the maximum life span has not.

Recent studies have shown that some features of the aging process can even be reversed: people

▲ A magnetic resonance imaging scan of a sagittal section through the brain of a 51-year old male, showing cerebral atrophy. Atrophy is the shrinkage and wasting away of tissue and occurs in the brain as a result of a stroke or of Alzheimer's disease, a common disease of old age. Patients with Alzheimer's suffer senile dementia as a result of the brain shrinking; the pink area at the top of the head shows the shrinkage that has occurred. The yellow area shows how much healthy brain is left.

who take up physical exercise even at the age of 70 can recover approximately 15 percent of their muscle strength.

The realization that environment and lifestyle often determine whether diseases develop in old age has had important ramifications for their prevention and treatment. People are no longer denied most medical and surgical treatments on the grounds that they are too old. It is now recognized that it is physiology that counts, rather than age, and that old people can recover perfectly well from, for example, open heart surgery.

Studies that appeared to show that the mental functions of elderly people were less good than those of their younger counterparts have been largely discounted. Research has shown that individuals do not show a corresponding decline in mental abilities as they age, except commonly in the 12 months before death. The differences found in tests came about because older people are from essentially a different culture. Much research has been conducted to account for these differences, which can create discrimination.

There is nevertheless increasingly good news for the elderly. There are even breakthroughs in Alzheimer's disease, once seen as an intractable condition. Research is increasingly pinpointing risk factors and producing new drugs to treat symptoms. Cholinesterase inhibitors are currently used, but other drugs such as Ampalex, which improves memory function in healthy patients, and Aricept, which can halt the progression of dementia, are undergoing trials. Scientists are also looking at whether stem cells—universal cells from which all other cells are derived—can help treat the disease.

It has also been discovered that head trauma appears to significantly increase the risk of getting Alzheimer's in later life. Further research has shown evidence that estrogen replacement therapy helps improve blood flow to areas involved in memory formation and may play a role in combating the disease in women. Therapies such as Vitamin E and the herb *Ginkgo biloba* have also been suggested as possibly helpful in preventing symptoms, although proof is yet to come.

FACT FILE

- *It may one day be possible to delay or even prevent some of the changes in the body that come about during aging by taking natural chemicals, such as hormones. For example, some studies have suggested that elderly men suffering from muscle weakness may be deficient in human growth hormone and that, if they take this hormone, it will build and strengthen their muscles.*

- *Tests on how growth hormone can help delay the effects of aging are still in their infancy. Before the treatment could be made available, doctors would have to prove beyond a doubt that the treatment was both safe and effective.*

- *Another hormonal treatment, hormone replacement therapy for women, is better established. Once a woman has passed menopause, her ovaries stop producing estrogen. As a result, her risk of heart disease rises, as does her risk of developing osteoporosis (thinning of the bones). Osteoporosis can lead to bone fractures, most commonly of the hip, which can sometimes be fatal.*

- *Gerontologists have discovered that hormone replacement therapy can protect against osteoporosis and associated fractures, as well as reducing a woman's risk of a heart attack. There may, however, be risks as well as benefits, according to research: some studies have shown an increased risk of breast cancer in women who are undertaking hormone replacement therapy.*

◀ Research shows that physical exercise can help people live longer and feel better in old age. This jogger is 90 years old.

SEE ALSO: BONES AND FRACTURE TREATMENT • CELL BIOLOGY • HORMONE • PHARMACOLOGY • SURGERY • TRANSPLANT

Glaciology

◀ Aerial view of one of the giant glaciers in Antarctica, the Liv Glacier in the Queen Maud range of the Transantarctic Mountains.

Glaciology is the study of glaciers, which are formed on the landmasses that extend into the polar regions and high up in mountains. Glaciers are formed by the accumulation of snow that with time becomes compacted and recrystallizes, pushing out more and more of the air between the crystals until it turns to solid ice. It can take 1,000 years for snow to turn to glacial ice at the South Pole, and at the point at which the transformation is complete, usually about 330 ft. (100 m) below the surface, the ice takes on a blue color.

When the resistance of the ice becomes exceeded by the weight of the snow accumulating on top of it, the glacier begins to move. Ice at the bottom of the glacier flows like honey under sufficient pressure, albeit very slowly. Most glaciers move only one or two inches per day and follow a pattern of advance and retreat according to changes in the climate. Glaciers can also move by basal sliding, which occurs when the pressure melting point is reached, turning some of the ice at the base of the glacier to water. Water can also infiltrate through cracks in the glacier or result from upstream melting.

Glaciers occur across a variety of climatic conditions. The most obvious are the polar glaciers, where the ice can form into sheets, caps, shelves, and valley glaciers. The temperature of ice in polar glaciers is always well below freezing, except for a small surface layer whose temperature rises to freezing point in summer. Although there is little precipitation at the poles because the air is very dry, the cold temperatures prevent too much ice from melting.

In temperate glaciers, such as those in southern Alaska, the main body of the glacier remains at freezing point, while only the surface layer drops below freezing in winter. Other glaciers have layers of subfreezing ice between layers that are at freezing point. Mountain, or alpine, glaciers tend to be small and flow down valleys like slow-moving rivers. As they move, glaciers have a profound effect on the landscape, sculpting the base rock and carrying material down the valley.

Environmental factors

Glaciers are built up in layers that mark each winter's snowfall and each summer's thaw. By drilling into a glacier it is possible to build up a picture of what the weather was like year by year, for thousands of years gone by.

Air bubbles are trapped in the ice as the glacier forms. Scientists are analyzing this air in their investigation of the greenhouse effect to see if increasing levels of carbon dioxide correlate with warmer weather. Cores of ice many hundreds of feet long are taken from the glacier and kept in giant freezers for later analysis. By examining the compaction of various layers, glaciologists may be able to obtain clues as to rates of precipitation and whether the climate was wetter or drier over periods of many hundreds of years.

Investigating glacial ice is not only of interest to terrestrial geologists. An experimental probe, called a cryobot, is being developed for use on Mars and on Europa, one of Jupiter's icy moons. Some of the instrumentation that will be incorporated into the cryobot will be tested in a unique project in Antarctica. Lake Vostok is a large sub-ice lake lying 2½ miles (4 km) beneath the surface that has never been explored and, as such, can provide clues to climatic and environmental changes thousands of years ago. Part of the challenge is to develop clean techniques that will not introduce any contamination into the lake, thereby giving false readings. However, the instruments will need to be robust enough to survive a long journey to a hostile environment and the sterilization processes needed to protect the results.

 SEE ALSO: CLIMATOLOGY • EROSION • GEOPHYSICS • WATER

Glass

Glass is not a solid—it is a molten liquid of sand, usually with added limestone and sodium carbonate, that has been cooled to ordinary temperatures, where it becomes very viscous and stiff with all the normal properties of a solid. When most liquids freeze they become crystalline, the crystal size depending on the rate of cooling. Glass, however, can be made so that it avoids crystallization in a process known as supercooling.

It is possible to make glass just from sand, which is crystalline silica or quartz, but the melting point is high (3092°F, 1700°C), and the result is still crystalline in nature. The high melting point and crystalline nature make this process unsuitable for normal sheet-glass purposes. This kind of glass, however, does have the advantage of being chemically inert and can withstand rapid changes in temperature. Adding about 10 percent limestone (calcium carbonate) and 15 percent soda (sodium carbonate) lowers the melting point to about 1569°F (850°C) and much reduces the tendency for the glass to crystallize (devitrification). Other components may also be added, their quantity depending on the type of glass needed.

Development

The first kind of glass made was formed by melting the surface of sand grains together with soda or potash. It was used for making beads and small decorations. The earliest known examples of these beads are Egyptian and date from 2500 B.C.E. In the second millennium B.C.E., the first true glass containers appeared. The Romans had cast window glass, but it was not particularly clear and was used just to let the light in and keep the weather out. The glass was cast in a flat sheet and rolled while it was still hot to make it thinner. Glass blowing is thought to have been invented first in Syria during the first century B.C.E. Glass began to be used in churches as early as the seventh century, but large sheets of transparent glass were not common until the 17th century.

Early processes involved either casting a sheet of glass, then rolling and polishing it, or blowing a globe of glass, then spinning it on the end of a rod so that it flattened out into a disk, already fire polished and smooth. Old glazing using this crown, or Normandy, glass requires small window frames, some of which contain the characteristic

▲ An attractive stained glass window from Durham Cathedral in the north of England. This window was made in the 20th century, but many of the finest stained glass windows in European cathedrals date from the 12th and 13th centuries.

central bullseye mark from the rod. Alternatively, in the broad glass process, the globe was swung so that it extended into a cylinder some 5 ft. (1.5 m) long by 18 in. (45 cm) in diameter. The ends were then removed, and the cylinder was slit lengthwise and flattened in a kiln.

This method, and a mechanized development of it, were used until the early 20th century, when two important processes were developed. In the Fourcault (1904) and Pittsburgh (1926) processes, a ribbon of glass is drawn vertically from the glass furnace up an annealing tower by powered asbestos rollers that grip the ribbon, as soon as it has cooled enough, a few feet above the furnace. The annealing lehr, or leer, allows the glass to cool slowly at a chosen rate. This step is necessary to prevent stresses caused by the surface cooling too rapidly. The glass is transparent with hard fire-polished surfaces but, because of the process, exhibits some distortion.

▲ A master glass blower adds a stem to the blown bubble of glass. The foot of the article is then put on by the deputy master blower, who shapes it as the glass turns, ending with a flat base.

◄ Humans were using glass even before they knew how to make it. This Neolithic arrowhead, found in Algeria, was carved out of naturally occurring glass (fused silica).

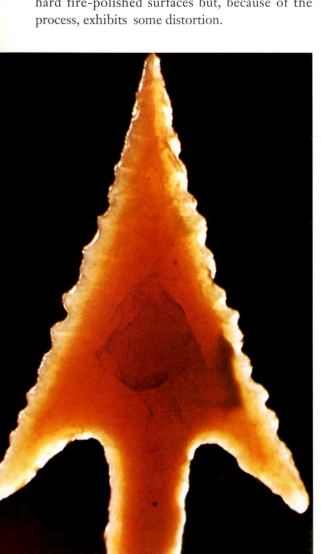

The float process

Since its introduction by the British firm of Pilkington in 1959, the float process has become the world's principal method of flat-glass manufacture. Previously, any flat plate glass had to be cast, rolled, and then polished to remove the distortions.

The float process, unlike previous developments in flat glass manufacture, did not evolve from predecessors. The advance was based on completely new technology.

To make polished plate, molten glass from a furnace was originally rolled into a continuous ribbon, but because there was glass-to-roller contact, the surfaces were marked. They had to be ground and polished to produce the parallel surfaces that bring optical perfection to the finished product. However, grinding and polishing incurred glass wastage amounting to 20 percent and involved high operating costs.

In the float process, a continuous ribbon of glass, up to 11 ft. (3.3 m) wide, moves out of the melting furnace and floats along the surface of a bath of molten tin. The ribbon is held in a chemically controlled atmosphere at a high enough temperature for a long enough time for the irregularities to melt out and for the surface to become flat and parallel. Because the surface of the molten tin is flat, the glass also becomes flat.

The ribbon is then cooled down while still advancing across the molten tin until the surfaces are hard enough for it to progress through the annealing lehr without the rollers marking the bottom surface. The glass produced has uniform thickness and bright fire-polished surfaces without the need for grinding and polishing.

After seven years' work—and after 14 months of unsuccessful operations on a full-scale plant—the float process was successfully making glass about ¼ in. (6 mm) thick. The natural forces within the float bath determined the glass thickness at about ¼ in. (6 mm)—a fortunate phenomenon since 50 percent of the market for quality flat glass is for this thickness.

The full potential of float could not have been realized without mastery of ribbon thickness. Just two years after float was announced, Pilkington developed a way of making a product half the thickness of the original float. The principle was to stretch the glass but in a controlled way so that none of the distortions arising in sheet-glass processes could occur.

In the next three years, thicker float was made. The spread of molten glass in the float bath is arrested and allowed to build up in thickness. The range of thicknesses now available commercially is ⅛ to 1 in. (4–25 mm) for the building trade, and glass down to ⅒ in. (2.5 mm) is manufactured for the automobile trade.

Other types of glass

Patterned glass is made by using rollers with surface patterns after the glass has emerged from the furnace. Wired glass, with a criss-cross pattern of wire set inside it, is made by rolling a ribbon of half the required thickness, overlaying it with wire, and adding a further ribbon of glass to fuse with the bottom one. To make the glass transparent, the surfaces must be ground and polished. The advantage of wired glass is that it holds together when broken by impact or heat.

Optical glass

Optical and ophthalmic glass is made in much the same way as other glasses with the important exceptions that the glass should be consistently homogeneous with no strain, striations, or discoloration. Small differences in chemical composition of heat treatment can have considerable effects on the optical properties. Common glass usually contains iron oxides that discolor the glass. Sand used in the manufacture of optical glass is purer, and the mix is modified by the addition of oxides of calcium, sodium, potassium, barium, or magnesium.

The bath is first melted, then the glass is refired by further raising the temperature. It is homogenized by being allowed to cool and then passed through a series of stirrers. The optical properties of the glass are preserved by the critical melting, refining, and stirring temperatures, but the cooling rate is even more important, since this has an important role in determining the refractive index of the glass. The cooling glass flows slowly down a delivery feeder and is sheared into globules or formed into a sheet or slab for further processing. The globules are then molded into lens blanks and passed into the annealing lehr.

Safety glass

There are many uses for particularly strong glass that will not shatter easily, for example car windshields, which must be able to withstand the impact of pebbles thrown up from the road. These products are made from annealed glass, which undergoes a further process of toughening or lamination. In the case of toughened, or tempered, glass, its temperature is uniformly raised until the glass is just beginning to become plastic.

The glass is quickly lifted out of the furnace, bent where necessary between matching tools, and then cooled uniformly all over by jets of cold air blown forcibly onto it. The surface then becomes very much stronger than normal and both withstands shattering forces better and contains the glass if it does break.

Laminated glass is made by sandwiching a layer of clear or tinted polyvinyl butyral between two pieces of annealed float glass. The sandwich is gently heated under vacuum, to evacuate all air from the laminate, and then heated to bonding temperature under pressure in an autoclave. No adhesives are required. A number of layers may be used for increased strength.

Heat-resistant glass

If boiling water is poured into an ordinary table glass, the inner surface layer will heat and expand rapidly. Glass is a good insulator, so deeper layers will remain at room temperature. The resulting distortion may easily shatter the glass. In order to make glassware that will withstand oven temperatures, a certain amount of boric oxide (B_2O_3) and alumina is added, reducing the expansion coefficient of the glass by a factor of three. Pure fused silica is particularly resistant to thermal expansion and so is used for the production of high-quality optical glass.

Light-sensitive glass

Light-sensitive glass is glass that will darken or become tinted when exposed to light. In photochromatic glass, the change is reversible, whereas in photosensitive glass, it is not. Also, photosensitive glass must be heated to develop the coloration.

◀ An image fixed in photosensitive glass by laying a leaf on the glass, exposing the glass to sunlight, and then reheating.

SEE ALSO: CRYSTALS AND CRYSTALLOGRAPHY • GLASS FIBER • LIGHT AND OPTICS • STAINED GLASS

Glass Fiber

▲ Cutting a sheet of glass-fiber mat, which can be used for insulation against heat or sound or to construct road vehicles, railroad engines, ships, and aircraft. Workers wear strong gloves when handling glass fiber, because it can irritate the skin.

The earliest Egyptian glass vessels, used as containers for oils, unguents, and perfumes, were built from glass fibers spun laboriously by hand around lightly glazed cores of clay. After the development of the technique of glass blowing in the first century B.C.E., glass fibers were used by glass blowers to enhance their wares. In the early 19th century, glass blowers would often spend idle moments making friggers, glass ornaments of elaborate design to testify to their skills. One such frigger in the Pilkington Glass Museum was made to represent a glass fountain with birds that trail long, silky tails of colored glass fibers.

At the beginning of the 20th century in Germany, a commercial process was developed for the production of glass silk. Deprived of access to supplies of asbestos during World War I, the Germans pioneered the use of glass insulation material. The first commercial production of glass fibers in Britain began in 1928, and after World War II, Britain produced glass fiber to help satisfy the postwar need for efficient insulation material. The continuing development of glass fiber reinforcement materials has complemented and accelerated the use of plastics.

Manufacture of glass fibers

In the manufacture of glass fibers, alumina, boric acid, and calcium oxide flux are added to the basic glassmaking mix of sand and soda ash. The batch is fed first into a continuous furnace where it becomes molten glass by the application of direct flame heating, and then into a fiber-drawing furnace, called a bushing. The glass fibers drawn from the bushing can be either continuous or discontinuous filaments, the latter being used in the manufacture of glass wool and glass tissue.

Glass wool is manufactured by the Crown process, in which a relatively thick stream of molten glass is allowed to flow by gravity from a bushing into a rapidly rotating steel-alloy dish with many hundreds of fine apertures around its edge. Glass is thrown out through these apertures by centrifugal force to form filaments, which are further extended into fine fibers by a high-velocity blast of hot gas. After being sprayed with a suitable bonding agent, the fibers are drawn by suction onto a horizontally moving conveyor positioned below the rotating dish. The mat of fibers formed on the conveyor is carried to curing ovens that cure the bonding agent and then on to the trimmers and guillotines that shape the final product, which is normally either a flexible mat or rigid board. The wool produced by the Crown process is of a very fine texture, the individual fibers having an average diameter of approximately 6.5 μm—less than one-tenth of the diameter of a human hair.

The manufacture of glass tissue differs from the Crown process in that, in this process, a num-

▶ Continuous-filament glass fibers being wound as bands onto a tube as reinforcement.

ber of small streams of molten glass are allowed to fall from bushings, but within an inch of the apertures, they are caught by a blast of superheated steam. The high speed of the blast grasps each tiny glass stream and by a whipping action, visible only in high-speed photographs, draws it out until it breaks away from the main stream and falls as a separate fiber into a forming hood. A binder is applied to the mat of fibers after they have fallen onto a collecting conveyor moving at relatively high speed. The resulting thin membrane, which is normally about 0.002 in. (0.05 mm) thick, can be either in plain form or reinforced with a continuous-filament fiber.

In continuous-filament manufacture, a continuous strand is produced, made up of a multitude of individual filaments. Molten glass is led from the furnace or tank through a forehearth to a series of bushings, each of which contains several hundred very accurately dimensioned forming nozzles. With a constant head of molten glass maintained in the tank, fine filaments of glass are drawn mechanically downward from the bushing nozzles at a speed of several thousand feet per minute, giving a filament diameter that may be as small as 5 µm, barely visible to the naked eye. The filaments from the bushing run to a common collecting point, where size (a protective and lubricating coating) is applied, and subsequently are brought together either as multiple or single strands on a high-speed winder. The strands are then further processed to produce specially treated rovings (continuous strands of fibers suitable for twisting into yarns), woven glass cloth, or chopped strands and mats for the reinforcement of composites. The strength of composites depends on the orientation of the fibers and the bonding agent.

Uses of glass fiber

Although the main use of glass wool is in the insulation of home attics, glass wool products are also used for heat and sound insulation of pipes, ducts, boilers, and tanks in all types of domestic and industrial applications and in road vehicles, railroad locomotives, ships, and aircraft. Glass tissue is used to reinforce the bituminous and coal tar protective coatings on buried oil, gas, and water pipes. It also provides the reinforcing membranes of damp courses and roofing mats. Continuous-filament glass fibers are used to reinforce thermosetting plastics and natural and synthetic rubbers. Glass-reinforced plastics may be used for a diverse range of products, such as car bodies, boat hulls, bath tubs, and various types of pipes and ducts. Special forms of glass-fiber reinforcement are also available for use in inorganic matri-

ces, such as autoclave calcium silicate, gypsum plaster, and cement.

The development of glass capable of resisting the alkaline conditions of Portland cement has led to the development of a completely new construction material, glass-reinforced cement (GRC). This material can be sprayed into flat sheets or onto a variety of shaped molds; the glass cement can also be premixed and then spread with a trowel, cast, spun, pumped, extruded, or injected. To give still further flexibility, thin flat GRC sheets can, while still green, or uncured, be folded or pressed into a wide variety of complex shapes. GRC has the tensile strength of reinforced concrete and yet is ten times lighter. Its uses seem virtually limitless, and applications already range from pipes and sewer lining to cladding panels for buildings, outside shutters, soil-retaining walls, and general street furniture such as bus shelters and benches. It is also used to make shells for low-cost modular housing and for integral door and window frames.

GLASS YARN FIBER

Borosilicate glass batch / Batch cans / Marble forming / Hopper / Electric furnace / Glass filament formation / Binder application / Yarn winding

◀ There are a number of steps in the production of glass yarn, used for making curtains and protective clothing. Borosilicate glass is used for its chemical and heat-resistant properties. First the glass is formed into marbles, then remelted. The molten glass passes through a bushing, a receptacle with numerous small holes, and emerges as filaments that are then coated with size. This coating helps to protect the filaments from abrasion. Finally, the yarn is wound onto a spool.

SEE ALSO: CEMENT MANUFACTURE • CONCRETE • FIBER OPTICS • FIBER, SYNTHETIC • GLASS • PLASTICS

Glider

A glider, or sailplane, is, in simple terms, an aircraft without an engine. Gliding as a sport originated just before World War I at the Wasserkuppe hill in the Rhön Mountains in Germany. Before this date, gliding had merely been an integral part of the efforts of humans to fly.

The first gliders were made by Sir George Cayley, who, after a series of models, constructed near Scarborough, Britain, gliders to carry a boy in 1849 and Cayley's coachman in 1853. Other gliders were made around the turn of the century by Otto Lilienthal in Germany, Percy Pilcher in Britain, and Wilbur and Orville Wright in the United States, culminating in the first flight of a powered aircraft on 16 December 1903. From that date, apart from people learning to fly, gliding was mainly ignored until competitions were organized at the Wasserkuppe in 1920 and 1921.

From these meetings, the sport of gliding grew throughout Europe, and the first international competition was held in Germany in 1937. During World War II, large transport gliders were built to carry up to 60 troops or small vehicles. After the war, sport gliding spread throughout the world, and international competitions have been held on a regular basis in the various continents since the 1948 competition in Switzerland.

Launching

There are two basic methods of launching a glider into the air. The first is winch launching, in which a long steel cable is wound onto a powered drum and the glider is pulled into the air in a manner similar to the launching of a kite. Special cable connections are used on gliders to ensure safety. The main cable is connected to a weak link that is designed to break at a preset load (normally 1,000 lbs., or 450 kg), thus preventing undue strain on the glider wings if it encounters an excessive force. The mechanism inside the glider that holds the cable ring is designed to automatically release it once the cable is vertical. Cables are normally released manually by pulling a yellow lever; this extra mechanism, called a back release, is a safety backup. Some winches incorporate additional mechanisms for cutting the cable if a glider gets into difficulties—remotely operated guillotines are safest, but hand axes may be provided as backups. Winch cables are equipped with parachutes between the weak line and the main body of the cable. They help the winch driver to reel the cable in smoothly and reduce the possibility of injury from falling cables.

The other launching method is using an aircraft to tow the glider up to any desired height.

▼ This single-seat high-performance sailplane is constructed from wood with aluminum alloy spars. This sailplane has a tail parachute fitted and a one-piece all-moving tailplane with antibalance tabs.

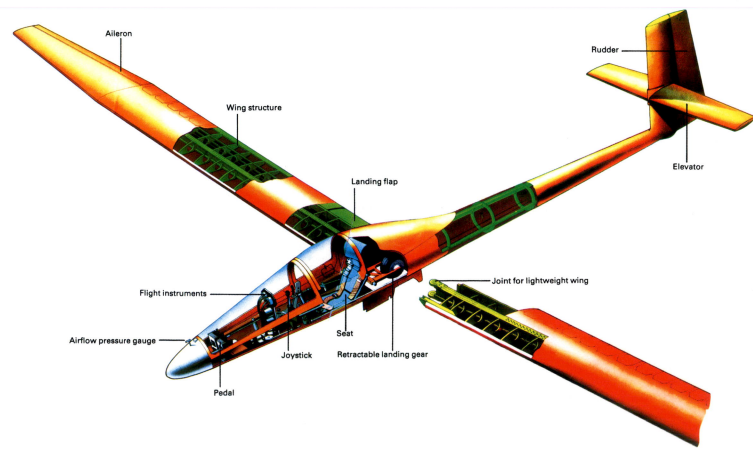

Labels: Aileron, Wing structure, Rudder, Landing flap, Elevator, Joint for lightweight wing, Flight instruments, Airflow pressure gauge, Seat, Joystick, Retractable landing gear, Pedal

An earlier method, using an elastic rope to catapult the glider into the air from the top edge of a cliff or high hill, is now rarely used.

Flying

Once in the air, a glider cannot maintain a steady horizontal flight path indefinitely, and the line of the flight path will slope downward relative to the horizon. The angle between the horizon and the flight path is known as the gliding angle, and the minimum value for each glider, known as the best gliding angle, is used to give a direct comparison as to the efficiency of each type of glider. Before World War II, a high-performance glider had a best gliding angle of about 4:100. By 1955 gliders had improved, and the average gliding angle of 2.9:100 was being achieved. This improvement was due to improved surface finishing and the use of laminar aerofoils, although the gliders were still made from the traditional wooden covering. Today, best gliding angles of 2:100 are being obtained, but the construction materials used are usually glass fibers with synthetic resins. These plastic materials give the very smooth surfaces necessary to suit the specialized aerofoils used on modern competition gliders in order to achieve the best gliding angles at higher speeds.

Minimum sink at high speeds is today very important in a glider, as competitions usually consist of triangular courses around which the competitor has to fly as quickly as possible. After launching, usually by aerotowing, the pilot has to find a thermal or any other air that is rising upward faster than the glider is sinking through it. Having thus climbed to a suitable height, the competitor sets off as fast as possible, gradually losing height until another thermal is found, and so on until the course is completed. In addition to thermals, other types of rising air currents can be found when air is blowing up the face of a steep hill or when waves are set up as air masses pass over mountainous countryside.

A glider is controlled in exactly the same manner as an aircraft, including the use of flaps when these are fitted. Most gliders are also fitted with air brakes or spoilers to limit the maximum speed and to assist landing the glider in small fields. Some gliders also have tail parachutes to act as air brakes. Competition gliders carry a very comprehensive range of flying instruments, including an airspeed indicator, an altimeter, and a variometer to show the vertical rise and sinking speeds. A basic variometer will consist of nothing more than a sealed container with some tubing attached to the pitot head. When the glider is climbing, air is expelled from the container through the tube causing a small green-colored weight to be

A modern sports glider about to land. The parachute acts as an air brake to slow down the glider and to enable it to land in a restricted space, such as a small field. Most sports gliders have removable wings so that they can be carried easily on small trailers.

pushed up; when the glider falls, air enters the container, pushing up a small red weight. Oxygen equipment and radios may be carried, as well as water ballast inside the wings to increase the speed when weather conditions are good and to achieve the best angle.

Types of glider

Several different types of glider are in use and are either single- or two-seat machines. The two-seat gliders are mainly used for instructional flying, either showing students how to operate the controls of the glider or how to make circuits of the airfield to be able to land correctly. Gliders used for this type of flying may be quite old wooden machines, although new motorized gliders have recently been introduced into some clubs for this purpose. The engine is quite small, but by using powered gliders, a club can offer instructional flying at any time regardless of the weather. Other two-seat gliders, of higher performance and built of light-alloy metal, are used to give lessons in advanced techniques of gliding.

There is constant research into improving the performance of competition gliders. One of the new generation of gliders is the SB-11, which has variable geometry wings to give greater wing area when needed for climbing in thermals. Another innovation is a water-filled ballast tank, which increases the aircraft's penetration and helps minimize speed loss while there are strong thermals during the day; this ballast can be dumped to reduce weight in the later, weaker thermals.

High-performance gliders may contain a lot of complex equipment; some even carry computers to keep track of thermals and calculate optimum flying speeds, but basic gliding can be enjoyed without any electronic equipment—a piece of yarn attached to the canopy can be used to tell the pilot if he is flying straight or sideways.

SEE ALSO: Aerodynamics • Aircraft design • Aviation, history of • Glass fiber • Helicopter • Navigation

Global Positioning System

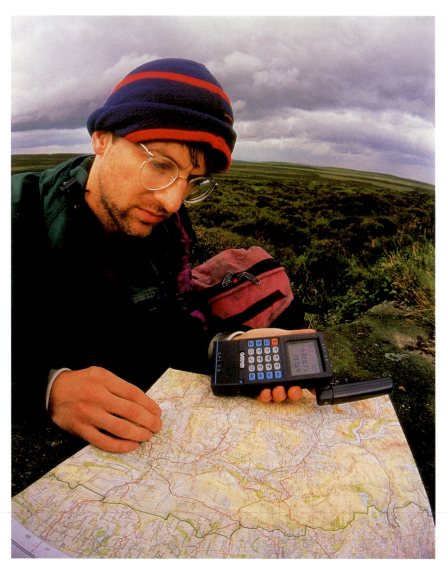

▲ Walkers can now find out exactly where they are by using a handheld satellite navigation receiver. The system uses signals sent by a network of 24 GPS satellites, each of which sends out a signal with its identity, position, and exact time. The receiver reads these data and can instantly calculate its position anywhere in the world to within 300 ft. (100 m). Portable systems like this are of enormous benefit to hikers, climbers, and sailboat enthusiasts.

A global positioning system is a means by which an observer can determine his or her position on Earth's surface by reference to objects whose positions are known at the time of measurement. Ancient travelers used the positions of stars to achieve this goal; their modern counterparts have access to receivers that calculate their positions using signals broadcast from satellites.

Early navigation aids

Ancient travelers used the position of prominent stars and constellations, such as the North Star and the Southern Cross, to gauge their approximate direction of travel. In the mid-18th century, this method was refined by the use of sextants—optical devices that help measure the precise angle of stars above the horizon. An observer could measure latitude or position north or south of the Equator by comparing the data from a sextant with charts of the stars' positions. A means of measuring longitude remained elusive for a while.

In 1761, the problem of measuring longitude was solved by the invention of the chronometer—an accurate timepiece that could be used aboard ships. By taking a chronometer with them, travelers had a way of keeping track of the time at home or in some place of reference. By noting the times of sunrise and sunset and comparing them with records of the times of the same events at the place of reference, travelers had a means of calculating their positions east or west of that place.

Since 1884, the principal time standard for travelers has been Greenwich Mean Time—the time kept by high-accuracy chronometers at the Royal Greenwich Observatory, England. The observatory is situated on the prime meridian, an imaginary north–south line of zero longitude. In the early 20th century, time signals broadcast by radio from Greenwich were the traveler's principal reference for calculating longitude.

Radio navigation

The main drawback in navigation based on star positions is its dependence on a clear night sky. Close-range navigation using sightings of beacons and other reference points suffers from a similar dependence on good visibility. Navigation using radio beacons was the first attempt to overcome such problems by using transmissions of low-frequency radiation that is not obscured by atmospheric conditions in the way that light is. Radio navigation has the weakness that it is difficult to determine the position of radio beacons with great precision over long distances.

Satellite GPS

In 1973, the U.S. government resolved to establish a network of satellite-mounted beacons that would beam high-frequency signals down to Earth as part of a high-technology replacement for navigation by stars. In fact, the first of these satellites were called Navstars, but the system later became known as GPS (Global Positioning System). The U.S. GPS is owned and operated by the Department of Defense, but most of its features are available for civilian use.

The first of the 10 development satellites that formed the so-called Block-I GPS was launched in 1978. Building on experience gleaned from the Block I project, a total of 24 Block-II satellites were put into orbit between 1989 and 1993. The satellites orbit 10,900 miles (17,500 km) above Earth's surface, giving them an orbital period of 12 hours. The orbits are coordinated so that most points on Earth's surface are in direct line of sight of six satellites at any given time. In fact, only three or four contacts are necessary to establish a position, but the extra satellites reduce the probability of the system being rendered useless by "outages" (failures) of several satellites all occurring at the same time.

Basic principals of GPS

Each satellite in a GPS constellation sends periodic transmissions that encode its position with the exact time of transmission according to its onboard timing system. The signal takes a finite amount of time to reach an observer on or above Earth's surface, and that time is equal to the distance between the observer and the satellite divided by the speed of light.

If the observer's detector had a timing system in exact synchrony with the satellite, then it could use the delay in receiving the signal to calculate its exact distance from the position of the satellite at the time of transmission. For an observer on Earth's surface, that information would be sufficient to define a circle on Earth's surface on which the observer must be situated.

Contact with a second satellite establishes a second circle that overlaps the first at two points, signifying the two possible locations that correspond to the satellite positions and distances. Also, the difference in delays between signals establishes the different distances between the observer and the two satellites, so the need for exact synchrony is eliminated.

Contact with a third satellite eliminates one of the possible locations established by the first two contacts and allows the detector to calculate its position with reasonable accuracy. A fourth contact enables a detector to establish its position in three dimensions, making it possible to determine the altitude of a location. Any further contacts can serve to confirm and improve the accuracy of the position as calculated by the principal contacts.

The satellites

The satellites and the launch vehicles that put them in orbit are sometimes referred to as the "space segment" of a GPS. The Block-II satellites were launched from Cape Canaveral, Florida, using Delta rockets. Future launches will take place as and when satellites have to be replaced.

Each of the Block-II satellites in the U.S. GPS constellation occupies an orbit at 55 degrees to the equator. This orbit ensures that in any 12-hour period, each satellite will trace a footprint that covers the North and South Poles and crosses the Equator twice.

The satellites carry atomic clocks that are accurate to within three-billionths of a second, a transmitter that broadcasts the satellite's signal to Earth, and a receiver that picks up signals from ground stations. The power for this equipment comes from a 50 sq. ft. (4.6 m^2) solar array that is capable of producing 700 watts. The array also supplies a battery that maintains the power supply when the satellite is in Earth's shadow.

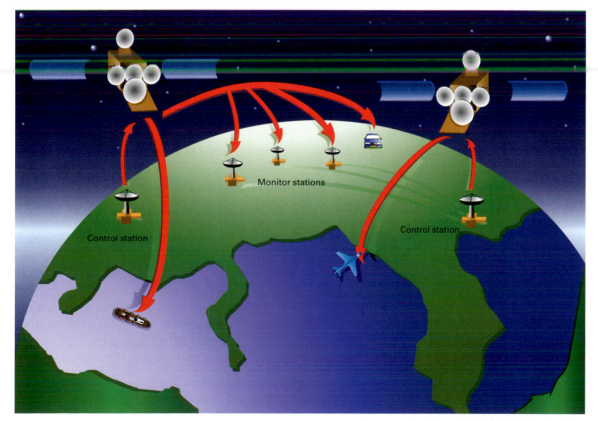

Monitor stations

Control station

Control station

◄ GPS systems can be used in a wide range of applications for accurate positioning. Time signals and correctional data are beamed to the satellites from central control stations. Monitor stations track the orbit of the satellites and relay the information back to the central control stations. By coordinating signals from three or more satellites, receivers in user vehicles, such as airplanes, ships, and automobiles, can pinpoint their position with reasonable accuracy.

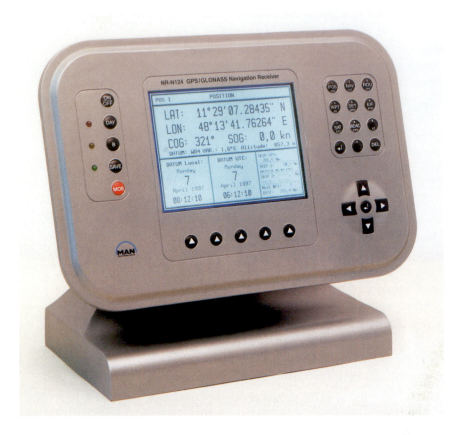

Receivers

Receivers are sometimes called the user segment of GPS. Their basic function is to receive and decode transmissions from satellites and interpret them to calculate location.

Most civilian receivers operate to the standards of the Standard Positioning Service (SPS), which gives a position on Earth's surface within an accuracy of around 110 yds. (100 m). The Precision Positioning Service (PPS) is accurate to within around 70 ft. (20 m) and is less susceptible to jamming attempts. PPS is generally restricted for use by authorized military receivers.

The accuracy of positioning can be greatly increased by referring the measuring receiver to a second receiver in a nearby location whose position is known exactly. The position of the second receiver is calculated from the difference between the two, so any inaccuracies in the GPS reception can be practically eliminated. Such inaccuracies might be caused by atmospheric distortions, for example, which will be essentially equal for both receivers provided they are not too far apart. This technique is called differential GPS, or DGPS.

The ground stations

GPS ground stations are sometimes called the control segment of the system. Their function is to pass three crucial pieces of information to each satellite as it passes overhead: the time, the satellite's location, and the precise path it is likely to take during the next orbit.

The time signal is dictated by the master control center at Falcon Air Force Base, Colorado. That base instructs unstaffed bases at Ascension Island in the Atlantic Ocean, Diego Garcia Atoll in the Indian Ocean, Hawaii in the Pacific Ocean, and Kwajalein in the South Pacific.

Each base tracks the orbits of the satellites in its scope and predicts the path of each one on the basis of that tracking. This information is passed to the satellite in an "uplink" (a transmission from Earth to satellite), together with the satellite's observed location at that time. Between uplinks, an onboard processor extrapolates from this data to calculate positional data for transmission.

Another important function of the control segment is in the management and remediation of outages. When a satellite is detected to be transmitting erroneous information, for example, the network can usually be instructed to inform receivers of the problem within a few seconds, thus preventing incorrect positional data from being displayed while the satellite is behaving incorrectly. Once such a problem is identified, the satellite can usually be reset and restored to normal working order within an hour.

▲ Safety at sea can be increased significantly by the use of maritime navigation systems such as the model above. This unit takes advantage of both the U.S. global positioning system and its Russian counterpart to double the number of satellites available for tracking to 48. The greater number of satellites can increase the positioning reliability by a factor of six compared with conventional GPS devices.

Applications of GPS

GPS was principally developed as a military tool, and it proved to be extremely useful to UN forces in Operation Desert Storm, which took place in early 1991 in Iraq and Kuwait. GPS receivers enabled units to coordinate their positions even when sandstorms reduced visibility to practically nil, thereby giving them a great strategic advantage over forces without GPS.

GPS has wide-ranging applications in air and sea navigation, where it can be used in conjunction with autopilot systems to ensure that craft stay on preprogrammed courses. Similar systems are used to direct land-based vehicles in remote or hazardous locations, such as quarries. High-accuracy GPS is used in surveying and in the execution of large-scale construction projects, such as the construction of the Channel Tunnel between Britain and France.

In conjunction with cellular-telephone networks, a GPS receiver can identify the position of a road vehicle and call up traffic and other information for that location. Other radio systems combine with GPS to monitor the positions of each unit in a fleet of emergency vehicles so that the closest unit can be identified when an incident arises. A similar system allows hijacked security vehicles to be tracked and recovered.

SEE ALSO: AIRCRAFT-CONTROL ENGINEERING • ELECTRONICS • NAVIGATION • SATELLITE, ARTIFICIAL • SURVEYING

Index